Normandy

Other books by James Bentley

Albert Schweitzer
Alsace
Bavaria
Between Marx and Christ
The Blue Guide to Germany and Berlin
A Calendar of Saints
A Children's Bible
A Guide to the Dordogne
A Guide to Tuscany
Languedoc
Life and Food in the Dordogne
The Loire
Martin Niemöller
Oberammergau and the Passion Play
The Rhine
Ritualism and Politics in Victorian Britain
Secrets of Mount Sinai
Umbria
Weekend Cities

NORMANDY

James Bentley

AURUM PRESS

A ma compagne, qui, depuis notre mariage,
m'a souvent encouragé dans les hauts et les bas
de mon métier

First published 1989 by Aurum Press Limited
33 Museum Street, London WC1A 1LD
Reprinted in paperback 1990

Copyright © 1989 by James Bentley

Photographs copyright © Joe Cornish
of Landscape Only 1989

Map by Richard Natkiel Associates
Decorative illustration by Joy FitzSimmons

British Library Cataloguing in Publication Data
Bentley, James, 1937–
1. France. Normandy – Visitors' guides
I. Title
914.4′204838
ISBN 1 85410 122 6

Typeset by Wyvern Typesetting Ltd, Bristol
Printed in Great Britain at The Bath Press, Bath, Avon

Contents

ENGLISH CHANNEL

Baie de la Seine

Barfleur

Beaumont

Martinvast   Cherbourg

St-Vaast-
la-Hougue

Valognes

Ste-Marie-
du-Mont

Grandcamp-Maisy

St-Laurent-sur-Mer

Colleville-sur-Mer

Port-en-Bessin

Arromanches-
les-Bains

Courseulles-sur-M

Bernières-sur

Langrun

Luc-su

Lion

St-Sauveur-
le-Vicomte

Carentan   Isigny-
sur-Mer

Asnelles

Ouistreham
Riva-Bella

Cerisy-
La-Forêt   Bayeux

Lessay

Balleroy   CAEN

MANCHE   ST-LÔ

Golfe de
St Malo

CALVAD

Coutances

Hambye

Clécy   Fal

Villedieu-
les-Poêles

Granville   Vire

St-Michel-
de-Montjoie   Tinchebray   Flers

Brécey   St Pois

Briouze

le Mont-
St-Michel   Avranches   Mortain   Lonlay
l'Abbaye   la Ferté-
Macé

Sélune   Domfront

Bagnoles-de-l'Orne   Ca

Pontorson   Tessé-la-Madeleine

Lassay

Mayenne

Richard Natkiel Assocs.

| 0 | Miles | | 50 |
| 0 | Kilometres | | 80 |

Evron

General map of Normandy

Preface

Anyone writing a travel book about Normandy has to contend with the powerful debunking spirit of one of its own greatest novelists, Émile Zola. His *Voyage circulaire* recounts the Normandy honeymoon of newly wed Parisian shopkeepers. Initially the serious young couple travel with their noses glued to a guide book. Then Zola charmingly charts their abandonment of textbook tourism in favour of *amour*.

Mindful of this, in describing the history, the art and the literature of Normandy, I have continually been aware of the desire of any tourist to see for him- or herself. In evoking both the Normandy countryside and its rich cuisine (wherever possible using the words of its great novelists and poets to do the work for me) my purpose has been to point my readers to places where they can see and taste for themselves.

Yet this is a personal book, covering all of the province but seen through my own eyes and often setting down what I have learned from talking to those who live there. 'Equilibrium' is the word that springs to the lips of the people of Normandy when you ask them to account for the beauty of their land, and others have concurred. Attempting to sum up the spirit of Normandy in 1837 the novelist Stendhal pointed to its little streams, its valleys, the leaves of its elms, its huge hedges and its apple trees, the view of the coastline as far as le Mont-Saint-Michel and 'the sea itself, without which no country can be dubbed truly beautiful'. Everything, he avowed, was obviously put together for a deep purpose and often the ensemble of village, farm, orchard and stream seemed to him to have been 'deliberately, finely and delicately calculated'. Today's inhabitants agree.

Hilaire Belloc in *The Hills and the Sea* brilliantly evoked their astonishing ancestors, 'bullet-headed men, vivacious and splendidly brave',who awoke all Europe, providing settled financial systems and settled governments of land, and were everywhere, from the Grampians to Mesopotamia, 'like steel when all other Christians were like wood or like lead'. Belloc judged that 'Some odd, transitory phenomenon of cross-breeding, a very lucky freak in the history of the European family, produced the only body of men who all were lords, and who in their collective action showed continually nothing but genius.'

Even before the time of William the Bastard, their history was intimately connected with ours and, as everyone knows, the Bastard became the Conqueror through conquering us. In the opening words of William Wordsworth's poem on the Norman Conquest:

> The woman-hearted Confessor prepares
> The evanescence of the Saxon line.

As my book reveals, this connection did not end here. It was, for instance, the English who in 1431 at Rouen made a martyr of France's patron saint.

British artists have sought inspiration in Normandy, and French painters refuge in Britain. The Channel defended Britain against Hitler after the fall of France, but in 1944 the British – along with their American and Canadian allies – fought their way back across it and on to the Normandy beaches. Rarely, in truth, has the Channel kept us out of Normandy. At the beginning of this century, rattling by railway train through wooded hills and deep green pastures and alongside ribbonlike streamlets, cosy homesteads, orchards and quaint village churches, an indefatigable lover of French cathedrals felt a sudden extra thrill as the train slackened speed when an ancient city with a fascinating galaxy of spires came into view, 'seated on a broad sparkling river crossed by bridges, bordered by busy quais, and with small poplar-grown islet patches breaking its sinuous course'. T. Frederick Bumpus added, 'The tract of goodly land is Normandy – that most enchanting, and to English most interesting, of all the provinces of fair France; the river is the Seine, and the spire-crowned city is Rouen.'

As often before in writing about France, I am much indebted to the kindness of Mrs Pauline Hallam, public relations director of the French government tourist board in London. And I cannot thank my daughter Emma-Jane sufficiently for coping with my incessant demands for translations of difficult pieces of French prose and poetry.

James Bentley
SEPTEMBER 1988

In the footsteps
of the Normans

To arrive at the port of Caen, which is called Ouistreham, is to be plunged instantly into the complex delights of Normandy. Here is a fortified Norman church, built in the twelfth century for the nuns of la Trinité, Caen, its west front a Romanesque masterpiece, its dedication – appropriate, in view of its mighty defensive aspect – to St-Samson. Ouistreham also boasts a marina and a casino, opposite which, as a reminder of the horrors and heroism of World War II, is a museum dedicated to the 4th French Commandos and to their exploits in 1944. Overlooking the bay, nowadays graced with elegant yachts, stands a German look-out post.

After a gentle walk along a cliff, the smell of fish brings one to the excellent restaurants of the little town and a leisurely lunch, which might include mussels or a salmon terrine in a piquant sauce, followed by a flounder fillet in a cider sauce (*filet de carrelet au cidre*, for this is the *département* of France known as Calvados and, like the whole of Normandy, is not wine but cider country). To emphasize our Anglo-Norman ties, one such restaurant is called la Britannia.

A swift drive takes you from Ouistreham to Caen itself, where William the Conqueror founded an abbey for men, and his wife one for women, and from Caen it is only half an hour's drive, or thirty-three kilometres, on a straight road (the N158) to the Conqueror's birthplace, Falaise. On the way you pass, in summer, trestle tables where the wives of Norman fishermen sell cockles, mussels and seafood in general, advertised as *fruits de mer*. The route traverses fortified villages and the Polish and Canadian war cemeteries.

At Cintheaux lie the remains of a Merovingian cemetery, as well as a lovely twelfth-century church with a seventeenth-century bell tower. Potigny, a little further on through the rich green countryside, boasts a thirteenth-century Gothic church, as does the next village of Solangy, whose church is further blessed with fine seventeenth-century furnishings. Next comes Aubigny. One might neglect its seventeenth-century church, but for the information that inside are six splendid kneeling statues of its former seigneurs; and just past the village, to remind us that we are not simply on a church-crawl, is a gorgeous classical château built at the turn of the sixteenth century – in style half Henri IV, half Louis XIII.

Thus Normandy instantly offers its charms to the visitor: seaside casinos and exquisite food, luxuriant countryside and magical architecture, as well as a history intimately connected not just with England but with much of the English-speaking world as well. All that is so far missing is superb art, alongside the writings of some of the greatest French poets and novelists.

South of Aubigny, as you enter Falaise – whose ramparts today cross the rue Georges Clemenceau – a spectacular view appears of the castle in which William, Duke of Normandy and King of England, was born, probably in the year 1027. In front of the town hall is an equestrian bronze of the Conqueror himself, William the Bastard, his charger prancing on its hind legs, the rider brandishing his standard, a gift of the Pope himself. Physically William was a giant. Rightly, then, his six ancestors, added around the base of the statue in 1865, are sculpted as smaller than the bastard. But these statues, of the Viking Rollo, William Longue-Épée, Richard I, Richard II, Richard III and William's father Robert the Magnificent (whom many dubbed Robert the Devil), are still fearsome.

The nearby church of the Holy Trinity, today in terrible condition (partly as a result of the bombardments of World War II, partly due to simple neglect), was begun in 1438. Building finished at the time of the Renaissance for lack of funds. Its splendid main doorway is Renaissance, its nave exquisitely Gothic. Another church in this tiny town is dedicated to St Gervais, and its Romanesque tower, with narrow slits for windows, sets the tone for the rest of the building, save for the flamboyant Gothic south aisle and the flying buttresses at the east end. If you go inside, a display of photographs reveals that the whole was savagely bombed, and restored only in 1980 – splendidly, save for the insipid stained-glass.

To the Briton's delight, this church was begun in 1066, the very year of the conquest of England by Falaise's most famous son. It was not consecrated till 1124, in the presence of King Henry Beauclerc. Even older is the little church of Saint Laurent, perched on a rock as you leave Falaise to the east, with a couple of bells hanging in an open belfry over the neat Romanesque west doorway.

Elsewhere in this book I describe Falaise in more detail; here I should like to recall the thrill I invariably feel on walking into the massive, half-ruined white-stone castle, past two old stone wheels for grinding corn, to reach the twelfth-century keep, which preserves the cell where William was allegedly born. The walls of this virtually square keep (twenty-seven metres by twenty-five) are four metres thick. The Conqueror's fourth son, Henry I Beauclerc, like his father King of England and Duke of Normandy, built it in 1123. From mid-June to early September an entrancing *son et lumière* performance in the château recalls the joint history of England and Normandy.

On the north-west side of the keep you find a relief by the sculptor Leblond on the so-called 'fountain of Arlette' set up in 1957 to the glory of William's washerwoman mother – though how the author of the inscription knew that her colour was like a rose, it is hard to know. In the bas-relief pretty Arlette washes away, the duke returns from the hunt and his castle perches in the background. Just behind this modern fountain is an ancient one, said to rise from the place where Arlette may have been washing her linen when Robert the Devil espied her and determined to make her his own.

As Régis Faucon in his *Sur les pas de Guillaume le Conquérant* slyly observes, today in the duke's château at Falaise the guide will show you the window through which, on his return from the hunt, the duke first saw the girl washing her linen in the river; though the guide will also add that the window in question was certainly constructed six centuries later. At any rate, although the duke would not make such a lowly woman his bride, he took her as his favourite. Arlette and Duke Robert were but seventeen years old when they met. With great pomp she was brought into his château, and at Falaise their bastard son was born. William grew proud of the description, so much so that he even signed himself *le Bâtard*.

The bastard succeeded his father as duke aged only seven, and with the aid of strong protectors and his own native cunning (not to mention a remarkable mixture of brutality and magnanimity) managed to establish himself as one of the most powerful rulers in Europe.

In the year 1066 an English monk recorded in the *Anglo-Saxon Chronicle* William's greatest exploit:

Count William came from Normandy into Pevensey on the eve of Michaelmas, and as soon as his men were able they constructed a fortification at the market of Hastings. This was told to King Harold and he then collected a large army and met William at the old apple tree, and William came upon him unexpectedly before his army was drawn up. Nevertheless, the king fought very hard with him together with the men who would stand by him, and there were many slain on either side. King Harold was killed there, and Earl Leofwine his brother, and Earl Gyrth his brother, and many good men, and the Frenchmen had possession of the field, as God granted them for the people's sins.

So William the Bastard of Normandy became King William the Conqueror of England, crowned in Westminster Abbey on Christmas Day 1066.

Yet his feat in that year was but one of a series of astounding conquests by his remarkable race. By the time he reached England, the Normans had already invaded and conquered both southern Italy and Sicily in the teeth of formidable opposition. In 1053, when Pope Leo IX allied himself with those Italians who resented their incursions, he had the misfortune to stand on the city walls of Civitate and watch his army routed by these Northmen.

The Normans were soon reconciled with the papacy. Before invading England, Duke William obtained not only the Pope's blessing but also a gift of several relics, as a sign of divine help, and a papal banner for his standard. Later Pope Gregory VII, who had encouraged his predecessor Leo IX to oppose Norman pretensions in Italy, was obliged to rely on the Normans for his own personal safety; for when the Emperor Frederick II invaded Italy and captured Rome, the Normans rescued the Pope. Today Gregory lies buried in their cathedral at Salerno.

Finally in November 1095, when Pope Urban II launched the first crusade, William the Conqueror's eldest son, Robert 'Curthose', Duke of Normandy, responded with an army that included perhaps a thousand knights; and the Italian Normans brought another army led by Bohemond of Taranto. When the city of Jerusalem fell to the crusaders four years later, Bohemond's nephew, Tancred of Hauteville, was one of the first to storm the walls. Meanwhile, on his way from Italy to Jerusalem, Bohemond himself had set up another Norman realm at Antioch.

Today Bayeux in Normandy offers the most delightful way of appreciating the military prowess of the Normans. There in the former Grand Séminaire, a splendid seventeenth-century building now known as the Centre Guillaume le Conquérant, hangs the so-called Bayeux Tapestry, which is not really a tapestry at all, but eight strips of embroidered linen around fifty centimetres (twenty inches) high, joined together to make a continuous strip nearly seventy metres (231 feet) long and telling the story of the Norman conquest of England.

Almost certainly embroidered in England scarcely fifteen years after the conquest itself, its first scene depicts Edward the Confessor, King of England, and his wife Emma, who was herself a Norman, daughter of Duke Richard I. Since he was childless, he needed to nominate an heir. William the Bastard of Normandy claimed that he was this nominee. His rival Harold, son of the Earl of Wessex, also claimed to have been nominated by Edward. Unfortunately for Harold, as the Bayeux Tapestry depicts, he set sail for Normandy where he was captured by Guy, Count of Ponthieu, who took him to the palace of Duke William.

Harold accompanies William on an expedition to Brittany, where they attack and conquer the troops of Conan of Dol, who surrenders to William the keys of Dinan. Then Harold is shown at Bayeux swearing an oath to William, before being allowed to set sail back to England. The Norman chroniclers affirm that such a visit to Normandy was made by Harold on Edward the Confessor's insistence, to confirm that William was the true heir to the English throne. None the less the Bayeux Tapestry shows Harold, immediately Edward the Confessor is dead and buried, crowned and on the English throne.

Harold was in fact crowned with haste on 6 January 1066 on the very day of his predecessor's funeral, and in Westminster Abbey where Edward was buried. The Bayeux Tapestry depicts events moving swiftly to bring about Harold's doom. A ship speeds to Normandy to report the news of the coronation to William, who, aided by his half-brothers Bishop Odo of Bayeux and Count Robert of Mortain, raises an army and constructs a fleet. On 27 September the winds were favourable at Saint-Valéry-sur-Somme, and the duke's fleet sailed for England.

Whoever designed the Bayeux Tapestry clearly relished the blood-thirsty slaughter involved in the subsequent battle. At the top and bottom of the scenes are margins frequently used to illustrate episodes from Aesop's fables: the envious fox; the sheep and the goat hunting alongside the lion; a crane removing a bone from the throat of a wolf, and so on – with occasional scenes of naked men and women making advances to each other. One curious scene that no one has yet satisfactorily explained shows a clergyman hitting a woman named Aelfgyva on the face. In the margin below crouches an explicitly naked male figure which, writes an expert on the tapestry, David M. Wilson of the British Museum, 'perhaps suggests a sexual subject'. (Perhaps!)

But now in the battle scenes the carnage spreads into this lower margin too. Men are decapitated or cut in two, horses tumble. Harold's brothers, Gyrth and Leofwine, are slain. Finally Harold himself falls, an arrow through his eye, and a Norman knight slices into his leg with a sword. The Bayeux Tapestry ends with the Normans on horseback pursuing the fleeing English.

A grisly parallel exists between the events surrounding William the Conqueror's own death at Rouen in 1087 and the scenes in the lower margin of the tapestry which depict the dead being stripped of their armour. In 1087 William's servants stripped his dead body and left it to fester for several days, before bringing the putrefying corpse to Saint Étienne, Caen. In the church itself the burial was delayed when a citizen who claimed that the grave was his had to be paid off. Finally the hole was found to be too narrow for the gross body, which exploded as the monks were trying to push the pungent remains of their former duke into his grave.

By contrast with this grotesque occasion the Bayeux Tapestry depicts William at his greatest. In one celebrated scene some of his followers are beginning to flee, supposing him dead, until William raises his helmet, crying (as the chronicler William of Poitiers records), 'Look at me. I still live, and with God's help shall conquer.' The whole is depicted in warm colours – green, terracotta, gold and blue. Above all, the artists of the tapestry relished depicting horses. As R. H. C. Davis has written:

In the eleventh century the most important element in any army was its knights, and the essence of a knight was that he fought on horseback. Consequently the most important item of his equipment was a horse. It had to be a horse of a very special sort. A draught horse would have been too cumbersome, and a palfry unable to bear the weight of the knight's armour. What was needed was a horse which was specially bred for strength and speed, which could manoeuvre easily, and which was trained not to panic in battle. Such a horse was called a destrier, apparently because it was led by the squire with his right hand, and was enormously expensive, about three times the cost of a palfrey.

So, as Professor Davis observes, with great pride and joy the artists of the Bayeux Tapestry depict horses galloping, horses tossing their heads, horses enjoying the sea trip, horses disembarking at Pevensey, Duke William's extremely virile Andalusian charger and, of course, horses in battle. In its seventy-two scenes appear no fewer than 202 of these superb animals, as well as fifty-five dogs, 505 other animals, forty-one ships and 623 human beings.

As well as being such superb fighters, the Normans were splendid builders and soon became possessed of a deep Christian spirituality. Throughout their realms their legacy can still be seen, both in churches and castles that have survived virtually unchanged: in Normandy itself, among much else, William the Conqueror's own castle at Falaise and the abbey church of Saint Étienne which he founded at Caen; in England, Durham and Norwich cathedrals, Pevensey castle and the Tower of London; in Sicily, the monastery of Monreale, the Norman palace at Palermo and Cefalù cathedral, with its remarkable apse mosaic depicting Christ in majesty; in Calabria, the still-impressive castle at San Marco Argentano; Trani cathedral, Saint Nicholas, Bari, and the shrine of St Michael the Archangel at Monte Sant'Angelo, all in Apulia; the two superb castles of Marquab and Crac des Chevaliers in Antioch, as well as the scarcely less impressive ruins at Bahgras, Bakas-Shoghr and Sahyum.

The tremendous impact made by these Normans tends to obscure the fact that their province existed long before their fearsome ships sailed up the Seine. Archaeologists have discovered that the valleys of the Seine and the Eure were inhabited in Stone Age times. At Ifs (some eight kilometres from Caen on the road to Falaise, and then reached to the right by the D235) you can see an early Iron Age necropolis. Drive or cycle on towards Falaise and at Lorguichon turn right along the D41 to reach Fontenay-le-Marmion for a guided tour of two yet finer prehistoric sites, the tumuli known as la Hogue and la Hoguette, evidence that Normandy possessed a sophisticated civilization 3,600 years before its invasion by Julius Caesar in 56 BC.

Numerous *oppida* dating back to the neolithic age dot the Norman countryside: at Limes near Dieppe, for example, at Caudebec-en-Caux, at Saint-Jean-de-Savigny eleven kilometres north-east of Saint-Lô and at Canada above Fécamp. A number of them, situated beside the Seine, clearly indicate a long-held desire to control the river passage. Later they were to offer a formidable resistance to Julius Caesar's legions.

When Julius Caesar's lieutenant Sabinius conquered Gaul, Normandy became part of the Roman Empire. At that time several Celtic Gaulish tribes lived here, some of whose names pleasingly survive in the present districts of the region. Caesar himself recorded that in Cotentin lived the Unelli, that the Caux district was the home of the Caleti, that the Vexin housed the Veliocassi and that the Lieuvin was inhabited by a tribe called the Lexovii. The Romans brought prosperity, and this prosperity enabled fine cities to be built, including Rouen (which the Romans called *Rotoma-gus*), Évreux (*Mediolanum*), Bayeux (*Augustodorum*), Avranches (*Abricates*) and Lillebonne (*Juliabona*).

Lillebonne, the chief town of the Caleti, lies four kilometres from the Seine and is today a centre for the petrochemical industry; but it also retains the most important Roman remains in Normandy – baths, an aqueduct, a forum and above all its splendid first- and second-century AD amphitheatre, a semi-ellipse whose axes measure eighty and 110 metres. (Its archaeological museum displays even older remains, both prehistoric and Gallo-Roman.) In the museum at Évreux you can see two splendid Roman bronzes, of Apollo and Jupiter, both discovered at Vieil-Évreux in 1840. The amphitheatre of Vieil-Évreux, still discernible in the village, seated 20,000 spectators.

Christianity came to the region in the third century AD, brought by St Mello (the first Bishop of Rouen around the year 260) and St Vitricius. Other pioneers of the faith in Normandy included St Floscel, martyred at Bayeux during the persecutions of the Emperor Maximin, and Saints Maxime and Vénérand, martyred at Acquiny in the mid-fourth century.

The legendary St Taurin founded the bishopric of Évreux in the fourth century, and his simple tomb survives in the crypt of his much rebuilt church. Among his exploits was a hand-to-hand combat with the devil himself, who had been bashing down the walls of this church. The redoubtable saint is said to have torn off one of the devil's horns, which was preserved at Évreux cathedral until the end of the eighteenth century. The faithful would place it to their ears and are said to have heard a melancholy demonic cry, 'Taurin, Taurin, give me back my horn.'

It has to be admitted that these bones may well not be precisely those of St Taurin. They were exhumed around the year 600 by St Landulf, one of his successors as Bishop of Évreux. The hagiographers record that long before he became bishop, Landulf had heard heavenly voices informing him of the whereabouts of Taurin's bones. On Landulf's consecration as bishop, a supernatural ray lit the precise spot where Taurin lay buried, and the new bishop promptly built a church over his predecessor's tomb.

In the century after St Taurin's mission the spread of Christianity was fostered by the Franks, who controlled the region after the year 486 and included it in the Merovingian Empire after Normandy was conquered by King Clovis. The organizational skills of these Christians equalled those later displayed by the Normans. Normandy was divided into seven dioceses, based on Rouen, Bayeux, Lisieux, Avranches, Coutances, Évreux and Sées – cities which retain their importance and beauty to this day.

These Christians also founded great abbeys, in particular those at Fontenelle founded by St Wandrille in 649, Rouen founded by St Ouen in 649, Jumièges founded by St Philibert in 654 and le Mont-Saint-Michel which St Aubert founded on a pagan site in 708. Then the Carolingians took the region in 751 and held it for two centuries. And these monarchs supported the Church. St Remy, the son of Charles Martel, became Archbishop of Rouen in the mid-eighth century; and the region prospered.

Perhaps the most charming of these abbeys is that situated in the Fontenelle valley and now known as Saint-Wandrille – an exquisite spot, not least because it still houses monks. Saint-Wandrille abbey lies three kilometres east of Caudebec-en-Caux (which is itself due east of Le Havre by way of Lillebonne), and opens to visitors between 10.00 and 12.00 and between 15.00 and 16.00. Nothing of the original foundation remains, for invading Northmen destroyed it before their conversion to Christianity (when they rebuilt it). Only then did the monastery take the name of its founder, who had been inspired by the Irish monasticism of St Columban, whom he had met at Bobbio in Italy.

The exquisite thirteenth-century abbey church of St Peter fell into romantic ruins when the monks were dispossessed at the time of the French Revolution, and it remains a ruin today, impressive and peaceful, with a choir of seventeen chapels and a magnificent seventeenth-century north doorway. When a new community was established here in 1931 the monks not only restored the twelfth-century refectory and the cloisters, which had begun in the fourteenth century and finished in the sixteenth; astonishingly, they also carefully demolished a thirteenth-century tithe barn at Canteloup and transported it, stone by carefully marked stone, for fifty kilometres or so to serve as their new church at Saint-Wandrille.

St Wandrille himself enriched his foundation with relics of another saint, Saturnin, the martyr of Toulouse. In the tenth century a new church was built over Saturnin's shrine, and you can reach it on foot in a ten-minute walk by following the Fontenelle valley in the direction of Rançon and then turning right along the abbey precincts.

An even more impressive ruin, the abbey of Jumièges, was not far away. Take the D982 east from Caudebec-en-Caux. The road, which passes through Le Trait (where you see a sixteenth-century church) and Yainville (with an even better Romanesque church), soon swings south following the loop of the Seine to reach the village of Jumièges. Here in the seventeenth-century château once lived the abbots of Jumièges.

A Viking named Oskar plundered and set fire to the first abbey after a raid on Rouen in 841. Abbot Thierry began building the new church in 1020. During the Wars of Religion the Huguenots sacked it, yet the secluded ruin remains one of the most moving monastic sites in Normandy. When Agnès Sorel, lover of King Charles VII and France's first official royal mistress, died in 1450 (possibly poisoned by the financier Jacques Coeur, who resented her influence on the king) she and the king were visiting the abbey. Her heart was buried here in the north transept. Legend has it that as a punishment two sons of Clovis, who rebelled against the authority of their mother while he was away in the Holy Land, were hamstrung and spent the rest of their days here. Their alleged stone tomb (the so-called tombeau des Énervés in the abbey museum) is more likely to be that of the Duke of Bavaria and his son Tassillon, whom Charlemagne captured and made monks of Jumièges.

The whole region is replete with such legends. Not far away St Philibert is said to have founded a convent for the holy women who used to wash the linen of the monks of Jumièges. One of the abbesses, St Austreberthe, trained a donkey to bring unaccompanied the dirty washing to her laundry. One day no donkey arrived. St Austreberthe went to look for it in the forest and found only bloodstained linen. Suddenly a chastened wolf appeared, knelt at her feet and confessed to killing the donkey. The resourceful abbess then trained him to take the donkey's place, and he in his turn transported the monks' washing back and forth for the rest of his life. At Jumièges no monks pray or soil linen today, but the ruined church, the remains of the twelfth-century chapter house and the other abbey buildings can be visited from 09.00 to noon and from 14.00 to 18.00

between April and September, opening one hour later and closing two hours earlier in the other months of the year.

Normandy prospered again once the Northmen had finished plundering the land and taken it over as their own. These Vikings (a word derived either from *vikingr*, which means pirate, *vising* or mariner, or else *vîk*, meaning bay), had begun ravaging the coast of France as part of a general depredation of Europe by pagan pirates from Iceland, Denmark and Norway which began in the eighth century. To these pirates the Seine was a vulnerable artery into France, and in 820 thirteen of their ships (or *dakkars*) first appeared at its estuary. On their next sortie into France the Seine's river guards, a force which had been set up by Charlemagne, killed five Vikings. But the raiders soon became more formidable and resourceful. In 851 for the first time they managed to stay in France for a whole winter, arriving by way of the Seine on 13 October and not leaving till 5 June the following year. They achieved the same feat the next winter, after which the monastic chronicles which relate these alarming facts peter out. Living on the banks of the Seine had become too dangerous for the monks.

Between 856 and 861, and then for the six years after 885, when they captured Rouen, the Northmen made raids and long expeditions up the river. In between times they were attempting the conquest of England, and tried again in the 890s. Failing to conquer the English, the Normans returned to the Seine, and in 911 at the treaty of Saint-Clair-sur-Epte the king of the Franks, Charles the Simple, ceded a large part of upper Normandy to a Viking leader named Rollo. Rollo took as his bride the king's daughter and, legend has it, arrogantly swore fealty to Charles, not by bowing his head but by raising the king's foot to his lips. His territory became known as the land of the Northmen, Northmannia and thus eventually Normandy.

Initially Rollo and his followers possessed only the dioceses of Évreux, Rouen and Lisieux. Taking advantage of Charles the Simple's problems with Raoul of Burgundy, Rollo summoned more Northmen from Scandinavia and these invaders speedily extended his territory, taking in most of lower Normandy between 933 and 944. With scant regard for the rights of those already living in these areas, the land was parcelled out between the new colonizers.

As we have already seen at Saint-Wandrille and at Jumièges, these pagan invaders at first destroyed most of the exquisite Christian monuments that they discovered in France. At Bayeux in 844 they martyred Bishop Sulpicius and did the same with his successor Bishop Baltfrid in 858. By the mid-tenth century, however, many of them had been converted to Christianity, and as reparation built some of the superb Christian monuments that today so embellish Normandy. Again at

Bayeux, for instance, Bishop Hugh, who reigned from 1015 to 1059, restored his cathedral and combatted paganism in his diocese by building village churches. Soon the Normans were using some of the booty derived from their campaigns to enrich the Church, and by the time of William the Bastard, his half-brother, the warlike Bishop Odo, was busily promoting religious reform throughout the dukedom.

Soon too the Normans were speaking French – although Scandinavian elements have survived, especially in Norman place-names. As you drive through Normandy today, indulge in a little etymology. *Tot*, for example, means field or land, and survives in such spots as Victot in the pays d'Auge, which today boasts an exquisite Renaissance château, Yvetot which Rollo gave to his Swedish ally Yvar, the nearby delicious village of Autretot, Critot where the Normans built a twelfth-century church and Valletot-sur-Mer on the coast between Dieppe and Le Havre. *Bec* derives from the Scandinavian word for a stream, and in Normandy it is preserved in the name of the celebrated abbey of Bec-Hellouin, at Bec-de-Mortagne where the medieval church nestles by the river of Ganzeville, in the forest-clad Caudebec-en-Caux which we have already visited, and at Caudebec-lès-Elbeuf near the place where Robert the Magnificent is thought to have communed with the devil. Again, *Torp* in Scandinavian means hamlet, a word paralleled in our English 'thorpe'. So the name of the village of Le Torps, for example, situated among splendid châteaux and massive farmhouses (known in Normandy as *manoir-fermes*) just west of the N158 between Calais and Falaise, indicates that the Scandinavians had settled here long before these impressive Renaissance and classical buildings were created.

The Norman dialect, followed by the French language itself, also took in other Scandinavian words. Fascinatingly, a good number of these relate either to the sea or to how you divide up conquered territories – *marsouin*, the French noun for a marine or a porpoise; *acre*, which is Scandinavian for a measure of land; *hogue* meaning mound or hillock; *mielle* which means dune; *hâ* for a dogfish; *quille* meaning keel; *cingler* in its sense of setting sail for a place; *bâbord*, the port-side of a ship; *tribord* for starboard; *aiguiller*, the Scandinavian verb to steer which now simply means to direct; *namp*, another measure of land.

Duke Rollo died in 927, as much a Frenchman as a Viking. His successor, William Longsword, was his son – though not by his marriage to the daughter of Charles the Simple. 'Longue-Épee' did homage both to Raoul of Burgundy and to the Carolingian King Louis IV d'Outremer. On 17 December 942 the Duke of Flanders assassinated him. His successor, Duke Richard I, was still a minor but soon learned the arts of combining with the King of France's enemies in order to enhance his own power. When King Louis IV made an expedition into Normandy, he was captured by the citizens of Rouen, who passed their prisoner into the care of Duke Hugh the Great. In 958 Richard I made a politic marriage with Hugh the Great's daughter.

Life remained as precarious for these magnates as it had proved for King Louis IV d'Outremer. Let me offer a brisk canter through such perils. When Richard I's son (also named Richard) succeeded his father in 906, a peasants' insurrection had to be put down. Such troubles paled beside the mutual hostility of Norman magnates. Richard II's successor, Duke Richard III, was almost certainly poisoned in 1027 by his brother and own successor Robert the Devil. Duke Robert the Devil was wise enough to support the French king, Henry I, against a royal brother who was attempting to usurp the throne in 1031, and as reward the Normans received Pontoise and the territory known as the Vexin. A ruthless quest for land and possessions obsessed them all. The tanner's daughter Arlette, on the night she bore him William the Bastard, is said in later legend to have declared, 'I dreamt that there grew from my womb a great tree which extended its branches so high and so wide that they shaded on one side Normandy and on the other the whole kingdom of England.'

In 1035 Robert the Devil died on a pilgrimage to Jerusalem, leaving his bastard son in the titular care of the king. In fact William spent much of his youth caring for his own safety, successfully escaping the daggers of his numerous enemies. Many of the young duke's rebellious vassals resented the Christian faith which Rollo and his successor had embraced. William is said to have fled by night from the castle at Falaise covered in the blood of his tutor Osbern, who slept in the same room and had been erroneously stabbed to death in William's place. He hid in forests and among peasants. Finally at the age of twenty he successfully solicited the king's help. Henry I's troops fought alongside William's Normans, defeating the insurgents at Val-des-Dunes near Caen in 1047. Thus began the training in war of one of the finest military leaders of the age.

William now devoted himself to enforcing his authority throughout his Norman territories and to centralizing the government. These Norman rulers were as superb at administration as at warfare. As the American scholar C. H. Haskins has described (inevitably simplifying the complex structures of our sophisticated past), in Normandy in the eleventh and twelfth centuries there were three classes:

those who fought, those who laboured and those who prayed, corresponding respectively to the nobles, the peasants and the clergy. Created by the simple needs of the feudal age, this primitive division of labour was even declared of divine origin and necessary to the harmonious life of man. It seemed right and natural that the nobles should defend the country and maintain order, the clergy lead men to salvation, the peasants support by their labour these two beneficent classes, as well as themselves.

C. H. Haskins observed that as an ideal this class system was open to obvious objections, 'not the least of which was the persistent killing and plundering of the peasants by the class whose function it was to protect and defend them'. Nevertheless, apart from a few sporadic uprisings, this peasant class had no choice but to accept meekly the powerful social system of medieval Normandy.

The duke ruled them all; it was a daunting task. According to the Norman poet Wace, on his death-bed William the Conqueror was to describe his subjects as brave, valiant, proud and boastful, fond of good cheer, extremely difficult to control and needing to be kept resolutely underfoot. To this end he did his best to keep his alliances secure, supporting the king against Geoffrey Martel, Count of Anjou. Together he and the king besieged Mouliherne. Then Geoffrey Martel took Alençon and William captured it back, along with Domfront.

In 1054 the future Conqueror married Mathilde, the daughter of Count Baldwin V of Flanders. She is said to have objected with the words, 'I should rather take the veil than marry a bastard.' William is reputed to have ridden to Lille and beaten her, which apparently changed her mind. The Pope also objected that the two were too closely related to be allowed to marry. When the monk Lanfranc pleaded William's cause at Rome, the Pope also changed his mind, on condition that William and Mathilde each build an abbey at Caen, the first (St Étienne) for men, the second (la Trinité) for women. These two memorials remain in all their splendour. The Abbaye-aux-Hommes, founded by William in 1065, was consecrated eleven years later with Lanfranc as its first abbot. Mathilde's Abbaye-aux-Dames, which took only six years to complete, was consecrated on 18 June 1066 when William was already preparing for his conquest of England.

Lanfranc's entry into this story indicates again the extraordinarily complex nature of the Norman character, and especially the genius of William the Bastard, for William's successor could not cope with the monk who had legitimized his father's marriage. Just as in the first half of the twelfth century the court of the Italian Norman ruler, Roger II, included a distinguished Arab geographer named al-Edrisi, so the wild William the Conqueror – who in a rage could put out the eyes of a humble messenger bringing bad news – also patronized one of the most sophisticated intellects of his era, the Italian monk Lanfranc.

Most churchmen fell foul of these Norman dukes, just as they frequently fell out with themselves. Lanfranc was no exception. Born at Pavia in the early years of the eleventh century, he studied civil law in his native city before entering the celebrated school of Berengarius at Tours. A brilliant dialectician, he set up his own school at Avranches in 1039, but suddenly renounced this career to become a disciple of Abbot Herluin, an inspired Benedictine who in 1034 had founded the monastery of le Bec-Hellouin in Normandy.

Lanfranc had become prior of the monastery by the time he was interceding with Pope Nicholas II on behalf of William the Bastard's consanguinous marriage. His inclinations as a teacher could not be suppressed, and at the school he started at Bec-Hellouin he taught some of the most distinguished prelates of the Norman age: as youths Pope Alexander II, Bishop Ivo of Chartres and above all St Anselm of Canterbury all sat at his feet.

His scholarly writings were revolutionary for their time. Commenting on the letters of St Paul, he insisted that a profound study of the text was necessary before the student could indulge in theological speculation. This belief was the legacy of his tutor Berengarius of Tours; but when Berengarius disputed the traditional views about the presence of the body and blood of Jesus in the Christian Eucharist, Lanfranc was ready to oppose him.

Lanfranc had no desire to become Archbishop of Canterbury, but the Pope insisted and in August 1070 he was consecrated. To his English Christians he brought a new insistence on the importance of an unmarried clergy, a fresh impetus to English monasteries and a defence of the ecclesiastical over the civil courts – all policies dear to the heart of the reforming Pope Gregory VII. Lanfranc also asserted the Archbishop of Canterbury's superiority over his fellow Archbishop of York.

After Lanfranc left France for Canterbury another brilliant Italian monk, St Anselm, became prior of Bec in his place. Abbot Herluin died in 1078 and Anselm was elected abbot, only to be forced to accept the Archbishopric of Canterbury fifteen years later, in spite of both his own reluctance and the opposition of his fellow monks in Normandy. In his later years Lanfranc had run foul of King William Rufus. So did his successor at Canterbury. The Norman king's insistence on interfering in the rights of the English Church now meant that Anselm spent many years in exile from his archbishopric.

William Rufus had deliberately left the episcopal see of Canterbury vacant for four years so as to appropriate its revenues. Only a serious illness led him to reconsider this policy of greed and appoint Anselm in 1093, another factor in Anselm's reluctance to accept the high office. The quarrel between the king and archbishop-elect was soon aggravated. William Rufus denied Anselm the privilege of visiting Rome to receive his archbishop's pallium from the Pope, on the grounds that Urban II had not been recognized in his office by the English. In 1095 Anselm called together a council of bishops and nobles to decide on the issue between himself and the king. They met at Rockingham, and the bishops proved more craven than the nobility, siding with William Rufus against their archbishop-elect. Only the support of the nobles prevented Anselm's instant removal from office.

Ultimately William Rufus was not strong enough to persist in his refusal to acknowledge Urban II as papal representative in England; but he none the less insisted that he himself must confer the pallium on his Archbishop of Canterbury. Rather than submit, Anselm left for Rome. He still hoped for a reconciliation with the king, pleading successfully at the council of Bari against a proposal to excommunicate William Rufus.

Anselm returned to France under the protection of the Archbishop of Lyons, and there in August 1100 learned that William Rufus had been killed in a hunting accident. The king's successor Henry I instantly invited Anselm back to England – but on condition that Anselm take an oath of allegiance. Anselm refused and spent another three years in exile. Only in 1106, thirteen years after his appointment as archbishop, did he return to England. The deal was this: Anselm agreed to consecrate bishops who had taken an oath of allegiance to Henry I, while the king gave up his own claims to invest the archbishop in his office. Alas, Anselm discovered that in his years of exile the Archbishop of York had revived those claims of equal status with Canterbury which Lanfranc had so vigorously contested.

Yet Anselm's years of exile were extraordinarily fruitful. He used the time to write a permanent masterpiece of Christian philosophy, *Cur Deus Homo?*, an attempt to answer the question why God should feel obliged to become man in the person of Jesus. And his disagreements with William Rufus only serve to emphasize the stature of the Conqueror in generously patronizing such men. St Anselm penned brilliant, godly and learned treatises on the Virgin Birth of Jesus (Anselm did not himself accept that Jesus's mother was born of a virgin too), on human free will, on the meaning of truth, on the nature of angels and so on, all treating traditional Christian subjects – but with a rigour yet more revolutionary than that of Anselm's tutor Lanfranc, for Anselm hoped (in vain?) to prove Christian truths by reason alone.

Anselm also invented the so-called 'ontological argument' for the existence of God, which I do not accept (though perhaps I should accept it if I understood it). As for his charming as well as austerely monastic character, we can still discern this in some 375 letters he wrote, which have survived to this day, as well as in three meditations and nineteen prayers composed by the saint – musings and desires through which we can look back 900 years into the mind of an Italian-Norman saint.

Small wonder with such predecessors that brilliant scholars proliferated in Normandy. The province even boasts the founder of modern mathematics and science, a bishop of Lisieux who was consecrated in 1378. Born in Normandy around the year 1320, Nicholas of Oresme became successively a theology student in Paris, grand master of the Collège de Navarre, canon and then dean of Rouen cathedral, chaplain to King Charles V and finally Bishop of Lisieux, where he died in 1382. The King of France commissioned him to translate works by Aristotle. He was also a resolute opponent of astrology.

His most innovative works extraordinarily foreshadow modern science. In his *Livre du ciel et du monde* and his *Traité de la sphère* Nicholas of Oresme insisted that God could well have created far more than one universe, and that the earth might more plausibly be considered to rotate rather than the heavens rotate around it. In addition he contributed to mathematics the concept of fractions and the rules by which they operate. He used graphs and algebra in a fashion that anticipates analytical geometry. Not content with all this, he wrote a treatise called *De origine, natura, jure, et mutationibus monetarum*, which for the first time in written history scientifically analysed the role of money. I understand Nicholas of Oresme's scientific treatises even less than I understand the theological writings of St Anselm.

Lanfranc's abbey church of St Étienne at Caen, especially its massive west front and the great austere nave, remains (in spite of a few later modifications and the addition of its spires) a major example of Norman art. As we have seen, William was buried here, and his wife lies in her Abbaye-aux-Dames. The Huguenots profaned the grave in 1562 during the Wars of Religion, and at the time of the Revolution most of what remained of him was thrown to the winds. In 1984 the tomb was again opened, more reverently this time, and a tibia was found – a bone of great size, confirming that William the Conqueror had been a man of unusually fine physique. On 9 September 1987, exactly 900 years after he fell mortally wounded in battle, a new tombstone was dedicated over William's grave.

Small wonder that not long after William the Bastard married Mathilde of Flanders, the King of France became increasingly alarmed at this giant duke's growing political strength and ambitions. The monarch gave his support to a revolt against William by the Counts of Eu and Montreuil. William defeated the rebels. Then in 1058 Henry I joined Geoffrey Martel in invading Normandy. William's troops beat them at the ford of Varaville. And William forced the Count of Maine, sometime vassal of Geoffrey Martel, to do him homage, to promise to marry one of William's daughters and to offer the hand of his own daughter to William's son Robert Curthose.

New problems soon arose. When the Count of Maine died in 1063, his subjects turned against the Norman duke, choosing as their new lord Walter of Mantes, who was Count of Vexin. It took William but one campaign to reclaim Maine. By now Normandy had reached more or less its present dimensions, which today comprise five *départements* set up at the time of the French Revolution, namely Eure, Manche, Seine-Maritime, Calvados and Orne. Three years later Duke William called together his barons and prelates in conference at the château of Lillebonne (where a plaque marks the occasion), persuading them to join him in his expedition to England, offering booty and English lands as reward. Bishop Odo of Conteville was the first to offer his support, promising 100 ships. The rest followed suit, and the Bastard's army and fleet successfully invaded England.

Now even his superb military talents failed him. His son Robert Curthose claimed Normandy and, aided by King Philippe I of France, defeated William in 1079 at the battle of Gerberoi. When William died his second son, William Rufus, became King of England, but Robert Curthose kept Normandy and Maine. By this time the English kings were determined to take back their duchy. William Rufus tried to reconquer it and failed in 1091. Five years later Robert set off on a crusade, pledging the duchy to his brother for 10,000 *livres*. He returned to find William Rufus dead and another brother, Henry Beauclerc, now Henry I of England and equally determined to win back Normandy, which he did by defeating Robert at Tinchebray in 1106 and keeping him prisoner till his death twenty-eight years later.

After the battle of Tinchebray Normandy remained united with England for ninety-eight years, save for a brief moment after Henry's own death in 1135. Orderic Vitalis's *Historia ecclesiastica* asserts that Henry had ruled his realms wisely and generously, protective both of the common folk and the Church. Soon Normandy was part of the great Angevin empire, which stretched from England into Aquitaine.

Henry Plantagenet, who became Henry II of England in 1154, was already not only Duke of Normandy but Count of Anjou and Duke of Aquitaine as well. His huge empire enormously threatened the French kings, but was ultimately unsustainable by the English monarchs. In 1204 King John, known as Lackland, lost the Norman part of this empire to the French king, Philippe Auguste II. It was an historic year for France, since the French monarchy now set about remodelling their kingdom along the far superior lines of Normandy. The English, however, were far from content to lose their Norman duchy. Yet slowly the French weakened the hold of the English. By the Treaty of Paris agreed between Louis IX of France and Henry III of England in 1259, Henry retained in continental Europe only Guyenne, paying homage to the French king and, more importantly for our story, relinquishing the duchy of Normandy.

Hostilities between England and France did not cease, and the Normans inevitably were involved in them. Norman and English ships fought briefly in 1293, setting off a struggle between the two nations –

with rebellious vassals of the French king frequently siding with his enemy – that was only resolved by the intervention of Pope Boniface VIII four years later. In 1381, in a show of independence, the city of Rouen rose up against the officials of Charles VI and set up in his stead a cloth merchant as their king. Only when Charles himself led troops against them was the insurrection suppressed.

Problems and rivalries were made more complex by the fact that the English kings were in truth also Frenchmen. In 1346 Edward III of England, grandson of the French king, Philippe le Bel, invaded the duchy of Normandy and went on to defeat the French army at Crécy. The Hundred Years War had begun and saw Normandy once again disputed between England and France. As he progressed from Caen, King Edward had laid waste to the duchy. Three years later the French conceded it to England by the Treaty of London, only to receive Normandy back one year later under the terms of the Treaty of Brétigny. Thenceforth they ruled most (though not all) of the duchy, until Henry V invaded in 1415.

On 10 August 1415 the English once again appeared on the estuary of the Seine when Henry V landed at Le Chef-de-Caux. His troops proceeded to take Harfleur before marching into Picardy, where they ruthlessly defeated a French army at Agincourt. Two years later Henry was back in Normandy with the intention of totally subjugating the duchy. With scarcely a struggle Caen, Alençon and Évreux were taken. Within five months Rouen was his, as were the whole of the Vexin region and the pays de Caux. Soon France was effectively controlled by three rulers, the dauphin, the Duke of Burgundy and the King of England, the last virtually supreme throughout Normandy and Guyenne.

The English in 1415 had conquered the army of the French king by means of a force of 60,000 men. Even so, Rouen held out from 28 July 1418 until 13 January 1419 – almost six months – and le Mont-Saint-Michel never surrendered. Henry V deemed it wise to entrust the rule of turbulent Normandy to a specially appointed council and built the fortified city of Granville to watch over it. Normandy was then declared English in 1420 by the Treaty of Troyes.

English rule lasted no more than thirty years. Twenty years after the battle of Agincourt the district of Caux was in revolt. The knights of le Mont-Saint-Michel took possession of Granville in 1442, and King Charles VII fortified it even further against the English who had built it.

Henry died in 1422, and the Norman territories of his infant son Henry VI were administered by John, Duke of Bedford. During his lifetime English ambitions were to be routed by the influence of a peasant girl, born in Domrémy and subsequently known as the Maid of Orléans or St Joan of Arc. Bedford had made an alliance with Burgundy, into whose hands Joan fell on 23 May 1430. The Burgundians sold her to the English, who one year later burned her to death as a witch and heretic in Normandy's chief city, Rouen, in the place du Vieux-Marché. Yet her spirit and patriotism had set in motion a French recovery which could not be checked.

In spite of (or maybe because of) Joan's martyrdom in 1431, the French reconquered their province, recapturing Rouen in October 1449. Alarmed, the English sent an army into Normandy. Commanded by Thomas Kyriel, it marched across the Cotentin to Bayeux, reaching Formigny on 18 April 1450, where the English were utterly routed by the French under the generalship of the Count of Clermont and the Conné-table de Richemont. Today if you drive along the *route nationale* 13 from Formigny along the valley formed by a little tributary of the River Aure you will reach the tiny chapel of St Louis, built by the Count of Clermont in 1486 to commemorate this victory. Inside are inscribed the names of those who distinguished themselves in the battle. Three hundred metres further on, to the right at the top of the slope, is an inscription denoting the site of the battlefield.

In the 1440s, helped by François I of Brittany, France began the final reconquest of Normandy. The dauphin, now King Charles VII, entered Rouen in 1449. Early the following year the English made their last sortie into their former duchy. They took Cherbourg and a few towns and castles in the Cotentin, but on 15 April 1450 their tiny army was no match for that of the French at the battle of Formigny. Normandy was at last for ever French (though until 1801 the sovereigns of England insisted that they were also kings of France).

Normandy once again found peace and with it a measure of prosperity. The English had founded a university at Caen; the French monarchy continued to endow it. At Rouen the Norman exchequer became a court of justice, sitting permanently in the Palais de Justice.

Good times do not last for ever. Troubles broke out again in the early sixteenth century when Calvinists preached in Normandy, with a Protestant named François Legay (who called himself Boisnormand) converting many to the Reformed faith at Rouen. Caen opted for the Reformation in 1531. The Wars of Religion which began in 1562 inevitably took their toll here. Rouen declared itself Protestant whereupon the Catholics immediately attacked and took it, placing the city under the control of Duke Alexander Farnese of Parma. In 1572 more than 500 Norman Huguenots were slaughtered here in the massacre of St Bartholomew's Day, and the Catholic League increasingly won back the province to the old religion.

Reading later Norman historians I feel that these slaughtered Protestants have not been given the sympathy due to them, though their own anti-Catholicism could at times be fanatical. Writing about the massacre of Huguenots at Lisieux on St Bartholomew's Day, as well as of the way these Protestants had earlier pillaged the cathedral, the nineteenth-century historian of the diocese, H. de Formeville, fatalistically and lugubriously agreed with Joseph de Maistre's dictum that war is the normal state of humanity. He was also at one with François-René de Chateaubriand's view that in this world the frightening truth is that every being recognizes only the law of the strongest.

Normandy in fact proved a decisive venue for Henri of Navarre's successful campaigns both to keep the throne of France and to protect French Protestants. After the massacre of 1572 he speedily (though temporarily) renounced his own Protestantism and fled with his new wife to Alençon. The city's own clergy and nobility had opted for the Reformed faith, only to be besieged and taken by the Catholics, who in their turn in 1568 successfully withstood the attacks of a force led by the Protestant leader Montgomery. There six years later, having repudiated his renunciation of the Reformed religion, Henri of Navarre put himself at the head of the French Huguenots.

In Normandy he was consistently victorious over the forces of the Catholic League. On 21 September 1589 at Arques-la-Bataille, six kilometres from where the River Varenne joins the River Béthune south of Dieppe, he defeated an army commanded by the Duke of Mayenne (hence the soubriquet 'la-Bataille'). Henri disposed of only 7,000 Protestant troops, as opposed to some 30,000 Catholics commanded by the duke. But he had captured the powerful château which still stands at Arques-la-Bataille. At the climax of the battle the cannons of the château, prevented from firing all morning by a thick mist, opened up and cut huge swathes through Mayenne's army. His surviving cavalry fled, many sinking in the neighbouring swamps as they tried to make their escape to Dieppe. The relief depicting a mounted Henri in the remains of the fifteenth-century château chapel dates from 1845.

Further south Ivry-la-Bataille in the valley of the River Eure similarly derives its own soubriquet 'la-Bataille' from Henri's second victory, on 14 March 1590, over the forces of the League, again commanded by Mayenne. Just over two centuries later Napoleon Bonaparte, having put down the royalist insurrectionists of the region, set up an obelisk seven kilometres north-west of Ivry (at Épieds) exactly marking the battlefield.

Yet Henri failed to take Paris. Three years after his victory at Ivry-la-Bataille he decided, in his famous phrase, that 'Paris was worth a mass' and finally embraced Catholicism. Meanwhile he ensured in the Edict of Nantes that the Huguenots were given complete toleration throughout his realm. Soon however the Capuchins, based at Rouen, at Les Andelys, at Alençon and at Bayeux were winning back Normandy for Catholicism. The seventeenth century saw countless new religious foundations as the Counter-Reformation spread. Trappists brought a new severity to the monastic life, modelling themselves at the abbey of Rancé on the ancient desert fathers. Extremely influential in reviving the monastic life in Normandy was the Benedictine congregation of St Maur – the Maurists – who flourished from 1621 until they were suppressed by the Revolutionaries in 1792. Their last superior-general, Dom Antoine Chevreux, was guillotined along with forty of his monks.

In the meantime nearly every French Benedictine monastery had joined the Maurists: 178 of them by 1675. Superb Maurist scholars published not just editions of the writings of the Church fathers and studies in Benedictine history, but also a virtually unprecedented literary history of France. Again and again as one reads the stories of the monasteries of Normandy the Maurists appear, spearheading a spiritual, architectural and intellectual transformation.

Although the military architect Vauban fortified parts of the northern coast, the English had still not given up their designs on the province, hopeless though these now were. During the Seven Years War, which lasted from 1756 to 1763, they made several abortive attempts to invade, notably when Admiral Anson tried to take Cherbourg in 1759 and the following year when Admiral Rodney bombarded Le Havre.

At the Revolution the two new *départements* of Orne and Manche turned out to be solidly republican. But many Normans, especially the Catholic peasantry, supported the deposed monarchy, even to the extent of taking up arms against the republicans of Paris. When the government introduced conscription, provoking the loyalist and Catholic insurrection of the Vendée in 1793, the peasant insurgents initially found little support here, and a government cannon foundry was set up at Villedieu-les-Poêles to strengthen the defences of the region. But loyalty to the republic was gradually eroded during Robespierre's reign of terror, especially in lower Normandy. The Norman peasants particularly hated paying heavy taxes to support the revolutionary armies. When Robespierre fell on 27 July 1794, the elimination of his allies brought fresh confidence to these parsimonious opponents of the Parisian revolutionaries. In the early months of 1795 bands of *chouans*, a dialect word meaning screech-owls, began gathering in the forests, gradually developing into what virtually amounted to an army. These *chouans* launched impressive operations at Briouze, Flers and la Ferté-Macé before the numerically superior forces of the republic forced them to retreat into the forests.

The vicissitudes of the *Directoire* set up in October 1795 revived the hopes of the Norman royalists and they took up arms again in 1798. More than 2,000 of them besieged Vire; others in the Cotentin and the pays de Caux intrigued with Britain against the Paris government; and their activities throughout the region seriously disturbed the authorities, using up scarce resources of cash and troops.

After Napoleon had toppled the *Directoire* in November 1799 the downfall of the Normandy *chouanerie* was inevitable. The First Consul, as he then became, could not tolerate a situation whereby an army of his royalist enemies had totally occupied a part of France. The *chouans* were brutally put down. Napoleon offered their leaders a safe conduct to Paris, where they were to be brought under the surveillance of no fewer than 1,800 troops commanded by General Chambarlhac de Laubespin. They never left Normandy, but were lined up and shot at Verneuil. Yet their peasant allies continued the struggle, a thorn in the side of Napoleon until the restoration of the French monarchy in 1815.

Napoleon also made some tactical errors, not the least being the appointment as primate of Normandy and Archbishop of Rouen of the brother of Cambacérès, who was Second Consul of France. The archbishop became a cardinal, but few of his subordinates were pleased at the rapid promotion of this placeman. He never commanded their respect, and his enemies – led by Abbé François Clément Dubois, former chaplain to the Carmelites of Dieppe – carried on a persistent campaign of hostility to the French government. Normandy was displaying its customary sturdy crustiness.

After 1815 came a new era of stability, with the railway built between Rouen and Paris in 1843 (extended to Le Havre five years later) contributing to a further burst of prosperity. Bathing resorts became fashionable, the celebrated Mme de Boignes in 1806 commissioning her brother to build the first horse-drawn covered bathing machine to trundle passengers into the sea at Dieppe. In the 1820s the regular elegant visits of the Duchesse de Berry made Dieppe yet more popular. Trouville was discovered by the élite in 1828, with no less a literary genius than Alexandre Dumas in charge of its publicity. In 1862 it was Deauville's turn to rule as the most modish of these resorts.

Meanwhile the political upheavals of the nineteenth century brought the Normans some discomfort. Charles X spent his exile after 1830 at Cherbourg. In 1843 King Louis Philippe ceremoniously met Queen Victoria at Eu and five years later left from Honfleur as an exile. The 1848 revolution saw rioting at Rouen but little else, and Normandy survived virtually unscathed the brief period of German occupation in 1871, at the end of the Franco-Prussian War.

None of this prepared Normandy for her sufferings in our own century. At the beginning of World War I the news of a general mobilization was slow to permeate the region and produced a general feeling of stupefaction, followed by the absurd hope that the war would be over by Christmas. During the conflict Norman military resolve became legendary. In Caen the 1914–18 war memorial in the place Maréchal Foch shows on the one side foot-weary soldiers and on the other a fearsome French cock besting the German eagle. Among its numerous laudatory inscriptions is a celebrated remark by Marshal Foch himself, uttered during the second battle of the Marne in 1918: 'Je suis tranquille, les Normands sont là' ('I am at ease, for the Normans are here'). Naturally too this race of seafarers contributed its sons to the French Navy.

The war industry paradoxically brought cash to the region as its menfolk were squandered on the battlefield. Normandy's first blast furnace went into production at Colombelles in Calvados on 9 August 1917. After 1918 much of this industry was no longer needed (though the iron works at Caen managed to survive by exporting to Britain). The population of the region had already begun to decline – deaths far exceeding births, save in the *département* of Seine-Maritime. Dieppe, inhabited by 231,000 people in 1866, had a population of only 195,000 sixty years later. By 1920 the government had become so anxious that it passed a law condemning contraception, a law which the Normans seem blithely to have disregarded, forcing their supposed rulers to welcome into the region supplementary workers from Flanders, Poland and even Yugoslavia. Yet strenuous efforts were made to reverse the industrial decline. Tourism became a new industry, with work beginning in 1923 on the first motorway between Paris and Deauville.

France capitulated to Hitler in 1940, and Normandy was occupied, waiting for the most massive military invasion of all time. The English had been driven out of Normandy in 1450, never to return until 1944, when they helped to drive out the Germans occupying France during World War II. This, however, was a war of liberation, not of conquest. And these Normandy landings, as well as the reconquest of the region, form the subject of another chapter of this book.

The luscious lie of the land

What makes Normandy a unified province of France? Is it the River Seine? Napoleon Bonaparte once said that 'Paris, Rouen and Le Havre are one city, and the Seine is its high street.' But Normandy is far more than Rouen, Le Havre and the Seine.

In one of her most evocative verses Lucie Delarue-Mardrus, the passionate Norman patriot who also achieved notoriety as a sapphist and a romantic novelist, acknowledged the rich diversity of her part of France:

> Who could deny your splendour, province of my birth,
> O Normandy, ever faithfully delighting my eyes,
> A piece of western France swirled around by the sea,
> A land tamed only by enormous labour!
>
> The hard stones of cathedral and the soft thatch of roof,
> Both over centuries have watched the harvests amass:
> Your cartloads of corn, your little boats of fish,
> Your cattle, succulent enough to feed a whole kingdom.
>
> The rich and peaceful business of your ports,
> Your famous and proud capital city,
> Every aspect of your life deeply rooted in history,
> Just as the roots of your beeches plunge into your earth.
>
> The brusque sea and the pallid, tender Seine,
> Apple trees dwarfed by triumphant steeples,
> So many facets reflected in the depths of your children,
> The hazy yet solid basis of their souls.

Their land today remains as yesterday.
No single labourer on any richly endowed farm
Is not happy and proud if he comes from Normandy stock,
For yours is the thoroughbred of all breeds.

Laud your spring, when the hawthorn blossoms,
Laud your summer crammed with seeds and greenery,
Praise to your yellow autumn when the apples are ripe,
To your bushy and frosty white winter.

'Gentleness and strength,' she continued, characterize Normandy 'where no season is harsh and there is nothing but pure air, fertility, exquisite fruit, fat beasts, noble cities standing alongside lovely waters and personalities that make you sing with joy'. And her poem ends:

Normandy, we love you,
Let your flavoursome accent flourish,
As well as your dense trees, dark against your pale skies,
O mother, rich in grasslands and cathedrals,
You who for ever flow in our blood!

Normandy, the guide books tell you, comprises five French *départements* set up at the time of the French Revolution: Eure, Manche, Seine-Maritime, Calvados and Orne. True enough, but the region is far more complex than this. Rich diversity, as Lucie Delarue-Mardrus's poem indicates, makes an overview of Normandy (as opposed, say, to the Dordogne where I have a home) impossible to sum up in one geographical paragraph, save to say that each region has its own particular succulence and that not one is boring or without exquisite charm. What holds the region all together, I sometimes think, is simply Norman patriotism.

Another factor has helped to create the varied countryside of this proud nation: the extraordinarily variable weather of the province. In Normandy always carry an umbrella in your car. As Émile Zola put it, this part of France offers you 'both superb weather and wild tempests, days when the sun beats down, nights such as make you believe you are in Naples, phosphorescent seas, and every change occurring so brusquely that I have never experienced such swift transformations of the scenery'.

The Normans themselves traditionally divide their own province not into five *départements* but into nine quite disparate regions. Starting at the north-east corner of Normandy, the first of these nine consists of the Bray country (or pays de Bray). Due south of the Bray country lie the Vexin and the plains of the River Eure (or Vexin et plaines de l'Eure). Due west from here is the country of the Auge, the Ouche and Rouen (or pays d'Auge, d'Ouche et du Roumois). North of this region lies the country of Caux (or pays de Caux) and south of it is the southernmost part of Normandy, an inverted triangle known as the Perche. North-west of the Perche you reach the interior Norman farmlands (or bocages normands intérieurs). Sandwiched between the Vexin and this region are the central plains of lower Normandy (the plaines centrales de la Basse-Normandie). North of these interior farmlands you reach the Bessin; and finally a long strip running down the western coast of the province forms the Normandy coastal farmlands (or bocages normands littoraux).

As an initial glimpse of the variety of these regions, consider their all-important farmhouses. In the Vexin and the plains around the River Eure, Normandy farmhouses can be massive, square, usually surrounding a courtyard and adorned with a monumental gateway. Nothing could be more different from these mighty enclosed farmhouses than those of the pays de Caux, which usually spread their many outbuildings amid vast pastures – sometimes scattering themselves over as many as three hectares. The whole ensemble is often planted with cider-orchards and surrounded by a high earth embankment (known as a *fossé*), which is itself surmounted by a double range of elms, oaks and beech trees. Whereas the farmers of the Vexin and the Eure plain build the thick walls of their homes out of chalky rubble and cover their roofs with tiles, most houses in the pays de Caux are half-timbered (apart from in the villages and market towns, where the favoured material is brick), though the major buildings are often stylishly made of flint and stone.

In the pays de Bray, by contrast, a good quarter of the farms date from the second half of the nineteenth century, when their owners needed to rebuild in order to incorporate byres for the growing herds of milch-cows and sties for the numerous pigs. Sturdy, brick-built, impressive, the farms logically adopted a U-shape, made up of a central dwelling house flanked by a couple of wings for the animals.

The Cotentin and the Bessin are regions of fortified seigneurial farms. Old Cotentin farmhouses are recognizably built of 'bluestone', a peculiarity of the schist around Cherbourg. Churches too were frequently tiled with this stone till 1350, when the English took the port and stopped the stone's diffusion throughout Normandy. The Caen plain boasts even greater farmhouses than those of the Cotentin and the Bessin, often some forty to sixty metres wide and sixty to a hundred metres long, invariably surrounding closed courtyards, whereas the farms of the bocage, though still embracing closed courtyards, are far smaller. Finally, in the Perche older farmhouses, which are often still thatched, have semi-closed court-yards, with the longest wall of the house almost always more than double the length of the end wall. Until the nineteenth century, when Perche farmhouses grew much bigger, this end wall was rarely more than eight metres wide.

Gustave Flaubert has his amiable dolts Bouvard and Pécuchet admire one such farm, and he magically evokes its interior as it was 100 years ago. 'All of the farm buildings were contiguous, occupying three sides of the courtyard,' he wrote. 'The bailiff drew their attention to little openings in the sheepfolds, level with the ground, and cunning doors in the pigsties which shut of their own accord. As for the barn, it was vaulted like a cathedral, its brick arches resting on stone walls.' The gem of the whole farm was its cattle shed. 'Wooden bars stretching straight up to the ceiling divided it into two sections, one for the animals, the other for those tending them. As all the shutters were closed, it was difficult to see in the gloom. Tethered by little chains, the oxen were eating, their bodies exhaling a warmth which was pressed down by the low ceiling.'

To the two Parisians the shafts of the cider-press seemed enormous, and the dairy positively astounded them. 'Taps in the corners enabled the slabs to be swilled down. Inside everything was surprisingly cool. Along the windows stood brown jars filled to the brim with milk. The cream was contained in pans made of earthenware. Massive rounds of butter seemed like slices from a copper pillar, and froth bubbled from tin pails which had just been filled and set down.' In the past 100 years farming techniques have inevitably developed here; but Normandy farmhouses still evoke the same wonder.

In exploring here the delights of these nine regions I plan to add leisurely tours, often of little-known towns with hidden gems, as well as some of the architectural masterpieces of the land – its superb churches, exquisite châteaux and majestic ruined abbeys.

Pays de Bray

The first of the regions, the deliciously hilly country known as the pays de Bray which occupies the north-eastern section of Normandy, is enlivened by a deep cleft, the Bray valley. It stretches between two splendid towns, Gourney-en-Bray and Forges-les-Eaux. Since the ground consists either of clay lying on chalk or of yet more infertile soils, this is a region where forestry has assumed singular importance. On either side of the Bray valley rise the forests of Bray, Hellet, Rouvray, the woodlands of l'Abbaye, l'Épinay and Vellozanne.

The much-patronized spa of Forges-les-Eaux stands on a 175-metre peak from which flow numerous streams and two rivers, the Epte and the Andelle. The combination of iron ore and water made this spot an important smelting centre 1,000 years ago. In 1632 its therapeutic waters brought here Louis XIII, Anne of Austria and Cardinal Richelieu. These notables spent three weeks at the spa, protected by 200 musketeers and

100 arquebusiers. They renamed the three springs 'la Royale', 'la Reinette' and 'la Cardinale'.

So Forges-les-Eaux became fashionable, and was frequented by Mme de Sévigné and Louis XV's son, the dauphin. Voltaire came, wrote *L'Indiscret* here and lost much money gambling. In the nineteenth century though, the spa went into decline. Then in the 1950s a gifted entrepreneur named Jan Herbetot transformed it into a stylish twentieth-century spa, laying out new parklands and a magnificent casino, as well as restoring the ancient streets of the town.

Today its three thermal springs, set among ten hectares of parklands and walks bordering the River Andelle, retain an iron-rich temperature of 45° F (7° C). The town hall boasts a pottery museum, with exemplary work produced here from the late eighteenth till the end of the nineteenth century. Another museum exhibits remarkable model vehicles. Drive four kilometres north and you reach Beaubec-la-Rosière with its half-ruined abbey and its eighteenth-century church, inside which you unexpectedly discover a fifteenth-century cross. Drive seven kilometres east and you will find at Pommereux a splendid wooden vaulted thirteenth-century church.

Gournay-en-Bray at the other end of the Bray valley is a lovely little town, with a late sixteenth-century gateway (the porte de Paris), old-fashioned Normandy houses in the rue de l'Église, the rue Notre-Dame and the rue Saint-Pierre-de-Ferières and an extremely stern twelfth-century church, dedicated to St Hildevert. (It was initially dedicated to St Stephen, until the bones of Bishop Hildevert of Meaux miraculously revealed their desire to rest here.) Inside the church you will find a splendid Renaissance organ-case dated 1526 and an eighteenth-century pulpit. Does the military starkness of this Romanesque church derive from the importance of this little town in defending Normandy against the French in the eleventh and twelfth centuries? A solitary ruined tower remains from the thirteenth-century fortifications to remind one of the turbulent past. Hugh the First of Gournay was one of William the Bastard's lieutenants in 1066 and as a reward became Count of Norfolk.

If you are lucky enough to reach Gournay-en-Bray on a Tuesday morning, your visit coincides with its main weekly market; and a little market selling mostly chickens and ducks takes place in the town every Friday morning. The annual Palm Sunday country fair is magnificent, especially if you wish to buy a cow or two.

The pays de Bray is also border country, on the edge of Picardy. Although the Romans garrisoned parts of it, the region was much fought over and scarcely hospitable to peaceful occupation before the thirteenth century. Only then were most settlements cleared – hence the villages here are much smaller than those elsewhere in Normandy, the hamlets often tiny, the farms less large, their fields ill-drained against the frequent rains, most of them surrounded by hedges of hawthorns and miniscule, sometimes straggling trees.

In the eighteenth century the economy of the pays de Bray suddenly boomed. The markets of Paris were opened up by better roads, and the farmers discovered that their cereal-producing land could be transformed into pasture rich enough to support cattle whose milk was profitably transformed into butter. Square, north-facing cellars, whose temperature remained stable at 47–50°F (8–10°C), kept this butter fresh. Increasing wealth and with it entrepreneurial confidence incited the farmers to add to their traditional cereal crops not only cider-orchards but also a sought-after cheese known as *le bondon*.

It is fascinating to trace the transformation of the agricultural fortunes of the pays de Bray throughout the nineteenth century. Farms still remained smaller than elsewhere – at no more than fifty hectares, with the majority around a mere twenty. But the building of the railway line to Beauvais in 1857 and the Paris–Dieppe line in 1873 opened up hitherto undreamed-of markets. A Gournay farmer inspired by a Parisian merchant invented a new cheese, *petit-suisse*; and the whey left over from cheese-making was used to feed fat pigs. The pays de Bray was becoming its present prosperous self.

The people of the region had long been accustomed to defending their homes from the heavy rains of their region by means of flat tiles. Now more serviceable, more expensive slates began to replace tiles on their roofs. Since Roman times the rich clay of the region had been used for pottery, the forests providing the necessary wood for the kilns. Medieval paving-stones in this deprived part of Normandy still survive.

In the eighteenth century English potters arrived, seeking here the white clay which would enable them to imitate Chinese porcelain. In 1797 one of them, Charles Wood, set up the first earthenware factory of the pays de Bray, at Forges-les-Bains. The products of this factory are now cherished period-pieces, their often naive subjects vividly painted on a background of yellow, green or blue. This pottery industry in the pays de Bray found a ready market throughout Normandy and in the markets of Paris, and flourished, especially with the advent of the railways and a growing use of coal-fired kilns, until the end of the nineteenth century.

The best view I know of the pays de Bray is from the little village of la Ferté, which rises on its 193-metre-high promontory and overlooks Forges-les-Eaux. Its tiny church is a remarkable survival from the tenth century. On its portal is carved a delightful wolf, licking chops. Don't miss either the so-called château of the reine Blanche, named after the queen of Philippe IV de Valois.

Then drive back into Forges-les-Eaux, visit its sweet park (with a well set-out museum that quaintly displays scale models of ancient vehicles) and, in one of its homely restaurants, eat an *escalope normande*, a dish that most likely will have been deglazed in cider and enriched with a touch of Calvados, saving till the end of the meal the remarkable savour of the town's unique local cheese.

The name of this cheese is *Coeur de Bray*, a fitting description of Forges-les-Eaux itself. To return to the main course, nothing to my taste is more succulent than an *escalope normande* accompanied by *carottes à la fermière* (that is, carrots cooked in butter and lard, mingled with little pieces of new potatoes and served with a dollop of *crème fraîche*). On the subject of cheese, later I wish to speak of the other delicious cheeses of the pays de Bray, but here is the place to give an additional mention to one that appears surreptitiously in a particular delicacy of this region of Normandy.

Les pommes de terre braytoises (a phrase often shortened on menus to *pommes braytoises*) are so easy to prepare that I bake them myself. For four people you need eight large potatoes, a half-litre of rich cream, the yolks of three eggs and a chunk (or *bondon*, as the French call it) of the cheese in question, *Neufchâtel*.

Wash the potatoes without peeling them, wrap them in aluminium and cook them in the oven. While they are cooking, grate the cheese. When the potatoes are done, take the pulp out of the skins, keeping these as intact as possible. The cheese, eggs and cream are then mixed with the mashed potatoes. Next the mash is put back into the potato skins and the whole popped back into the oven for browning. Normandy chefs usually twirl a little of the mash on top of each potato, like whipped cream on a sundae. Usually, too, a Normandy restaurant serves each person only one *pomme de terre braytoise*, but if you bake your own there is no reason not to guzzle two or three.

Vexin et plaines de l'Eure

The Vexin and the Eure plain lie south of the pays de Bray and together
with it constitute the easternmost part of Normandy. Here are plateaux
ringed with forests, dotted with villages and boasting fine countryside,
their base of chalk supporting flint, sandstone and a coating of alluvial
soils. In consequence this forms the start of those great plains stretching
south towards the Île-de-France and growing sugar-beet, wheat, maize
and barley.

As you travel south-west the farms grow larger: around fifty hectares in
the Neubourg plain, twice as large in the plain of Saint-André, and
averaging a colossal 200 hectares in the Vexin to the east of the River
Seine. Over 10,000 hectares of forest grow on the vast plateau of the
Vexin, situated between the Rivers Seine, Oise and Andelle. Much prized
and fought over, by the treaty of Saint-Clair-sur-Epte the region was cut
in two, divided between France and Normandy.

Fine towns have blossomed as agricultural centres, Etrépagny in
particular gaining its living from manufacturing and selling agricultural
implements. Four rivers, the Eure, the Iton, the Andelle and the Epte,
have cut their way through the plateaux. Metallurgy, the chemical
industry and textiles vie with orchards and cultivated land as you follow
the meandering Seine on its route to Rouen and on to Paris. And the
charm of the land, as well as the proximity of these two great cities, has
made it a haven for secondary homes, their roughcast walls almost, but
not quite, harmonizing with the varied stones, timbers and brick of the
traditional homes of this region.

Of the fascinating towns in this region Ivry-la-Bataille we have already
visited. Drive due north along the D386 to reach a gem: Menilles, whose
church of 1562 and château beautifully dovetail. Overlooking the village,
the brick and stone château dates from the second half of the sixteenth
century, and the church houses a fifteenth-century font. A kilometre or so
further north you reach Cocherel, in whose cemetery (which half-circles a
sixteenth- and eighteenth-century church) lies Aristide Briand, the
President of France who died in 1932. And here on 16 May 1364 the forces
of England and Navarre commanded by Jean de Grailly, captal de Buch,
were defeated by a French force under the direction of the brilliant du
Guesclin.

The D386 north from here constitutes one of the prettiest châteaux
routes in France. Drive along it by the riverside to reach the early
seventeenth-century château de Chambray, a delicious confection of
brick and stone, close to which stands a sixteenth-century church hosting
some splendid contemporary statues. Further north you come upon an
equally splendid early seventeenth-century château at la Croix-Saint-

Leufroy, flanked by manor houses and a former tithe barn.

Drive on to Acquigny for a yet greater Renaissance château which Anne de Laval, maid-of-honour to Catherine de Medici, commissioned in 1557. The parish church of Acquigny is quite as remarkable, built in the sixteenth century and crammed with treasures of ecclesiastical art.

Pays d'Auge, d'Ouche et du Roumois

North of the Perche and stretching as far as the lower valley of the Seine is a diverse region of Normandy which includes the pays d'Ouche, the pays d'Auge and the region around Rouen known as the Roumois. Here the land slopes towards the river valley, gradually descending from 320 to 100 metres above sea-level. Half-timbered and brick houses nestle among farmland criss-crossed by lines of trees and hedges.

To one's surprise the southernmost part of this region, the pays d'Ouche, is the starkest, with a cold and frequently damp climate brought about by the altitude. The humid weather and the area's lack of alluvial soil, with sandstone alternating with a sandy topsoil, account for the vast forests of Beaumont, Saint-Évroult, Conches and Breteil which characterize the pays d'Ouche. Today the first of these, the Beaumont forest, covers no more than 3,600 hectares, but when the King of France gave it to the Duke de Bouillon in 1651 it covered a vast 24,000 hectares. Stags and wild boar still freely roam its dusky dank stretches. All of the forests of the pays d'Ouche are latticed with walks, and hikers and pony-trekkers vie with huntsmen during the tourist and hunting seasons.

Villages and towns sheltered by these forests are often exquisite, such as la Ferrière-sur-Risle in the Beaumont forest, blessed with half-timbered houses, a fourteenth-century covered market and a magnificent thirteenth-century church (don't miss its gilded retable). Directly north-west along the D140 lies Beaumesnil, whose marvellous baroque château was built out of brick and stone for Count Jacques of Nonant in the early seventeenth century. Superb chimneys and dormer windows, a remarkably ornate staircase in the central pavilion, monumental eighteenth-century furnishings and a stupendous park make Beaumesnil unmissable. Here is all the arrogance of the early years of Louis XIV, viewed amid trees across the huge artificial lake.

From Beaumesnil the D26 runs north-east to Beaumont-le-Roger. Although some 60 per cent of the town was destroyed during the last war, the lovely fifteenth-century glass of the church of Saint-Nicolas and, above all, the romantic ruins of its medieval priory amply reward the visitor to this town on the river Risle.

For the most part I describe the entrancing towns of the pays d'Auge

(Trouville, Deauville, Cabourg, Honfleur, Lisieux, Pont l'Évêque) elsewhere in this book, so here I shall concentrate on the quiddities of the pays d'Ouche. The starkness of the climate did not prevent its occupation by prehistoric men and women, as the dolmen at Ambenay on the bank of the Risle indicates. Yet this starkness once matched an antagonism between the peasant farmer, scratching his living amid his oats, his beet, his buckwheat and his miserable sheep, and the inhabitants of the fine châteaux who usually exploited him. Since the clergy were frequently parasites on (or at least supporters of) the grands seigneurs, a tradition of anti-clericalism long survived among the poor farmers, craftsmen and forgers of the pays d'Ouche.

Today much has changed, though I am not so sure about the anti-clericalism. Richer cattle graze on well-fertilized pastures; corn-growing receives its government subsidies; and the smallish towns of Rugles, Conches-en-Ouche and L'Aigle are industrial centres. Not that they are ugly or to be avoided – quite the contrary.

Rugles derives its name from the abundant traces of metal in its soil (which the Romans called *regulae*) and from this inheritance makes pins and needles. The town suffered considerably from the fifteenth to the seventeenth century, occupied by the English between 1417 and 1449, a haunt of the Catholic League in the 1590s and pillaged by the Frondeurs during the mid-seventeenth-century civil war.

Yet it retains one of the oldest churches in France, Notre-Dame-Outre-l'Eau, pre-Romanesque in origin though the west front was rebuilt in the sixteenth century. Its wooden ceiling is delightfully sculpted with faces, masks and animals. The parish church of Saint-Germain at Rugles is equally pleasing, with a splendid tower decorated with statues and a Renaissance choir, on the right of which opens a magically carved Renaissance chapel. Finally Rugles boasts no fewer than three châteaux: one in the rue des Forges known as le Petit Château and recently entirely restored by the town fathers; the moated fifteenth-century château de l'Écureuil; and the eighteenth-century château de Rugles, which today houses the town orphanage.

Conches-en-Ouche, like Rugles, had a stormy past, taken and retaken for centuries by the English and French. Faithful to the Protestant Henri IV, it was sacked and pillaged by the Catholics in 1590. The ruins of its eleventh-century château now enclose a peaceful garden from which rises the stone keep, square at its base, circular above. Once Conches-en-Ouche possessed four splendid medieval churches. Sainte-Foy alone remains, a masterpiece almost entirely rebuilt in the fifteenth century, surmounted with a fifty-six-metre-high spire and containing some of the finest sixteenth-century stained glass in Normandy.

At L'Aigle, as at Conches-en-Ouche, half-timbered houses front its parish church. L'Aigle derives its name from the legend that its first lord, Fulbert de Beira, discovered an eagle's nest on the spot he had chosen for his château and decided to embody the bird in his coat of arms. Today this town, like Rugles, manufactures pins, needles and knitting needles; but it is also a thriving centre for tourists who come to enjoy the superb surrounding countryside. Every Wednesday L'Aigle hosts an enjoyable market, and around the Feast of the Ascension it is the venue for a tremendous four-day fair.

To the north-west of this region the countryside blossoms in the warm pays d'Auge. The valleys that cut into the chalk and the loess-covered plateaux offer a sweeter life. Hedges protect huge stretches of meadowland, interspersed with apple orchards – cider has long been a staple source of income. The pays d'Auge profited from an agricultural revolution in the eighteenth century. Pastures created at the end of that century and the beginning of the nineteenth raised large, chubby cattle destined to be eaten during the winter or to churn out milk for the production of succulent cheeses.

Fine cheeses and creamy milk depend on lush grass. André Gide's *L'Immoraliste* describes the countryside of the wide valley of the Auge, situated between Lisieux and Pont-L'Évêque as:

the shadiest, wettest country I know. Countless narrow combes and gentle rounded hills reach as far as the valley, which then stretches in an uninterrupted plain as far as the sea. You see no horizon, but only a few copses, filled with mysterious shade, a few cornfields, but chiefly pasture, soft, quietly sloping meadows, where the rich grass is mown twice yearly, where when the sun is low the apple trees give deep shadows, where untended flocks of sheep and herds of cows graze. Every hollow is filled with water: pond, pool, river. On every side streams constantly murmur.

Gide continually stresses the richness of this countryside. His protagonists Michel and Marceline rejoice to see on every side 'great oxen and fat cows grazing in opulent meadows, and apple trees planted in order on the sunniest slopes of the hillsides, giving promise of a magnificent summer crop'. Gide wrote *L'Immoraliste* in 1902. His descriptions have not dated.

As Lisieux reveals, a city of 30,000 inhabitants can survive by producing milk and by living on the forestry industry. And during the second Empire the seaside resort of Deauville brought not one, but two, new lively elements into the economy of the pays d'Auge: fashionable holidays and the breeding of racehorses, which remain – apart from farming – its staple means of subsistence.

As for the Roumois, situated between the Rivers Risle and Seine, on no account should you miss, leaving aside Rouen itself, Brionne,

Bosguérard, Boissey-le-Châtel, Ecaquelon and the fantastic ruins of the abbey of le Bec-Hellouin.

You reach Brionne by way of the N13 north-west from Évreux and then take the D130 directly north. The town has a long and fairly turbulent history, and it straddles two Roman roads which met here. Even earlier the Celts had established a settlement at this crossroads on the lovely banks of the River Risle. Traces of the Roman camp have been excavated on a hill overlooking Brionne. After the arrival of the Normans, Duke Richard I of Normandy gave the town to his son Godefroy, elevating him to the rank of Count of Brionne. In 1044 William the Bastard decided to take possession of the town and managed to do so only after a three-year-long siege. A hundred and fifty years later the King of France, Philippe Auguste, cast envious eyes on the splendid town and took it.

The Risle proved an invaluable aid to textile production. Wool and cloth from Brionne were greatly enriching the town in the sixteenth century, and even the pillaging Protestants, who set fire to parts of Brionne in 1562, failed to dent its steady aggrandisement. In the twentieth century Brionne remains the most important centre for weaving cloth in Normandy, and has expanded this industry into the manufacture of synthetic fabrics as well.

All this rich history is visible today in the architectural impact of the town. The old château was set on fire and destroyed when Philippe Auguste was besieging Brionne, but you can walk up to the square keep of the Norman castle built in its place by Robert de Meulan at the end of the eleventh century. Oddly enough, at the very moment that the eighteenth-century Dukes of Lorraine were building their charming brick and stone château in the middle of the town, they were also dismantling parts of Robert de Meulan's eleventh-century castle.

The city fathers of Brionne deserve enormous credit for beautifully reconstructing the church of Saint-Denis after the Allies' bombs smashed it down in 1944. The transepts date from the sixteenth century and the nave windows from the fourteenth; but the church is basically a twelfth- and thirteenth-century jewel. The church of Saint-Martin is equally worth visiting. Its spire, graced with pretty dormer windows, rests on a fifteenth-century tower, the chapel of the Virgin dates from the 1690s and the rest of the church – including the splendid panelled ceiling in the choir – dates from the late fourteenth century (save for the side-aisles, which were added in 1870, and the innocuous modern stained glass by G. Loire).

What makes a visit to this church mandatory, however, is its furnishing, in particular the fifteenth- and sixteenth-century statues and the magical eighteenth-century high altar, all of which came from the ancient abbey of le Bec-Hellouin. The altar and the chapel of the Virgin are both the work of a celebrated monk and architect, Guillaume de la Tremblaye.

Drive north-east from Brionne along the N138, crossing the River Bec and reaching the crossroads with the D124, where you turn right to reach Bosguérard-de-Marcouville. Here Catholic Normandy has benefited from the wealth and taste of a Dutch Protestant named (improbably, it seems to me) Jacques Scot. In 1695 he bought the château de Mésangère at Bosguérard-de-Marcouville and then employed France's greatest landscape gardener, Le Nôtre, to create a superb park, sown with classical statues and now filled with magnificent full-grown trees. Another shadow roams this park, that of La Fontaine, for Jacques Scot's son Guillaume married his patroness, Mme de la Sablière. In her park La Fontaine was inspired to write his celebrated fables of the two pigeons, and of the frogs who wanted a king. He is said to have dreamed the first of these fables sleeping under one of the trees.

At Bosguérard-de-Marcouville you cannot miss the so-called Virgin's oak, an immense tree planted over 400 years ago. Make sure you also don't miss the exquisite medieval crucifix, carved at the beginning of the sixteenth century, in the cemetery of the church of Saint-Pierre-de-Bosguérard.

Return along the D124 to Boissey-le-Châtel, whose church of Saint-Jean-l'Évangeliste appears boring, save for the fact that inside are some astonishingly beautiful statues sculpted in the fifteenth century. Just north of the town is another magnificent château. The château-de-Tilly is a masterpiece of Renaissance architecture built in the first half of the sixteenth century for a counsellor in the Normandy *parlement* named Guillaume le Roux. A mighty round tower with a pepperpot hat at one corner is matched by a much more delicate slender tower at the other. In between, pretty dormer windows with Renaissance decorations rise above classical windows, with smaller delicate dormers in between them.

Continue along the D124 looking out for the sign on the right to Écaquelon. Even if church-crawling isn't your favourite occupation, please go inside the church of Notre-Dame et Saint-Jacques, founded in 1248 by Archbishop Eudes Rigaud of Rouen but today dating basically from the fifteenth and sixteenth centuries. The panelling of the nave includes seventy-six splendid carvings; here also hang three superb eighteenth-century tapestries. These masterpieces pale, however, alongside Écaquelon's treasured alabaster altarpiece, a fifteenth-century carved retable – possibly made in England, some scholars think – depicting in seven panels the passion of Jesus. Nothing is in perspective here. The angel catching Christ's blood in a chalice at the foot of the cross is tiny compared with the rough Roman soldier who is about to confess 'Truly this was the son of God', yet the apparent simplicity is deceptive. This retable is one of the most moving in Normandy. Notice the skeletal arms of the dead Saviour as the holy women lay him in the tomb, helped by St James who wears his pilgrim's hat and cockleshell-decorated bag.

Écaquelon also boasts a fine château built around 1700. Far more imposing is the ruined Norman château at Montfort-sur-Risle, which you reach by taking the D130 from Écaquelon. Saint-Philbert-sur-Risle lies due west, where you find not only a twelfth-century priory founded by Abbot Boson of Bec but also one of France's curiosities, a former church which is now private property, this one dedicated to St-Ouen and built in the thirteenth and sixteenth centuries.

The D130 and then the D39 from Pont-Authou takes you south from Saint-Philbert-sur-Risle to the Benedictine abbey of le Bec-Hellouin, situated beside a serpentine stream which eventually flows into the Risle. The knight named Herluin who founded the abbey in 1034 (though initially at Pont-Authou a little further north) was born at nearby Brionne. Since the monastery later fell into disrepair until the Maurists took over (see Maurists and le Bec-Hellouin in the index to this book) and was then completely abandoned by the monks at the time of the Revolution – when it became a cavalry barracks – little remains of the medieval buildings, save for the strong tower of St Nicolas, dating from 1467, and the Norman chapterhouse.

Guillaume de la Tremblaye's lovely cloisters with their elegant pool also happily survive, as do the fine and sober eighteenth-century buildings left by the Maurists. Look out in the abbey church for the fourteenth-century statues of the four doctors of the church, Sts Augustine, Jerome, Gregory and Ambrose, as well as a charming statue of the Virgin Mary from the same century. Since 1948 le Bec-Hellouin has once more been inhabited and splendidly restored by Benedictine monks. Visiting a working monastery means guided tours, but le Bec-Hellouin is open every day except Tuesday, and if you arrive just after a tour has begun you can while away the time till the next one by visiting the motor museum just outside the abbey gates.

Monasteries brought work and a measure of wealth to those who lived around them, and le Bec-Hellouin is situated near a charming village with a good number of extremely pretty half-timbered houses. Having visited the monastery, you may balk at looking inside the village's fourteenth-century parish church, in which case you will miss a cornucopia of statues in wood, terracotta and stone, dating from the fourteenth to the eighteenth century and mostly taken from the abbey itself. Then the journey from here back to Brionne is a mere four kilometres.

Pays de Caux

In *Madame Bovary* Gustave Flaubert describes the sea breeze as it plays over the Norman countryside, especially that of the pays de Caux. 'Sometimes the wind would begin to blow in strong gusts which came from the sea and swept across the plateau of the Caux region, filling the whole countryside with cool salt air. The rushes would hiss, flattened against the ground, and the quivering beech trees would rustle loudly while the tops of the trees swayed and murmured.'

The boundary of the pays de Caux stretches from Dieppe south-west along the Normandy coastline as far as Le Havre and due east as far as the D151, where it turns due north again to the coast. Bordering on the industrialized region of the lower Seine, its chalky plateau rises between 100 and 150 metres above sea-level as a barrier against the west winds. Much of the scenic excitement of this plateau is created by its deep, narrow valleys, which descend either to the Seine or to the Channel. This white chalk also creates the picturesque cliffs of the coastline and of the left bank of the great ambulating river, where they look across to wooded terraces. It rarely emerges on the plateau itself, being covered with flinty clay and loess, sown from time to time with blocks of sandstone.

This exposed land is well-watered. Each year between 800 and 900 millimetres of rain fall on the pays de Caux. Ironically, much of it instantly seeps away into the flint-pitted ground and the porous chalk. Until recent technology enabled us to drill deep into the land, those who lived here had to depend for their water on clay-lined ponds, and in summer they were obliged to venture further afield to fetch water from the neighbouring valleys.

The pays de Caux is unique in Normandy for its pattern of population and for its farming. Local custom has resisted the French habit of dividing up an inheritance among all the sons, so that here farms have remained as large as eighty hectares in size and the smallest comprise at least twenty-five hectares. In consequence the countryside is cultivated in fields which are sometimes massive, and elsewhere long and divided into sizeable individual chunks. Screens of trees add their charm to the whole region. Copses and groves turn out to shelter villages, hamlets and isolated farms. Sometimes a great tree will stand isolated on the plateau, and apart from the copses there are few forests, save to the east.

Rouen, and to a lesser extent Le Havre and Dieppe, have inevitably influenced the economy of this region. Today those who live around these conurbations frequently commute daily to the cities to earn their living. But in the past trade was in the other direction. Rouen in particular promoted the cottage industries of spinning and weaving in the pays de Caux, with the same workers often earning a living as farm labourers as

well. In the eighteenth century the cotton industry blossomed here, and
more than half the population is said to have lived off weaving.

In such a society children are a necessary boon, and from the
eighteenth to the twentieth century the people of the Caux so enthusiastically bred them that nowadays every square kilometre of land supports
nearly 100 inhabitants. These countryfolk needed to buy and sell, and the
effect of the semi-industrial boom, as well as the agricultural fecundity of
the pays de Caux and the varying needs of a growing population, can still
be seen in the countless entrancing little market towns which are disper-
sed over the plateau, as well as in the remarkable number of villages
boasting a market square.

Traditional societies need protection from the developments of the
twentieth century, and that of the pays de Caux, especially in the Seine
valley, is threatened by the petrol, chemical and steel industries, as well
as by the profits to be made from exploiting sand and gravel. A partial
answer in this region has been the establishing of the Brotonne national
park, whose beeches are renowned. The forest is sown with exquisite
villages: Notre-Dame-de-Bliquetuit boasts an eleventh-century church;
Vatteville-la-Rue is enhanced by the ruins of a château and a seventeenth-
century windmill; at the centre of Heurreville stands a tithe barn whose
wooden roof dates from the twelfth century; Saint-Maurice-d'Ételan is
blessed with a superb view of the river and the forest, as well as a chapel
dedicated to St Madeleine in which gleam sixteenth-century stained-glass
windows.

One of the most elegant towns in the Brotonne national park is
Quilleboeuf. Its Romanesque church stands squat and proud, every arch
rounded, with not a single exterior concession to the Gothic – though
inside the choir, the pointed arches date from the sixteenth century. The
modern bridge at Tancarville, the last one to span the Seine, is a
technological masterpiece, joining the *département* of the Eure with that of
the Seine-Maritime.

Le Tréport, Dieppe, Varengeville-sur-Mer, Saint-Valéry-en-Caux,
Fécamp, and Étretat are the delicious coastal resorts of the pays de Caux.
Inland you should not miss Yvetot, Caudebec-en-Caux and Saint-Wan-
drille. All these places I describe elsewhere in this book.

The forest of Eawy shelters the attractive town of Neufchâtel, whose
splendid Renaissance château (le château de Mesnières), built for the
most part in the first half of the sixteenth century, is open to vistors from
April to September on Wednesdays and at weekends from 14.00 to 18.00.
'Autumn has its charms here,' wrote André Gide at Neufchâtel in 1894.
'This evening I went up to the woods which dominate the town. I
followed a road which was overlooked on one side by red limes and
walnut trees. There was a warm breeze.' In the autumn of 1986 I

wandered among these same woods and felt this same cheering breeze warming my own neck.

Le Perche

Covering altogether 4,780 square kilometres, the Perche is far vaster than simply the tip which forms the southernmost part of Normandy and here consists of not quite 2,000 square kilometres. Yet some of its loveliest aspects belong to this province, not least its forests – de Bellême, de Longny, de Réno-Valdieu – and its rich meadowlands, in part the consequence of the fact that something between 800 and 830 millimetres of rain waters the Perche every year.

As a boy I spent much of my spare time farming, sitting on the backs of huge horses, steering them and the haycart through narrow gates or staggering behind them with a hand-held plough, and I used to dream of one of the greatest work-horses of all time, the beautiful dappled percheron. Until the 1930s the principal industry of the Perche was breeding these horses – a breed which had achieved fame in the eighteenth century, drew carriages in the nineteenth, became a post-horse after 1850 and then developed into one of the mightiest, most magnificent beasts of burden, weighing as much as 900 kilos and certainly 600. The percheron stud-book was begun in 1873 and the *Société hippique percheron* ten years later. Until World War II at least one pair of percherons was the prized possession of virtually every farm in the Perche, and thousands were exported either abroad or to the rest of France. Loyally toiling by day, these tremendous horses rested from their work in noble stables. Then the tractor replaced them. Today the percheron is bred only for horse butchers. When I last drove through the Perche I saw, to my regret, not a single one.

Almost as sad is the sight of the mostly abandoned stables which once sheltered these gentle beasts. The long, low farms of the Perche, with their pairs of gables and their outbuildings, none the less fit beautifully into the lush countryside, their sandy roughcast or brick walls supporting steep orange or brown tiles (roofs scarcely found in the towns, where slate has become the rule). And as with the pays d'Auge, the Normandy Perche is close enough to Paris for countless city-dwellers to flock here each weekend and during the summer to their second homes.

North of the Perche forest you can find the abbey of la Trappe, founded in 1140. Trappist monks still live here, and they will tell you that in the seventeenth century one of Richelieu's godsons, after a life of debauchery, came here as abbot and is the hero of Chateaubriand's *Vie de Rancé*. In the seventeenth century many French families emigrated from

Mortagne-au-Perche to Canada. Today they return nostalgically to their roots. Between the huge flamboyant Gothic church of Notre-Dame and the place du Palais the ancient town retains much of its former quaintness.

Longny-au-Perche is almost as delightful, its fifteenth-century church of Saint-Martin instantly drawing attention to itself by its complex half-flamboyant, half-classical belfry, tempting one to venture inside to marvel at the religious statuary. Bellême is yet finer, superbly situated on a peak, surrounded by forests, ringed with a splendid promenade that runs all the way round the town. Bellême also boasts the rich classical church of Saint-Sauveur and the noble seventeenth- and eighteenth-century houses of the so-called 'Ville Close'. And if you want a breath-taking view of the Perche, drive eleven kilometres west to the hilltop village of La Perrière, with its picturesque old houses, its pines and the remains of its medieval fortifications.

Bocages normands intérieurs

The huge square tract of farmland to the west of the Bessin, and stretching from the south of Normandy almost as far north as Rouen, is known as the interior bocage. This hilly region, undulating more than any other part of the province, includes to the north the area not surprisingly dubbed 'Swiss Normandy', where the hills reach some 360 metres above sea-level, culminating in the peaks of Mont Robin and Mont Pinçon. Further south the Écouves forest and hills push up another fifty metres. La Suisse normande consists of rocky escarpments, valleys and lively rivers – including the mid-course of the Orne and the little valley of the Noireau north of Flers. The Rivers Orne, Vire, Varenne and Cance have carved deep gorges through the plateaux, which endures a hard climate, matching the granite and sandstone of its terrain. Not surprisingly this part of Normandy was not cultivated and was only sparsely inhabited until the end of the Hundred Years War. In the forests the inhabitants eked out a living as charcoal-burners, shapers of wooden clogs and smiths.

Not until the eighteenth century did the farmers of this region achieve a measure of prosperity, and even today alongside the fields of buckwheat, rye and oats which surround the isolated farms and hamlets you see great stretches of uncultivated land.

Yet there are gentler, more fertile parts. The nineteenth century brought an unexpected prosperity, when wheat replaced inferior crops and the increased wealth of the farmers enabled them to clear vast meadowlands. Polyculture brought to this interior bocage cereals and apples, vegetables and milch-cattle. Around Domfront pears intersperse with apples, and the liqueurs brewed in this pretty town are now renowned. And since World War II the neighbourhood of Flers, of Condé-sur-Noireau and of la Ferté-Macé have seen the development of small industrial complexes. That they are small remains important for the charm of this region. What Flaubert wrote to a friend in the 1870s still holds true: 'The banks of the Orne between Condé-sur-Noireau and Caen are – forgive the word – picturesque. Everywhere are rocks and from time to time a great cliff rises amidst the greenery.'

Even so, the inhospitable inheritance of the region means that here the farms are far smaller than elsewhere in Normandy. Nowadays people leave this area for more prosperous parts of France, and you come across numerous abandoned homesteads. Around Briouze the houses are half-timbered and more substantial than anywhere else in this part of Normandy. Of course a peasant community may be poor and at the same time enchanting to the tourist. Here thatched cottages bespeak the late development of the interior bocage and at the same time charm those who do not have to live in them.

In short, there is much to relish in the interior bocage. Vire, the *sous-préfecture* of Calvados, is graced by a thirteenth-century gateway, a fifteenth-century clock tower and the thirteenth-century church of Notre-Dame, whose choir rises higher than the nave and whose side chapel of 1764 is filled with contemporary sculptures. Look for the eighteenth-century château de Cotin. The local museum in the former town hospice is devoted to Normandy customs and costumes. And a rocky perch supports the keep of a château built in 1123 by Henry I of England. Vire is noted for a celebrated sausage, the *andouille de Vire*, which I find virtually inedible but which you should certainly sample once. In the fourteenth century this town also gave us the word vaudeville, when a clockmaker named Olivier Bassin amassed a collection of bawdy lyrics which were later published as 'les Vaux de Vire'.

Although Domfront, la Ferté-Macé, Condé-sur-Noireau, Saint-Lô and Briouze have become important industrial centres, they also preserve a fine architectural heritage. Domfront rises above the River Varenne on its promontory, from which your eyes can overlook the old moat to glimpse in the distance the rocks of Mortain. Two walls of its ancient château still stand. I am not sure what I think of its art deco church, built of cement, dedicated to St Julian and designed by an architect named Guilbert in 1925. It is undoubtedly surpassed by the lovely church of Notre-Dame-sur-l'Eau, made of granite but this time built in 1020 and housing no fewer than thirty-seven seventeenth-century tombstones. In this cider country Domfront surprises you by running a beer festival each July.

The church of la Ferté-Macé is basically nineteenth-century, but it preserves a Romanesque tower and a couple of Romanesque spans in its choir. The charming town hall, now the municipal museum, dates from the fifteenth century. Condé-sur-Noireau, which was almost totally demolished in 1944, has been meticulously restored, and its light industry in no way interferes with tourism. Its church, modern inside, preserves an authentically medieval exterior, and in the suburb of Saint-Martin you will find another church with a thirteenth-century choir. As for Saint-Lô, named after a fifth-century bishop of Coutances, the town was savagely bombed on 6 June 1944, yet the church of Notre-Dame managed to save some glowing fifteenth- and sixteenth-century stained-glass windows. The sadly damaged spires of its cathedral remind one of the folly of World War II, but the church of Sainte-Croix has been rebuilt (with a concrete belfry!) and its Romanesque portal restored.

Once an important defensive town (some of its ramparts still survive), Saint-Lô belonged to the princes of Monaco, whose portraits you can see in the municipal museum. Today the town caters for its tourists by sponsoring international horse races in May and an international fishing competition the following month. Finally, Briouze hosts no fewer than thirteen annual fairs, and also retains a late twelfth-century priory church whose delicious choir is built of granite and sandstone.

Plaines centrales de la Basse-Normandie

The plains of lower Normandy stretch from Alençon as far as the estuary of the River Orne and thus include two spots connected with William the Bastard, Falaise and Caen. Generous in climate, these plains were occupied by our ancestors in the third millennium before the Christian era.

Historians speculate whether the rigid social order imposed by the Normans has affected the pattern of its farming. What always strikes me about this area is its diversity, attribute it to what you will: industry; sugar-beet and flax; meat and milch-cattle; sheep; cereals; and, as the historians tell us, draught- and racehorses until World War I. What saddens one is the massive destruction of traditional houses during World War II. The onslaughts of the Allies in 1944 damaged 27 per cent of the buildings around Caen and Falaise, completely destroying nearly 10,000 and partly ruining another 50,000. Yet somehow the charm of this region remains. Though many of the houses have been rebuilt in a modern style, ancient villages retain medieval houses clustered round the parish church. Great farmhouses partly or totally surround their court-yards, their limestone walls embellished with cut stone (and, around Alençon, with granite), with sometimes a brick house or a half-timbered building adding variety.

Argentan is where the battle of Normandy ended on 19 August 1944. Here too Henry II learned that Thomas à Becket had excommunicated him, provoking the king to an oath which inspired four Norman knights to murder the archbishop. The church of Saint-Germain, with its lantern tower and flamboyant north doorway, and the seventeenth-century church of Saint-Martin both survived the war, although much damaged, and have been well-restored. Happily, Saint-Martin's lovely sixteenth-century stained-glass windows were saved. Argentan's palais de justice occupies the former fourteenth-century château, which boasts a machi-colated tour Sainte-Marguerite.

Alençon is equally charming and, like Argentan, is dedicated to lace-making. It also boasts as its jail a fifteenth-century château, not to mention the church of Notre-Dame, whose flamboyant west end is outrageously beautiful. After a fire, its choir and bell tower were rebuilt in the mid-eighteenth century in a half-classical, half-baroque style. Alençon was the birthplace of St Thérèse of the Infant Jesus, and the pious visit her former home. As well as a goodly number of seventeenth- and eighteenth-century houses, the town possesses a fine museum crammed with splendid pieces of lace.

This too is racehorse country. In 1823 races first began at la Bergerie. And twelve kilometres east of Argentan is the Haras-du-Pin, France's national stud, founded by Colbert in 1665. This must be the most beautiful stud-farm in the world, set amid 1,112 hectares comprising woodlands, pasture, exercise grounds and racecourses. The buildings are magnificent, designed by François Mansart, and the gardens were laid out by Le Nôtre. Today some eighty stallions are cared for here, and you can visit the stud-farm every half-hour during the working day from mid-May to mid-September between 09.00 and 12.00 and between 14.00 and 18.00.

Le Bessin

As for the Bessin, without knowing it those of us who have travelled along the landing beaches of 1944, west of the ferry-station of Ouistreham as far as the estuary where the River Vire pours into the baie des Veys, have been running along the Bessin coast. The Bessin and the neighbour-ing plain are two tiny agricultural regions of Normandy separated by the marshlands of Carentan and watered by lovely rivers: the Seulles, Taute, Douve, Merderet and Aure, its tributary the Drôme, and the Vire itself.

Great elms, willows and pruned oak trees dot the countryside. The willows indicate the unique nature of the Bessin, for the rivers, which flood the surrounding fields in wintertime, create the rich *prés-marais* or marsh fields which are subsequently drained to provide succulent pasture. Along the coast the flint and clay is covered with peat.

Thus this is rich country, long known for its salted butter which, since the eighteenth century, has been exported from the ports of Isigny-sur-Mer and Carentan. The farmland is covered with a rich alluvial soil, partly chalky, partly decomposed marl, which lusciously retains water. As a result the farmland of the Bessin is unusually well-drained. Outside the villages, little parcels of land betray a centuries-long peasant ownership, while elsewhere huge ploughed fields, extensive pastures and powerful isolated, beautifully constructed farmhouses represent ancient wealth. Over the centuries these farmers have bred the characteristic brown and white fecund cattle of Normandy.

The southern pebbled slopes of the Bessin merge into the forests of Cerisy, le Tranquay and le Molay. Willow from the Lozon valley, peat farming, pottery factories around Airel and the reclamation of land around the baie des Veys complete the economic picture of this part of Normandy. Bayeux, lying on the Aure, is the capital of the Bessin. Carentan is its next greatest town, and both appear elsewhere in this book. Isigny-sur-Mer is its major coastal resort, devoted above all else to producing butter. Its town hall is a seventeenth-century château, and on most days (not Saturday mornings or Sundays) you are welcomed to a guided tour of Isigny's sumptuous dairies.

Bocages normands littoraux

A line running due south from Isigny-sur-Mer separates the coastal farmlands of Normandy, the bocages normands littoraux, from the rest of this region. Inevitably the coastal farmlands have been marked by the neighbouring ocean, its winds and its showers. Houses are beautifully situated here to shelter from the west wind, turning their backs on it, hiding behind copses and little slopes.

Tourism is inevitably a major industry around the Channel coast, based on Granville and Cherbourg and to a lesser extent Coutances. Inevitably too, since the assault of 1944 when much was destroyed, there has been considerable rebuilding here in non-traditional style. Much also remains from the past. Around Coutances the Normans traditionally build in lovely stone, with splendid manor houses enclosing courtyards, with two-storeyed dwellings boasting dormer windows, and to the west, whence the sharp winds blow, with windowless gable-ends. By contrast the region around Avranches is graced with fine brick houses mostly roofed in grey slate.

All this is determined by the natural materials available – schist, granite, sandstone and chalk offering their varied characteristics to the peasant-builders, as well as to the grander architects of the region. The granite region *par excellence* is the promontory of the Hague. Here and in the Saire valley traditional houses built of stone or rubble are often enhanced with granite and with bluestone or thatched roofs.

Driving north-west from Cherbourg along the Hague promontory you reach Querqueville, a resonant Viking name recalling our own word 'kirk' and boasting a pre-Romanesque church dedicated to St-Germain, an eighteenth-century château (now the town hall) and a fortified sixteenth-century manor house. By the shore is a defensive battery set up in 1788. The need to protect the coast of Normandy is revealed in the next town, reached by the D46 from Querqueville. Urville-Nacqueville is defended both by the fortified château de Due-Écu, built at the end of the sixteenth century, and by the splendid château de Nacqueville of roughly the same date, the latter rendered yet more picturesque by its twin-towered gateway and drawbridge. Both châteaux welcome visitors.

Almost at the furthermost point of the promontory is Saint-German-des-Vaux with its six windmills. Then you turn south along the D901 to reach Jobourg, with its magnificent rocks and twelfth-century church. The 'nez de Jobourg' juts out into the sea, and at 128 metres is the highest such promontory in Europe. The road runs on south-easterly to Beaumont-Hague, where one realizes that war is no modern invention, for here are the celebrated Iron Age fortifications known as the Hague-Dick. Finally you take the D318 south to Vauville, where once again you discover a mighty château founded in the Middle Ages, as well as a priory built by a companion of William the Conqueror, Richard de Vauville, on his return from England in 1070. The whole of this little region is remarkable for its birdlife, and has been designated a protected site.

This then is Normandy, not in a nutshell, for Normandy cannot be so reduced. I return to the notion that its unity derives only from the fierce patriotism of its citizens. As the nineteenth-century savant Émile de la Bedollière put it, 'Normandy is neither a province nor an assemblage of *départements*. Normandy is a nation.' It is a nation beloved by many other Frenchmen too. In Normandy the weather may be uncertain, with rain sometimes pouring down in autumn and occasionally becoming torrential in October, but Parisians revere the region and many other Frenchmen and women nostalgically sing 'Ma Normandie':

> *Quand tout renaît à l'espérance,*
> *Et que l'hiver fut loin de nous,*
> *Sous le beau ciel de notre France,*
> *Quand le soleil revient plus doux*
> *Quand la nature est reverdie,*

Quand l'hirondelle est de retour,
J'aime à revoir ma Normandie,
C'est le pays qui ma donné le jour.

(When hope once again springs in my breast,
And when winter has flown far away,
Beneath the beautiful sky of our France,
The gentle sun returns;
When nature is covered with new verdure,
And the swallows have once more returned,
I long to see my Normandy again,
The land where I was born.)

From
le Mont-Saint-Michel
to Trouville

'On the whole, all that I would call pretty in Normandy, buried under its honeysuckles, doesn't mean much to me,' Marcel Proust once told his friend Madame Strauss. It is not the prettified Normandy that I plan to describe in this tour. Instead my chapter offers a drive throughout Normandy, attempting to distil its varied flavours. The tour runs from le Mont-Saint-Michel to Trouville by way of towns, countryside and villages which (though any thrusting traveller could rush through them in two days) require, in my view, at least fifteen days to savour – especially if you are to eat well of an evening and also strike off my route from time to time on your own accord, to discover the enchanting villages in those neighbouring parts of Normandy which I have here not space to describe.

One of Guy de Maupassant's finest short stories, *Notre Coeur* ('Our Hearts'), describes the superb Gothic abbey of le Mont-Saint-Michel as standing 'lonely on the limitless sands'. The sands still seem limitless; the Gothic abbey is still superb; but it is not 'lonely'. Le Mont-Saint-Michel daily bursts its seams with tourists.

Guy de Maupassant's description of driving up to the mount remains thrillingly true, though, whether you ride today in a car or as he did in an open coach. 'Still the great abbey seemed to loom higher and higher towards the azure sky against which every detail was projected,' he wrote, 'its crest decorated with steeples and little towers as well as the grimacing gargoyles with which our ancestors delighted to embellish their Gothic sanctuaries.' The abbey, carried on the summit of the huge granite mount and defended by a massive battlemented wall with its platforms and watchtowers, surmounts a medieval town whose ancient houses crowd upon each other. 'Above them, apparently miraculously suspended in the sky, rose a massive tangle of spires and belfries, of granite sculpted into flowers, of flying buttresses, of arches stretching from one tower to another, a stunning masterpiece of massive yet delicate architectural lace, adorned with a crazy army of menacing gargoyles with animal faces.'

So it is today. In Guy de Maupassant's *Notre Coeur* the hero and heroine are advised to join a guided party to venture out on to the sand-dunes, which seem secure but can be treacherously soft. 'From here the abbey changes its appearance from that of a maritime cathedral to that of a feudal château,' observed de Maupassant, 'as if it planned to put fear into the invading ocean by menacing it with a crenellated wall pierced with slits for arrows and sustained by huge buttresses.'

So many of the greatest novelists and travel writers have brilliantly described le Mont-Saint-Michel that I feel anxious (frightened, in fact) at trying to evoke its uniqueness myself without first quoting another of them. 'Le Mont-Saint-Michel issues from the waves like an island with the shape of a pyramid,' wrote Stendhal. 'It is an equilateral triangle of increasingly brilliant red verging on rose and standing out against a background of grey.' The area around it is flat enough for easy cycling, and the flatness of the green fields, as well as the symmetry of the granite rock on which the abbey stands, makes the great finger pointing at the sky even more impressive.

The rock was a shrine long before the Christians came to France, almost certainly dedicated to the cult of Mithras. In the eighth century St Michael the Archangel is said to have appeared to Bishop Aubert of Avranches instructing him to build a chapel in his honour on the rock. Aubert awoke and supposed he had simply been dreaming. He did nothing, at which St Michael appeared in a second dream, repeating his command. Bishop Aubert again supposed the vision was but a figment of his sleepy imagination. The Archangel's third appearance left him in no doubt that the vision was real, for this time St Michael vigorously hit the bishop's skull with his forefinger. For fear of yet more damage (for, if you visit the crypt of Saint-Gervais in Rouen it will be pointed out that Aubert's skull, kept there in its fine reliquary, was in truth slightly poked in by the heavenly finger), Aubert set to work and built a chapel of prayer on the rock.

Michael the Archangel was the patron saint of France, and for the seafaring Normans the notion that Lucifer's conqueror hovered over and around this rock, set virtually in the ocean itself, gave them a powerful impetus to treat le Mont-Saint-Michel as a place of pilgrimage. From the fourteenth century onwards groups of children would toil to this spot, hoping for salvation. In our secular age it is still a place of pilgrimage, for after Paris and Versailles more tourists visit le Mont-Saint-Michel than any other site in France. There are religious pilgrimages too, on the first Sunday in May and around the Feast of St Michael and All Angels. To cope with the press of visitors, medieval pilgrims' hostels and traders soon set themselves up on the mount beneath Aubert's oratory. Within two centuries the oratory itself proved too small for the throng of pilgrims, and a new church replaced it.

As we have seen, the Normans enthusiastically threw their energies into supporting the reforming zeal of the reforming papacy – in return, of course, for papal support of their conquests. In 966 Duke Richard-Sans-Peur expelled the canons of le Mont-Saint-Michel, replacing them with progressive Benedictines from Montecassino. The patronage of William the Bastard's grandfather, Duke Richard II, enabled them to start building a new abbey church in 1020 under the rule of Abbot Hildebert. By 1058 the four massive piers (still impressively there today) were complete, designed to hold up the mighty central tower. The church itself was finished in 1135.

Abbot Hildebert built his church at the peak of the rock, 73.6 metres above sea-level. On every side his masons created massive foundations to support the walls. Hildebert's successors perilously enlarged the abbey, extending out from the apex of the mount. Then Abbot Roger de Torigny, who ruled the monastery 150 years after Hildebert's death, overreached himself. The trusted adviser of Henry II Plantagenet, his political counsel was better than his architectural nous. He decided to rebuild the whole west front of the abbey church, flanking it with two mighty towers, which proved too heavy for the vaulting that was supposed to support them. In 1300 one of them collapsed. In 1618 the entire façade began to lean dangerously. By 1776 the monks had no option but to demolish not only the façade but also three spans of the arched nave.

One other disaster proved a paradoxical boon to the abbey on le Mont-Saint-Michel. At the beginning of the thirteenth century its inhabitants had chosen to support English pretensions in France. In consequence the French set fire to their town in 1203, incidentally burning down part of the abbey as well. By way of recompense King Philippe Auguste generously financed its rebuilding in so splendid a Gothic style that the new complex became known as the 'Merveille'. It included new guest chambers, a knightly hall, a refectory and lovely cloisters.

Soon laxity prevailed here; as elsewhere in French monasteries, followed by the anti-clericalism of the Revolution when the abbey was transformed into a jail. Maybe the fact that the first prisoners were recalcitrant clerics preserved the abbey church as a place of worship. Under Napoleon III less bigoted views prevailed. The Bishop of Avranches once more became spiritual head of le Mont-Saint-Michel, and soon the French nation realized that here was a remarkable piece of their patrimony. Restoration of le Mont-Saint-Michel began.

Today you visit a superb and living monument, inevitably packed with tourists herded along in guided tours, but still exceedingly moving. Go early in the morning (the tours begin at 09.00), so as to find a parking spot close enough to the sole entrance, the porte de l'Avancée, and avoid the intolerable crush. Between this defensive gate and a second one, the porte du Boulevard, is a little square flanked by the early sixteenth-century guard house and guarded by a couple of cannons and some piles of stone cannon-balls. A third gate, the porte du Roi, which retains its ancient portcullis, beckons you up into the village on the rock.

The gateways are steeply tiled. Half-timbered houses overhang the Grande Rue. Windows and turrets add charm to blatantly touristic shops, restaurants and bars, and nothing can spoil the tall houses on either side of the narrow twisting street. In the restaurants the inflated prices are almost justified by superb views over the sea. Here and there are dotted museums and historical waxworks. In summer the doors of dark houses are open to let in the air, their owners sitting on stools by the walls and peering out at the throngs of tourists. Over the entrances of these homes you sometimes spot inscriptions, such as 'Le vieux Logis XIVème siècle'. One noted house here was the home of du Guesclin's wife, Tiphaine Raguenel. The colour of the stone changes from honey to darker hues, but always it is rich – including greens, deep browns and maroons – the stones sometimes almost as thin as slates, 150–170 cm (six or seven inches) long and 50–70 cm (two to three inches) wide.

On the second Sunday in July, I pushed my way through the crowds thronging le Mont-Saint-Michel to attend Mass in the lower church of Saint-Pierre. Today its eleventh-century stone pillars are joined together by sixteenth-century arches. Three sixteenth-century altars speak of the eternal. That Sunday, as le Mont-Saint-Michel sweltered under its mass of tourists, a mere twenty-five of us gathered in the cool church and remembered that sacrifice on the cross in honour of which this whole monastic edifice was erected.

Beyond the church of Saint-Pierre steep steps, now lined with trees and shrubs and flanked by a rose garden, lead up through more defences to the abbey itself. There instead of savouring the Middle Ages at will you must submit yourself to a guided tour, in French, English or German. The cool and elegant almonry has become a bookshop, enlivened with carved frescos and painted representations of St Michael at work. He kills devils, thrusts Lucifer out of heaven and weighs saved and damned souls in a balance. Here you can buy your own cardboard construction kit of le Mont-Saint-Michel. Last year I bought one, but its intricacy defeated me.

A far from arduous staircase (*le grand degré extérieur*) twists up to the outer balcony of the abbey, which is flanked by two fine towers. Take the escalier du gouffre from here to the thirteenth-century guard house, enriched by a monster fifteenth-century fireplace and a fine vaulted ceiling. Then take the inner staircase (*le grand degré intérieur*) to reach the magical abbey church itself. The Romanesque nave is topped by a lovely wooden barrel vault. By contrast, the chancel gleams flamboyantly. The abbey church is honeycombed with numerous crypts – for countless relics were given to the monks, and in addition they needed an ossuary for their own bones after death. Look for the marvellous lace stairway and the exquisitely carved foliage in the *chevet*, finished in the early 1520s.

Then walk into the 'Merveille'. First the cloisters, with their delicate little columns and green men's and women's faces peering through carved foliage remind you of the wonder of medieval monasticism, an organization that allowed countless religious to meditate, write, pray and live in peace. Next comes the refectory, its narrow windows lighting the monks' mealtimes, again used for spiritual reflection, for no one spoke, save the lector chosen to read holy books or the Scriptures as his fellow monks ate. The guest chamber underneath is sumptuous by comparison, for the monks of le Mont-Saint-Michel welcomed the great men and women of the world as well as the humble. Thin pillars divide it into two, and two fireplaces cooked for the monks and their illustrious visitors. As for the knights' hall, whose round Norman arches support simple and charming Gothic arches, in truth it never housed knights. Its name derives from the order of Saint-Michael, which Louis XI of France founded, and which inscribed on their chains of office the words *immensi tremor oceani*, a reference to the fear of the tremendous ocean. This, in fact, is where the monks worked, their scriptorium and their warming room.

Walk along the ramparts to look out across the bay. At low tide pony-trekkers are safely guided over the mud flats. You can see from here over into Brittany and across the bay to the right as far as Avranches. Avranches is our next stop, reached by running back along the causeway from le Mont-Saint-Michel (thoughtfully constructed in 1879) along the D976 to Pontorson and there turning north-east to drive along the N175.

En route Pontorson, on the edge of Brittany, is not to be neglected. Its strategic importance in the Middle Ages is indicated by its appearance in the Bayeux Tapestry itself, in a scene where William the Bastard fights the Bretons. Today do not miss the twelfth-century Norman church of Notre-Dame, sternly built of sandstone and granite and housing delicately carved seventeenth-century choir stalls.

Avranches is set on hills at the estuary of the Sée, twenty-two kilometres from le Mont-Saint-Michel. General Patton's advance into France in 1944 left three-quarters of the city ruined, yet it remains lovely. Try not to miss the Saturday market in the place du Marché. During the first week of August, Avranches is the glamorous setting for an annual antiques fair.

On the corner of the rue d'Islande and the place d'Estouteville in Avranches rises a ruined château. Built in brown stone, this château is guarded by two scowling towers, a round one and an elliptical one, their stern selves contrasting with the charm of the gardens that have been built around them. Part of the château today houses the *sous-préfecture*. Quaint half-timbered houses and a pedestrianized way lead to a church with a modern tower. Then you reach the town market, from which the rue Saint-Gervais takes you as far as the church of Saint-Gervais. The interior of this church is extremely pleasant, classical and simple, with impressive Doric columns, all built in the mid-nineteenth century, when the citizens of Avranches decided that their former church of the same name was too small. Twenty-three bells playing tunes every quarter-hour hang in the belfry, which rises to a height of seventy-four metres. Normally I shrink from recommending visitors to explore the treasury of a church, for such delights are a rather peculiar pleasure. But that of Saint-Gervais is unmissable, crammed with spiritual masterpieces, including the reliquary which houses the cranium of St Aubert himself. Did I say that the Archangel's forefinger dented it? On a second look, St Michael's digit seems actually to have pierced the holy skull.

Avranches has retained much of its medieval street pattern. The bookshop opposite the church of Saint-Gervais has lovingly reconstructed the former half-timbered façade. Walk south along the rue Saint-Gervais to the place Angot and then turn right, to stroll west along the enticing rue Belle-Étoile, and you reach place Carnot. Here there is a church dedicated to Notre-Dame-des-Champs, before which even the most virulent opponent of nineteenth-century Gothic will pale. Notre-Dame-des-Champs overlooks a wide, broad square, shaded with diversely delightful trees and housing one of the city's two tourist offices.

Across the square once stood a Capuchin convent. Its gardens remain, reconstructed by an eighteenth-century botanist named Perrin. Cedars of Lebanon, Japanese gingkos, banana trees and huge pines shelter the plants, shady walks and lawns. The view of le Mont-Saint-Michel across the bay is breathtaking. And to the north of this exquisite botanical garden you will find a theatre and cultural centre, which once were the cloisters and abbey church of Sainte-Anne-des-Moutons, founded by Louis XIII in 1635.

People continue to describe Avranches as a city, even though cities only qualify as such by virtue of possessing a cathedral. Today no cathedral graces a spot which was made famous by Aubert, the founder of le Mont-Saint-Michel, and immortalized by the school of Lanfranc. Avranches lost its bishop in 1792. Two years later the cathedral caved in and was never rebuilt. Walk north from the abbey of Sainte-Anne-des-Moutons to the former site of this cathedral. A stele informs you that here Henry II of England did penance for the murder of Thomas à Becket in 1172.

Across the square is Avranches' city museum. Its treasures include many priceless manuscripts created at le Mont-Saint-Michel between the eighth and the fourteenth centuries, among them a gold and grey register dating from the late 1150s. Folio 4 depicts the Archangel Michael in the year 708 hitting a sleeping St Aubert with his forefinger, to prove that the saint is not dreaming. As further proof that this is no dream, the saint sleeps with his eyes open. Opposite this museum rise the remains of the former bishop's palace, built in the fifteenth century and partly burned down in a fire a hundred or so years later.

This is cattle country, beef and milch-cattle. As you divine from the numerous advertisements for horse races, the farmers in the neighbour-hood of Avranches also breed superb mounts. You drive roughly east along the D911 to Brécey (which boasts a pretty brick and stone seven-teenth-century château), travelling through the rolling bocage where fierce bulls are tethered in fields separate from the cows, and you are grateful for the high hedges of the secondary roads which offer some protection against these malevolent males. We are traversing the Sée valley, noted for its succulent trout and salmon. I have eaten here a filet of salmon baked in puff pastry and served with a sharp sauce Hollandaise, which indicates to me that the cuisine of Normandy from time to time can accept a boost from other elements of the French culinary art, while still utilizing its own rich fish. At Brécey you can visit a château built at the very centre of the seventeenth century, whose park, with its successive terraces and sumptuous main doorway, is delicious.

Follow the D39 to Saint-Pois. This is granite country, and at Saint-Michel-de-Montjoie another three kilometres along the route you can even visit, next to a quarry, an open-air granite museum displaying the varied uses of this powerful material. The charm of its usage is contradic-ted four kilometres along the D39 at Gathemo. Here, at the crossroads, a new church has been constructed entirely of granite, and it seems very queer indeed. Ugly is the word that occurs to me.

For a welcome contrast, turn north-east and drive twelve kilometres to Vire itself. Welcoming and warm, Vire is entered through the arch of a thirteenth-century doorway, flanked with two mighty towers and sup-porting an elegant late fifteenth-century square clock tower. This is the porte-Horloge, bearing a statue of the Virgin Mary and her child, enriched with a prayer adding Mary's personal protection to the strength of the town defences. Not far to the left you can see down the street yet another powerful machicolated tower defending Vire.

Drive past the porte-Horloge and park in the rue Saulnière (unless it is Friday morning, when your car will conflict with a market), then explore the rest of this pretty town on foot. This parking spot abuts on to the semi-fortified Gothic church of Notre-Dame, again warm brown granite outside, with a thirteenth-century tower and a superbly lofty interior. Here the lighter brown granite is magically mottled, the carvings of the apse displaying a virtuosity that reveals just how well you can sculpt this hard stone. Notre-Dame at Vire has three aisles, whose slender round pillars grow more complex as you walk towards the east end and deambulatory. The nave dates from the thirteenth century, the aisles from the fifteenth, the choir and deambulatory from a century later. The process of enrichment, as Gothic architecture developed in Normandy, is shown with absolute lucidity in this unduly neglected church. Who remembers that the mason who created the hair-raisingly beautiful keystones of the choir was he who built the 'Merveille' at le Mont-Saint-Michel? Do not miss also a more modern delight – the mid-eighteenth-century baroque altarpiece created for a chapel of 1764 in the south transept. In the chapel opposite is a very pretty and surprisingly effective modern organ.

Beyond the church is the wide place Nationale, whose fountain is usually flower-bedecked. The slender column topped with a bust of Marianne, symbol of la France, was set up here by the citizens of Vire in 1889 to commemorate the centenary of the French Revolution. Cross the place Nationale and you reach a park lined with lime trees (with larger trees behind them), under which are benches where you can sit and picnic or simply enjoy the shade, the bandstand, a square, ruined keep and views of what remains of the ancient city walls, as well as fine panoramas of the surrounding bocage. Five towers of the city ramparts have survived. As for the keep, it belonged to a Norman château built in 1123 by King Henry I of England and demolished, on the orders of Cardinal Richelieu, in 1630 as part of his plan to subjugate this unruly region to the French monarchy.

As well as enjoying picnics here I have eaten well in the restaurants of Vire, always taking care to avoid their famous chitterling sausages (*andouilles*). If you relish Normandy costumes, before leaving the city pay a visit to the city museum in the former hospice (a pretty eighteenth-century building), which is devoted to the arts and traditions of this part of the bocage. Then follow the D524 through open and rich countryside fifteen kilometres south-east as far as Tinchebray, which lies on the edge of la Suisse normande. Twelfth- and thirteenth-century towers rise picturesquely above the town as you drive down into Tinchebray. The most spectacular is surrounded by nineteenth-century abbey buildings, next to which is a hideous chocolate factory.

Here in 1106 the forces of Henry I faced and defeated those of his brother Robert Courthose (who was away on a crusade), thus once again bringing the duchy of Normandy temporarily under English rule. All that remains of their château is its chapel, now the church of Saint-Remi, unusually heavily fortified for Normandy and decorated with fourteenth-century frescos. Tinchebray's museum of local furniture and art is housed in the former royal prison, a formidable enough eighteenth-century building. And to see the skills of local iron-forgers, visit the seventeenth-century cemetery chapel of Notre-Dame-des-Montiers, with its splendid choir screens and a completely panelled ceiling.

Fifteen kilometres east of Tinchebray the D924 reaches the town of Flers. Its château is now the town hall, a sweet, tower-flanked classical building whose narrow windows climb three storeys and are topped by pretty dormers. A little stream separates the front of the building from a flowery children's play park. The children slide and swing, while their grandmothers doze or chatter under the trees. Over every seat is a canopy protecting you from the heat of the afternoon. Swans swim in the moat of the château, whose long, low stables are now the town's museum and art gallery. I was delighted and surprised to find works by J.-B. Corot and Charles-François Daubigny among a good collection of paintings by the Barbizon group, as well as a couple of Boudins. And since Flers has seen a good many battles (at the time of the Revolution a centre of *chouan* resistance; sacrificing her sons in 1870 and in World War I; taken by Rommel in 1940), an interesting section of the museum is devoted to the impact of these wars on the town.

Beyond this gallery is a splendid park, with massive ancient beech trees and a huge lake where tourists and townsfolk sail canoes. Though much of the town was grievously damaged by American bombers at the end of World War II, its enormous nineteenth-century church of Saint-Germain, built of granite by Paul Hulot, was spared. In the place Saint-Jean is an entertaining curiosity: the motor museum of lower Normandy, where in the afternoons (from 14.00 to 19.00) you can inspect forty or more historic vehicles, including Marshal Joffre's Delaunay-Belleville.

The drive south from Flers to Domfront (eighteen kilometres along the D962) runs up and down hills and through forests of evergreens, firs, pines and deciduous trees. The grey-walled city rises above us as we approach, its classical town hall clearly visible. As its name suggests, Domfront was founded in the sixth century by the celebrated hermit from Périgord, St Front. I live in Périgord and am pleased that one of us has so signally improved the formerly savage Normans of Domfront.

Drive along the stepped walls and arches of the town, making for the signposted Centre ancien, past medieval granite houses, some of them with balconies, others overhanging the road. To explore the town's narrow one-way streets and spy its charming irregular private courtyards you must park and walk. The town walls retain seven fourteenth-century towers. An odd intruder into this medieval and Renaissance glamour is the art deco church of Saint-Julien, built in 1926. Manors and half-timbered houses, with numerous stepped streets, lead up to the ruins of the eleventh-century château (demolished in 1610 on the orders of Henri IV), which is now surrounded by a little park. Old ladies sit under the trees on benches here, and from the esplanade you can see the gorges of the Varenne (known as the valley of the rocks), the surrounding lakes and forests, as well as (near the railway station) the Romanesque church of Notre-Dame-sur-l'Eau which stands beside the River Varenne.

Notre-Dame-sur-l'Eau dates from 1120, and inside are no fewer than thirty-seven seventeenth- and eighteenth-century knightly tombs, as well as a fine statue of the Virgin Mary sculpted in the fourteenth century. Notre-Dame-sur-l'Eau also conserves some rare, faded Romanesque wall-paintings, as well as a Romanesque altar. Small wonder that here in 1178 Chrétien de Troyes was inspired to compose the first ever Arthurian romance, *Lancelot du Lac.*

Tourism flourishes at Domfront alongside local traditional ways, with horse races at the end of July, a Saturday market, canoeing, fishing and pigeon-fancying. Another favourite trip is to the nearby Benedictine abbey of Lonlay, founded on the green banks of the River Égrenne in 1017, today partly ruined – but magically so. You are continually invited to sample the local pear brandy – and should, in my view – save at the beginning of July when Domfront celebrates its annual beer festival.

The D908 runs east from Domfront through the thick Andaines forest for twenty-one kilometres as far as la Ferté-Macé. This route is dubbed by the local tourist boards the path of the three forests, since the Andaines forest is prolonged by the forests of Magny and de la Motte. Saint-Michel-des-Andaines on the way to la Ferté-Macé is a hiking, fishing and horseriding centre. Guarding the west door of its nineteenth-century church are statues of St Michael and the Blessed Virgin Mary. Opposite the church stands the château with a fearsome central tower and elegant extensions, part of its stables now housing the motorized brigade of the *gendarmerie nationale*, everything built out of brown granite.

We are now in the Normandy-Maine nature park, which covers altogether 234,000 hectares and is dedicated not just to the survival of Normandy's superb flora and fauna but also to nurturing its ancient culture and cuisine. Fittingly, therefore, the first thing you see on entering la Ferté-Macé is a tripe shop. Next comes a museum of old farm implements, and third a basically nineteenth-century church with a flat *chevet* dating from an earlier Romanesque building. Inside is a mighty Cavailé-Coll organ. La Ferté-Macé earns a decent living from small industries, but it remains unspoilt, with a number of fifteenth-century houses and a couple of châteaux. Throughout the year its restaurants ply the local delicacy, *tripes en brochette*, and, inevitably, each year on 22 April la Ferté-Macé makes merry with a tripe fair.

From la Ferté-Macé take the D908 north-east for thirteen kilometres as far as Rânes. In the middle of Rânes rises a Renaissance and classical château, with a two-storeyed machicolated keep. Thirty French knights and thirty English ones fought against each other here in a celebrated battle of 1432. The church of Notre-Dame was first built in the fifteenth century and then rebuilt 200 years later.

Rânes lies eleven kilometres north-west of Carrouges. En route you pass the little village of Sainte-Marguerite-de-Carrouges, over the doorways of whose granite houses the dates of their construction are incised. The entrancing church at Rânes has a Romanesque doorway with a sixteenth-century statue of St Sebastian, as well as a seventeenth-century pulpit that must have made the preacher swell with pride the moment he was allowed to climb into it. If you are not a natural churchgoer, look out for the secular concerts regularly held in this sacred venue.

Carrouges is the chief town of the massive Écouves forest, covering some 14,000 hectares. Its moated château rises impressively on a promontory, built of brick and granite in an irregular quadrilateral. The square keep dates from the fourteenth century. You can visit the château for a guided tour and should not miss its splendid kitchens and the sumptuous seventeenth- and eighteenth-century décor and furnishings. Its park is equally attractive, terraced, graced with forged iron gates and balustrades.

As you drive for twenty-six kilometres alongside the Écouves forest east along the D908 to Sées, granite is replaced by stone, a sign that the countryside is changing its character. The church at la Ferrière-Béchet, just over halfway to Sées, with its wainscotting for a roof contains some exquisite statues, in particular a beautiful painted wooden sculpture of St John the Baptist. Sées itself is marvellous. Its promotional literature describes the city as a 'gastronomic stopover'. As well as that, Sées is also an architectural paradise. Its glorious cathedral, with two crocketed symmetrical west spires, flying buttresses and gargoyles (one of them grotesquely seeming to vomit the rainwater), rises where stood a Gallo-Roman sanctuary three centuries before the arrival of the Normans. Notre-Dame de Sées is a thirteenth-century masterpiece, still immaculate despite the savage depredations of the Hundred Years War and two more mutilations, in 1450 and 1793. The seven arches of its nave support a twenty-four-metre-high vault spanning an elegant forty-two metres.

Is there in France another thirteenth-century choir to compete with this one? The grace of its deambulatory is matched by few others. High in the apse gleam stained-glass windows. At the cusp of the arches which support the crossing tower, and in the choir, you spot carved foliage, mannequins, merry animals, a monk with a bottle, pigs, saints and fools. Two exquisite rose windows bring the colour of their glass to the north and south transepts. In the centre of the north rose, Jesus hangs on the cross against the blue sky. In the glass surrounding this crucifixion are depictions of the events of his earthly ministry as, for instance, when he sits in a blue gown among a couple of pink-clad disciples celebrating the Last Supper. Opposite, in the south transept, he sits enthroned in glory, backed by blood-red glass and surrounded by effigies of his twelve apostles, themselves ringed by the great saints that he inspired as well as by the prophets and Jewish kings who came before him. Each of them carries an identifying emblem or, as in the case of wise King Solomon, a scroll bearing his or her name.

In such a masterpiece one easily neglects apparently minor works of art, which are in truth magnificent: the seventy-eight Renaissance carvings on the choir stalls; a marble bas-relief of 1784 depicting the discovery of the bodies of Saints Gervais and Protais (to whom the cathedral was once dedicated); a thirteenth-century statue of the Virgin; the seventeenth-century eagle lectern and altar; the thirty-eight voices of Cavaillé-Coll's organ. Walk round the deambulatory from the south side. In the first chapel the middle two lights show a soldier on horseback piercing Jesus's side with a lance – all set against a brilliant blue background. This is in fact modern glass, as one can spot from the fact that the lance crosses from one light to another, which no medieval glassmaker would allow. Yet it is good glass. The next chapel is dedicated to St Augustine, and in the stained-glass of its windows we find him teaching, studying, theologizing.

The windows of the next chapel contain on the left two entrancingly matched windows from 1375. Both show saintly teachers. In one St Nicholas, Bishop of Myra, is instructing a disciple. In the next St Anne, mother of the Virgin Mary, instructs her most blessed daughter. The disciple of Nicholas and the Virgin Mary both humbly kneel. The symmetry of the stained-glass artist's vision extends to the dress of the windows' subjects. Mary's blue gown is matched by St Nicholas's chasuble. His disciple's chasuble glows with the same rose-pink hue as the dress of St Anne.

The history of Sées cathedral is depicted in music and light every Saturday during the tourist season. 'Construction, destruction and reconstruction' are the themes of the show. The cathedral also offers concerts and musical evenings in an accoustically splendid building.

To the north of this church is what everyone calls the former chapter house, though to me it seems to be a perfect thirteenth-century tithe barn. It has become a museum of religious art and displays the most exquisite liturgical vestments. Ancient wooden beams support the roof of a shady walkway around the museum. From here look back at the powerful flying buttresses added to the cathedral in the nineteenth century to stop its tower falling down – the sole change in its structure since 1330.

Sées has preserved the church of Notre-Dame-de-la-Place, which houses twelve sixteenth-century gilded and painted reliefs depicting the life of the Virgin Mary, as well as a splendid eighteenth-century episcopal palace, classically regular, three storeys high, reached by the rue d'Argentré from the right of the cathedral. The monsignor who built it scarcely lacked money, since he combined his episcopal duties with the office of royal tax collector.

Stroll down the rue de la République south of the cathedral to find the remains of the church of Saint-Pierre, its tower and three of its arches still standing forlornly in an exquisite garden. Opposite rises an old people's hospice. Through its eighteenth-century arched doorway you can see old men sitting in the shade at the side of the courtyard, flowers everywhere and a decorated well in the middle of the grass. After dinner in the hôtel du Cheval Blanc (at no. 1, place Saint-Pierre) I once accepted the chef's invitation to sample a *kir normand* (having earlier declined his *andouille chaud*) and slept soundly till 8 a.m. the following morning. Then I obeyed the sign which points from the corner of the square along the D224 to the abbey of Saint-Martin, another gorgeous eighteenth-century group of buildings, which is now a medical institution but can be visited if you persist.

Sées is twenty-three kilometres south-east of Argentan, which you reach along the N158 by way of two unmissable châteaux: château d'O and château Sassy. Turn right at Mortrée for the château d'O, which is open to the public every afternoon. Its gay Renaissance wing contrasts vividly with the sober earlier part, though this heavyweight section is balanced by a moat which transforms itself into a leisurely lake. And nothing can dull the Italianate lustre of its turrets, pavilions and sharply pointed roofs. Jean I d'O, who began building the château, was Charles VIII's chamberlain. His grandson, François d'O, enriched the family still further as master of the wardrobe and chancellor of the exchequer to Henri III and Henri IV. Yet he was an utterly incompetent financier and eventually died penniless. The loveliest decoration of his former home is, in my view, the fresco of Apollo and the muses in the so-called salon des Muses. The massive farm attached to the château d'O has now been turned into a restaurant.

To visit château Sassy, return to the D158 and turn right towards

Argentan. Six kilometres further on a notice directs you left to the mid-eighteenth-century château (which opens daily from 15.00 to 18.00). Perfectly symmetrical, built in red brick and white stone, it rises above formally descending terraces. Its library is rich, brought here in 1850 by a member of the Pasquier family (who still own and live in the château Sassy). Five Aubusson tapestries adorn its apartments.

Back on the D158 you drive the remaining ten kilometres to Argentan, situated just above the point where the River Orne meets the River Ure. The road enters the town in classically French fashion, by way of a tree-lined avenue flat enough to host a little aerodrome. Much bombed in 1944 – the Allies destroyed nearly 90 per cent of the town, while the retreating Germans were mining the rest – the ensemble of Argentan's central square has been prettily restored. Its mighty flamboyant and Gothic church of Saint-Germain is enhanced by a delicious classical tower, and houses a stone high altar of 1680: baroque, magnificent, among a plethora of treasures.

The church of Saint-Martin has been equally beautifully restored, and seven splendid early sixteenth-century stained-glass windows were happily saved. They represent Judas betraying Jesus before Pontius Pilate, Jesus carrying his cross to Golgotha, the crucifixion, the deposition of the Saviour and the Day of Pentecost. Alas, the damage to the medieval town walls could not be similarly repaired, but remnants remain of the formerly powerful ramparts. A twelfth-century keep, some medieval and classical houses and a ducal château of 1370 add to the town's charm.

Follow the signs east out of Argentan for l'Aigle, taking the N26. We are still in the Normandy-Maine nature park, and our route skirts the forest of Gouffron, with the forest du petite Gouffron on our right. The countryside scarcely knows whether it is plain or bocage. Manors and châteaux, as well as powerful farms, dot the land. After eight kilometres, just beyond le Bourg Saint-Léonard (which boasts an eighteenth-century château and a couple of classical churches), turn left along the D14 for Gacé. The road winds, climbing and descending for fifteen kilometres through bosky fields and beside stud farms – the finest, of course, being the Haras du Pin based on the village of Nonant-le-Pin. We drive through Exmes, whose ruined château still glowers down from its rocky perch and whose church boasts a Romanesque nave and a flamboyant choir which was never entirely finished.

The Gauls called Gacé 'Waccium'. This agricultural town on the banks of the River Touques retains its fourteenth-century château, partly rebuilt in the seventeenth century and standing where the English built its predecessor 600 years earlier. The most direct road from here to Lisieux is left along the D979; but a far more picturesque route is to fork right here, that is to say, not towards Lisieux but towards Rouen.

The land now becomes more diverse. Gorges and valleys, dips and rises, a pine forest, cultivated fields with the farmers selling their luscious apples by the roadside, soon give way to wide fields of corn and small fenced meadows, interspersed with woodlands and grazing cattle, studded with brick houses, half-timbered cottages, manors and stately châteaux. You drive straight as an arrow for twenty-three kilometres, with orchards everywhere, until the road finally winds down through the bois de Broglie into Broglie itself.

This half-timbered little town seems an apparently minor spot today, yet it boasts a medieval château rebuilt in brick and stone in the eighteenth century and enshrining Mme de Stäel's library, not to speak of a sixteenth-century church (begun in the eleventh century), with fine contemporary stained-glass windows.

Here is where, if you have time, you should not drive directly on to Bernay but instead turn off the straight N138, forking right on the D49 across the River Charentonne and immediately left along the D33. This narrow road runs for twelve delicious kilometres to Bernay, through a countryside of wild flowers, especially delicate orchids. On the far side of the stream rise manor houses and mini-châteaux. The route winds through Saint-Quentin-des-Isles with its derelict eighteenth-century cotton mill asleep by the river, its seigneurial nineteenth-century château, its low four-arched bridge, its tiny church and no one seeming alive here save a few chickens. Then you reach Bernay, with its Gothic cemetery chapel high on your left.

In Bernay's parish church you find an almost unique glimpse of Normandy before the arrival of the Vikings. Rich in half-timbered houses, the town is also blessed with the oldest standing Romanesque church in Normandy, Notre-Dame-de-Bernay, founded in 996, much altered over the centuries but retaining its sculpted medieval capitals. As if this were not enough for a tiny town, the church of Sainte-Croix, begun in 1374, is packed with ecclesiastical treasures brought from the ruined abbey of le Bec-Hellouin and boasts a fine fifteenth-century tower, while the church of Notre-Dame-de-la-Couture has a flamboyant doorway which shimmers like flames.

Medieval streets lead you out of Bernay along the D138 for twelve kilometres to Thiberville, with its own little winding streets and half-timbered houses. Take the rue de Lisieux out of the village to find the N13, which runs due west through l'Hôtellerie to Lisieux. Orchards and distilleries creating the exquisitely lethal Calvados liqueur line the road.

One nostalgic, sometimes distressing, but often pleasingly musty task of a travel writer is to read neglected and out-of-date books which history has outstripped. The literature of Lisieux, capital of the pays d'Auge and today the home of some 17,000 Normans, offers many examples of the genre. Louis Serbat's *Lisieux* was published in 1926 and enthuses over the fifteenth- and sixteenth-century houses in the rue aux Fèvres, the Grande Rue and the place des Boucheries. Even in his time one of these ancient dwellings, on the corner of the rue du Paradis, had just been demolished. Henri de Formeville's *Histoire de l'ancien Évêché-Comté de Lisieux*, published in 1873, is even more poignant. Much of their texts is devoted to priceless houses transformed into rubble by no fewer than thirteen air attacks between 6 June and 13 July 1944. Yet as well as depicting a city long gone, such books describe a Lisieux still recognizable.

The city lies amid the rich apple orchards of the Touques valley at the confluence of the Cirieux and the Orbiquet. A venerable Gaulish centre destroyed by the Romans, and next a Roman station pillaged in the third century AD by the vicious barbarians, Lisieux rose from the ashes in the Christian era. The first bishop we know by name was Theudebaud, who reigned from 538 to 549. The city achieved fame as the venue of a council in 1055, which deposed a recalcitrant Archbishop of Rouen. Here in 1152 Henry II of England married Eléanor of Aquitaine and triggered the Hundred Years War. Seventeen years later Bishop Arnulf of Lisieux felt strong enough to offer shelter to Thomas à Becket during his deadly quarrel with the English sovereign. Arnulf's second great achievement was to rebuild his cathedral in the Gothic style, the first such in Normandy.

Lisieux flourished, only to be devastated by plague and famine at the end of the Middle Ages. None the less medieval treasures survive. You can still visit its former cathedral, close by the exquisite public gardens. Dedicated to St Peter, it was begun in 1170. The statues on its façade were despoiled long ago, but its thirteenth-century grace, along with the richly decorated towers of the church, entice one inside. Once there you find powerful cylindrical pillars, sculpted with Romanesque foliage, as well as ogive vaulting and a choir displaying all the majesty of Normandy Gothic. The choir stalls date from the fourteenth century. The notorious Bishop Pierre II Cauchon, who condemned Joan of Arc, paid for the flamboyant reconstruction of the chapel of the Blessed Virgin in the fifteenth century, and there he now lies buried. Oddly enough, the plainer of the two towers of the cathedral of Saint-Pierre dates from the sixteenth century, while the ornate Gothic spire was built 300 years previously.

Sometimes I have been enthralled on entering this church by hearing a voluntary played on the organ which Aristide Cavailé-Coll built in 1874. Don't miss the thirteenth-century stained-glass in the south transept. Next door to the cathedral stands the episcopal palace, built of brick and stone in the early sixteenth century, commissioned by Bishop P. Cospeau.

The canons of Lisieux grew rich, witness the arrogant classical hôtel du

Doyenne which they commissioned as their home in 1769. In addition, Lisieux's public library contains a magnificent 47,000 manuscripts, incunabula and priceless historical documents. To find superb Renaissance houses in Lisieux follow rue Henri-Chéron, rue du Docteur-Degrenne, rue Paul-Banaston and the quai des Remparts. The flamboyant church of Saint-Jacques should on no account be missed. Begun in 1498 it was finished a mere three years later – and though, alas, its superb stained-glass windows were turned into splintered fragments in 1944, the church managed to save its magnificent classical choir stalls and retables. The architect of Saint-Jacques was Guillemot de Samaison. To my regret, the church no longer flourishes as a place of worship; you can eulogize over Saint-Jacques only when it is being used as a concert hall, for no one today celebrates Mass here.

None of this explains the extraordinary twentieth-century blossoming of Lisieux. Piety and religion have given the town a worldwide reputation. On 2 January 1873 a girl, baptized Marie-Françoise-Thérèse, was born at Alençon, the youngest of nine children, daughter of a watchmaker and his wife Zélie. Four years later her father was widowed, and moved with his little child to Lisieux.

Deeply distressed at her mother's death, Thérèse entered the Benedictine abbey school and soon fell seriously ill. Comas, hallucinations and convulsions attacked her frail body. After three months she sought in prayer the help of the mother of Jesus, represented in a statue dubbed Our Lady of Victories. As Thérèse later testified, the statue smiled at her and she was instantly healed. But suffering had changed her. Thérèse now conceived the notion that she might endure suffering not as a burden but as a gift which she might offer to God Himself. She felt that the best way to achieve this would be to enter the Carmelite convent at Lisieux, where two of her elder sisters were already nuns.

Of course she was too young to do so. The superior of the Carmelites, Abbess Delatroette, told her to wait until she was twenty-one. But potential saints are tough. Thérèse, her father and her sister Céline made a pilgrimage to Rome, to be presented to Pope Leo XIII. On such occasions custom requires one to be penitentially silent in the presence of His Holiness, just as one does not speak to the Queen of England unless she first speaks to you. Thérèse had no time for such protocol. Boldly she asked Pope Leo if she might be admitted into the Carmelite convent of Lisieux at the age of fifteen. The courteous pontiff hesitated, and then responded that if God willed it, she could do so. Aged fifteen, Thérèse duly entered the nunnery, a red-brick, slightly dull building in the rue de Liverot, Lisieux.

She had fewer than ten years to live. The mother-superior, Marie de Gonzague, had not the slightest subtlety at coping with a spiritual genius in the midst of her nuns, let alone at uniting a disparate group of religious women with volatile temperaments. The convent was riven with divisions; Thérèse ignored them all. For her last four years on earth she cared for the convent's novices, secretly writing her *Little Way to God*. It saw the light of day in three parts: one was a present to her sister Pauline on her feast day; the next she gave to her sister Marie; and the third she offered to Marie de Gonzague.

In 1896 Thérèse developed tuberculosis. Miserably tormented with pain, she spent her last months in the convent infirmary. 'I had not thought it possible to suffer so terribly,' she once exclaimed. But her dying words were, 'My God, I love you.' Normally Carmelites send round to their sister-convents an obituary notice when one of their nuns dies. In Thérèse's case the sisters of Lisieux decided to circulate her *Little Way to God*. Its effect was electrifying. Nuns demanded more and more copies; the meditations were printed, translated as *The story of a soul* and sold well over a million copies within fifteen years. As Pope Pius XI remarked, Marie-Françoise-Thérèse Martin blew 'a hurricane of glory' throughout the Christian world. Her convent was besieged with visitors and letters. Countless believers attributed miracles of healing to her intercessions with her Saviour. They still do.

Thérèse died in 1897. 'I considered that I was born for glory,' she had written, 'and God made me understand that my glory would not be evident to mortal eyes, but would consist in becoming a great saint, raising me to himself and clothing me in his own infinite merits.' She was both right and wrong. Thérèse became a saint, and lesser mortals did perceive her glory. Eight weeks before her death she wrote to her adopted missionary brother, 'Oh how glad I am to die, for soon I shall be much more useful to other people than I am living here below.'

Sometimes Thérèse's piety overflowed into sickliness. Vita Sackville-West described one such moment, the day the saint designed a coat of arms for herself and Jesus:

It is most elaborately drawn and blazoned; two shields, side by side, are surmounted by the respective initials J.H.S. and M.F.T. (Marie-Françoise-Thérèse). The Holy Child lies on a pillow, playing with a bunch of grapes which represents Thérèse's own desire to offer herself first as a plaything to His every whim and then as a means of of quenching his thirst. On Thérèse's shield amongst other symbols appears the inevitable little flower turning up its face to some rays of light.

Yet she possessed an authentic Christian spirituality. 'Jesus gives me exactly what I can bear at each moment, and no more,' she wrote; 'and if a second later he increases my suffering, he also increases my strength.' Again, she observed, 'To pick up a pin off the floor can be an act of love.'

Such apparently trivial actions were, for St Thérèse, of eternal signifi-
cance, as was her own insignificance. As she put it, 'Precisely because I
was small and feeble, Our Lord stooped down to me and graciously
taught me the secrets of his love.' Today, as then, the Catholic church
almost invariably insists on delaying for fifty years any decision about the
sanctification of its heroes and heroines. In her case the waiting period
was abandoned. Investigations into the sanctity of the girl were begun by
the diocesan tribunal of Bayeux in 1901. The pious began to see visions of
the young child. She appeared to, and cured, a sick woman in London in
1908. In Glasgow in the same year hundreds of people wrote claiming to
have been vouchsafed a vision of the holy child, and two years later she
healed a Glasgow woman of a cancer. Three years after that a Donegal
woman was miraculously healed of terminal septicaemia, allegedly
through the intervention of Thérèse of Lisieux. In 1923 a Dublin girl,
dying of acute nephritis, sought her help in prayer and was cured.

These were but a few of the miraculous interventions that persuaded
the Holy See to consider her case. She had been particularly active in Italy,
handing over money to an impoverished Carmelite priory in Sicily,
helping poor fishermen at Porto Recanati to a superabundant catch, and
kindly filling the kitchen boiler of a Carmelite cook who was weary with
incessantly carrying water from the convent well. And whenever the
Carmelite nuns of Lisieux were despondent, Thérèse would comfort
them with the delicious scent of roses.

Marie-Françoise-Thérèse Martin was beatified in 1923. On 17 May 1925
in St Peter's in Rome, Pius XI declared her a saint. As the Pope observed,
Jesus once said that you cannot enter the kingdom of God without
becoming a child again. Thus the path of the child-saint, he added, paved
the way for all of us to be saved. The great basilica was decorated with
Thérèse's favourite flower. As the Pope finished speaking, five rose
petals detached themselves and slowly floated down on to the
congregation.

As you drive into Lisieux on my zigzag route through Normandy,
watch for the sign on the left which directs you to St Thérèse's massive
basilica. Every evening during the months from June to September the
little saint's words are relayed here from 9.30 onwards. Thirty-eight
grandiloquent steps lead to the entrance of the basilica (there is an easier
way in for the infirm), dedicated to a girl whose humility has become
legendary. Its architect, whose name was Cordonnier, drew up the plans
in 1929. By the time the basilica was consecrated in 1954, both his son and
his grandson had continued his work. Romanesque-byzantine in style, its
dome rises almost 100 metres. The interior is decorated with marble and
with mosaics by Jean and Pierre Gaudin. The saint's right arm lies in a
reliquary given by Pope Pius XI and is displayed annually on the day of

her death. (The rest of her body lies in the Carmelite convent.) In the undercroft you can see a thirty-minute film show about her life.

Saint Thérèse's parents lie buried behind her basilica, at the foot of the sculpted way of the cross. I cannot help thinking that a much more fitting memorial to such a charming saint is their former home, le Buissoners, where Thérèse lived from the age of four till she entered the convent. Her own room has been transformed into an oratory and in another stands her bed and some of her possessions.

From Lisieux do not omit an easy and entrancing tour of some of the finest manors and châteaux in the pays d'Auge. Follow the D579 south-west, looking on the right for the signs directing you to the village of Saint-Martin-de-la-Lieue, just off the main road. Here is the fifteenth-century brick and stone manor of Saint-Hippolyte-du-Bout-des-Prés, with a splendid wooden dovecote in the middle of its courtyard. Further along the D579 you reach an Italianate gem, the château de Saint-Germain-de-Livet. Pale-blue, white, turreted and tiled, it is washed by a tributary of the Touques. Jean de Tournebu and his wife Marie de Croixmare built it btween 1561 and 1584. Today (except on Tuesdays) you can visit its sumptuous Renaissance rooms, filled with tapestries from Flanders and furniture from the seventeenth century to the restoration.

As an extra treat, the church at Saint-Germain-de-Livet is also well worth seeing, with its Tournebu tombs and eighteenth- and nineteenth-century retables. Follow the D579 further south-west as far as its cross-road with the D273, where you turn right and then take the D47 north-west to reach the exquisite half-timbered manor of Coupesarte, reflected in the calm waters of its moat, its side turret precariously held up by a couple of struts.

We are now in the valley of the River Vie, and the D269 takes us further north-west from Coupesarte to the massive brick and stone château de Grandchamp, which you can see standing one and a half kilometres from the road. A mélange of half-timbered medieval, seventeenth-century Renaissance and eighteenth-century classical architecture, all built on the site of a Norman castle, château de Grandchamp is surrounded by a most elegant garden.

Drive on, still running north-west and along the D154 to the D16, where a right turn leads to Crèvecoeur-en-Auge. The route is studded with half-timbered manors, and just after le Mesnil-Mauges – whose eighteenth-century church boasts a Romanesque tower topped by a slate flèche – le Mont de la Vigne rises up, offering a stunning panorama from its summit and also topped by its own fifteenth-century manor and chapel. The château at Crèvecoeur-en-Auge dates from the twelfth century. Its keep and parts of its defences still stand, as do its twelfth-century chapel and another superb fifteenth-century dovecote. Today this château houses the Schlumberger museum, devoted both to Normandy's half-timbered architecture and to the quest for petroleum!

The N13 takes us back east to Lisieux by way of Notre-Dame-de-Livaye, which boasts a thirteenth-century church and next to it an imposing fifteenth-century château. Back in Lisieux find the cathedral square (place Thiers) and the signpost directing you north along the D48 to Pont-l'Évêque, but seventeen kilometres away. En route you pass a huge lake surrounded by leisure centres, as well as stations for horseback riding.

Pont-l'Évêque lies where the River Touques meets the Rivers Calonne and Tvie. Its name derives from a bridge thrown over the first of these rivers by a bishop of Lisieux. Once again appear pretty half-timbered houses, though these are only the ones spared by the bombs of 1944, prior to which Pont-l'Évêque boasted many more. The mighty church of Saint-Martin is slightly disfigured by its modern stained-glass (by a glassmaker from Lisieux named Chapuis) and tantalizingly offers inside a small display of the fragments of the ancient glass it replaces, shattered in those same 1944 air-raids. The church itself has been beautifully restored, a flamboyant Gothic masterpiece begun in 1483 and finished some three decades later. The hôtel Montpensier nearby dates from the early seventeenth century, and the mid-eighteenth-century brick and stone hôtel de Brilly adds further to the town's charms.

On Monday mornings the market at Pont-l'Évêque offers pungent smells of fish, for we are near the sea, as well as apples, fruit and cheese. From here the N177 takes you to Deauville and Trouville through stud-farms and pony clubs. The thatched houses and inns of Canapville on the way are outmatched by a stunning fifteenth-century bishop's manor house next door to the parish church. This protected village is totally unspoilt. Touques, which comes next, describes itself as a medieval village, and so it mostly is, though you will not believe this unless you drive to the centre to discover two churches: Saint-Thomas (whose foundation stone was laid by Thomas à Becket) with its twelfth-century nave and magical flamboyant choir; and the yet finer Romanesque church of Saint-Pierre.

Touques is only two and a half kilometres from the pretty port of Trouville, with its racetrack and sophisticated classical casino, its turn-of-the-century mock medieval hotels whose balconies face the sea, and other buildings which will be for ever associated with the name of Marcel Proust. Trouville remains an active fishing port as well as a tourist centre. Today it is totally contiguous with its sister-resort, situated at the foot of Mount Canisy and on the left bank of the River Touques, and boasting an extraordinary casino (modelled on the Trianon of Versailles but built in 1912), little shipyards and the welcoming, healthful savour of the sea.

Passionate pen
and ink

At Bonneville-sur-Touques which, as its name suggests, lies above the port of Touques itself, the dukes of Normandy in the eleventh century built a formidable château to command the estuary. Unlike their château at Falaise it was not impregnable. Taken five times between 1200 and the mid-thirteenth century, it surprisingly still preserves its circular defences, including five powerful towers, the remains of its mighty keep and living quarters built in the thirteenth century, all protected by a deep ditch.

On summer afternoons you are welcome to visit these historic remains, not only to imagine the feelings of William the Bastard on his return here from conquering England, but also to reflect on one of Émile Zola's most fascinating novels, *La Joie de vivre* (*Zest for Life*). The title itself is fascinating, for when Zola began the book, to outward appearances his career had become one of remarkable success. *Nana* had made him famous. He had recently moved into a sumptuously furnished house at Médan. Having survived deep poverty he was now rich. Yet overwork had left him profoundly nervous and distressed. In 1880 Gustave Flaubert, the man Zola most revered in his profession – despite their disagreements – had died. Then his mother, fallen ill in Paris, came to Médan where she too died. She had always resented Zola's wife Alexandrine. Now, at the end of her life, she openly expressed this hatred, even refusing Alexandrine's food, claiming that her daughter-in-law was poisoning her.

As Zola told a confidant, at night both he and Alexandrine, tender to one another but unhappily childless, would lie awake each knowing that the other was brooding on death. On his mother's death, because of the narrow stairs, her coffin had to be lowered through the window of his Médan home, and now the novelist became obsessed with the shortness of the time left before his own coffin would follow the same route. For some time he had to abandon any attempt to finish *Zest for Life*, beginning work on it again only in 1883 and publishing the finished novel a year later.

Whereas Zola's masterpiece *La Bête humaine* occupies a more or less mythical part of France between Paris and Le Havre, he set his *Zest for Life* in a real place, Bonneville, but a Bonneville which seems a far cry from today's pretty spot. Instead Zola depicted a downtrodden fishing village, with a main road steeply descending between two cliffs and thirty or fewer seamen's hovels, which every tide threatened to crush against the hillside. Such a miserable wreck of a village seems utterly unlike anything you see in today's excellently preserved Normandy; but other nineteenth-century witnesses confirm that many parts of the region, even including some of its great cities, were similarly decrepit.

Writing of Normandy's greatest city, Flaubert, in *Madame Bovary* for example, describes a brook called the Eau-de-Robec, which, he added, 'makes its part of Rouen a kind of sordid little Venice'. To cite another witness: 'Normandy was a vision mingling loveliness and ruin,' commented the novelist Stendhal (Marie-Henri Beyle) in his *Mémoires d'un Touriste* of 1838. 'At Caen I visited the cathedral, then a shambles. I clambered over piles of rain-soaked stone and eased inside where I could feel the cold earth through the soles of my shoes and where for a while I seemed engulfed in a damp, musty rot.' Again, after a night in a bug-ridden Normandy hotel in Pontorson in 1836, Victor Hugo complained that he had 'paid five francs not to have eaten but to have been eaten'. Despite the proximity of the sea, not a single fish had been featured on the menu. Instead he and his mistress Juliette Drouet had been offered the remains of a half-eaten leg of mutton, served on a table lit by a single, precariously balanced candle which dripped wax on to the plates of the diners. In a hotel on le Mont-Saint-Michel he noted with gloom that the only dish which the ancient and swarthy landlady, Madame Laloi, could serve them was 'a fish that had rotted while still in the depths of the sea'.

Zola, whose *Zest for Life* triggered this brief historical excursion into nineteenth-century Normandy grottiness, had first visited the Normandy coast in 1875, staying at the small village of Saint-Aubin. His initial response was that he could scarcely imagine anything uglier, and this impression was undoubtedly incorporated into *Zest for Life*. Soon, however, the splendour of the sea began to overwhelm the novelist. 'The view is superb,' he wrote, 'the sea, always the sea! A tempestuous wind has been driving the waves almost as far as our door. Nothing could be grander, especially during the night. This sea is something totally different from the Mediterranean, at one and the same time mean and great.'

In the village overlooking this sea he set his remarkable tale, which has frequently been described as encapsulating in nineteenth-century fashion rivalries equalling those of the Montagues and Capulets. Zola's hero in *Zest for Life* (if hero is the word) is a neurotic young man named Lazare, who at first seems absorbed only in music, but soon dreams of building a redoubt with jetties and breakwaters at Bonneville in order to 'defeat' the sea. Instead the sea defeats his jetty, as the spring tide not only demolishes it but also carries away three fishermen's hovels. Finally the sea destroys the whole village.

Yet in Zola's novel all is not pessimism. He portrays the Norman fisherfolk as a proud race, clinging like limpets to the rocks with an almost stupid obstinacy, proud even when their boats are smashed by the waves and their fellow mariners drowned. Zola himself clearly relished the dangerous sea and the coastal storms. But he also made them menacing, even malevolent. Zola's Normandy sea is mythical, symbolizing the animality of the peasant people, often subdued by the bourgeoisie but never finally tamed by them.

The sea and the storms of Normandy also seemed to exorcise his own melancholy. In lines which also describe some of today's Normandy storms, he wrote:

In the livid sky huge black sooty clouds were being driven above the waters by the west wind. This was one of the storms which blow up here in March, as the tides of the equinox angrily batter the coast. The sea was just starting to come in and could be seen only as a thin and distant line of foam, a white band on the horizon. As for the beach itself, it was completely exposed as a long stretch of gloomy rocks and seaweed, a bare plain dirtied with puddles and miserable black patches. Under the increasingly dark and panic-stricken clouds its aspect was one of dreadful melancholy.

The roads were so bad that when Zola's heroine Pauline, in *Zest for Life*, travels by coach from Paris, the journey from Bayeux to Bonneville takes nearly two hours. Pauline is the antithesis of Lazare. The novelist Angus Wilson has acutely observed that the brilliant yet pessimistic young man, who in the end comes to nothing, 'is the embodiment of the decadent end of nineteenth-century prosperity' whereas Pauline, the young and healthy daughter of a plump, sensual pork butcher, is 'one of the most complete women in nineteenth-century fiction'. Filled with animal pleasure, she finds fulfilment and meaning in a simple life of service and good works.

The sea obsesses her too, and from leaving the beach at Arromanches on her journey to Bonneville she continually thrusts her head out of the carriage window in defiance of the wind to gaze at the water, finally watching its enormous white crests at the foot of the Bonneville cliffs. The sea, wrote Zola, 'appeared a being that belonged to her. Slowly with her eyes she seemed to be making it her own.'

Everything Lazare attempts – not just his redoubt but also music, the study of medicine and the opening of a factory – ends in failure. Boredom makes him profoundly unhappy. Bored both with leisure and with work, with himself and everyone else, he also becomes ashamed of his idleness, considering it a disgrace that a man of his age is 'wasting the best years of his life in wretched Bonneville'. What sustains him in his attempt to build the jetties is not a desire to better the lot of the fisherfolk but resentment, especially resentment against the sea.

Although the vicious sea wins, Zola's message is no longer one of total despair. To quote Angus Wilson again, 'In the character of Lazare, he fought the neurotic side of himself and won.' Pauline's joy in living is matched by the remarkable behaviour of the fishermen even when the sea is finally overwhelming their village. 'Bonneville,' Zola writes as he begins to describe this terrifying event, 'had lately endured unprecedented misery. The great storms of May had crushed its last three houses against the cliff. That was the end. After centuries of continuous onslaught the spring tides, which had encroached every year on another stretch of land, were all that was left on the shingle as they wiped out even the traces of the ruins.' The fishermen had been forced to build a new Bonneville, higher up the cliff. Then one day when the wind blows from the north, the sea finishes its work of destruction by sweeping away Lazare's redoubt, his jetties and his breakwaters. Lazare stays on his terrace watching its fury, but the excited fishermen run down the hill 'brimming over with terror and pride', as he shakes his fist at them, 'roaring in unison with the roaring sea, gesticulating and dancing like savages, drunk with the wind and the water and giving themselves up to the horror of it all'.

If this entrancing Norman novel by Zola is not his greatest, Zola's master Gustave Flaubert devoted to the region his acknowledged masterpiece. Flaubert was born the son of a Rouen surgeon in 1821. On a visit to Trouville in 1836 he met and fell hopelessly in love with a Madame de Schlésinger, and with a true novelist's skill at not losing any possible experience used her as the model for the heroines of several of his works. *Madame Bovary* appeared in 1856 as a magazine serial five years after Flaubert began writing it. His explicit account of the sexual life of a frustrated provincial wife married to a well-meaning, but boring, doctor was bound to offend. In contemporary, and frequently hypocritical, eyes Emma Bovary's ultimate suicide did not expiate her sexual adventures. After the publication of the novel Flaubert was put on trial for 'committing an outrage against public and religious morality'. His lawyer, Maître

Marie-Antoine-Jules Bernard, successfully defended the author, and it was to Bernard that *Madame Bovary* was dedicated when it was published in book form the following year.

Yet Flaubert's *Madame Bovary* is truly provocative. As he cunningly phrased it, 'She revelled in every malicious irony of her triumphant adultery, and her former virtue now seemed to her a crime.' The more she succumbed to her lover Rodolphe, the more she began to regard her husband with repugnance.

The more excessively she gave herself to the one, the more she loathed the other. Charles had never seemed so disagreeable to her, his fingers never so blunt, his mind never so dull and his manners never so crude as when she saw him after she had met Rodolphe. As she performed her role as a wife – but merely as an actress – she would passionately imagine the black hairs which curled down over her lover's tanned forehead. She would think of his powerful and yet graceful body, his mature mind and his hot-blooded temperament.

One night, after Madame Bovary had cruelly repulsed the tenderness of her despairing husband, Rodolphe arrived in the garden of their home. He found Emma waiting at the foot of the steps. 'They embraced,' wrote Flaubert, 'and like snow all their rancour melted in the warmth of their embrace.'

The coast of Normandy forms in Flaubert's masterpiece an exquisite backcloth to his heroine's guilty love. She and Rodolphe stay for three days at the hôtel de Boulogne on the waterfront, sipping iced fruit juices when not making love, hiring a covered boat to take dinner on an island, listening to the rumble of carts and the sound of caulkers' mallets striking against the hulls in the shipyards. Flaubert offended conventional morality even more by describing these three full, exquisite and sinful days as 'truly a honeymoon'.

Whereas *Zest for Life* enthuses over the sea, *Madame Bovary* relishes the Norman countryside, especially the farms of the pays de Caux. 'Alongside the farm buildings lay a wide, steaming manure pile; among the chickens and turkeys pecking at its surface were five or six peacocks, a favourite luxury in the barnyards of the Caux region. The sheepfold was long and the barn was high, with walls as smooth as your hand.'

In a moment I must return to *Madame Bovary*, but Flaubert's nose for manure reminds me of what, in my view, is his other masterpiece, the oddly neglected *Bouvard and Pécuchet*, which he wrote between 1862 and his death in 1880 and which was published posthumously the following year. In her *Souvenirs Intimes*, Mme Caroline Commanvile recounts how Flaubert conceived of the novel. Sitting on a bench in Rouen with his dear friend the poet Bouilhet, he spotted the workhouse opposite and began to muse on the fact that one day they might end up as two daft old codgers living there. Flaubert and Bouilhet then animatedly began to conjure up the story of a couple of decrepit former clerks living in penury inside this workhouse, their lives declining into gloom as their ambitions faded. Initially Flaubert conceived their names as Dubolard and Bécuchet, then as Bolard and Manichet and finally as the delightfully daft Bouvard and Pécuchet.

In his last tale these two mock-heroes start out as Parisian copying-clerks, grow dissatisfied with their lives and boldly try out virtually everything imaginable. Not one project succeeds. By error, as gardeners, they plant passion-flowers in the shade and pansies in the sun. They foolishly water the lilies after they have flowered, cut the rhododendrons back and so destroy them, try to stimulate the fuchsias with glue, fatally expose a pomegranate tree to the kitchen fire and kill hyacinths by smothering them with dung. Not surprisingly, Bouvard and Pécuchet end their days once again as copying clerks.

'I shall place my *Bouvard and Pécuchet* between the valley of the Orne and the valley of the Auge, on a comical plateau between Caen and Falaise,' Flaubert wrote in 1874. Three years later, what the author described as an 'archaeological-geological-picturesque' journey, in the company of his friend Edmond Laporte, took them by way of Argentan to the environs of Caen, Bayeux and Falaise and then back to Domfront, enabling him to soak up the atmosphere of the region which was to form the background for his burlesque.

But for Flaubert the setting of any novel was no simple backdrop. The Normandy landscape in *Bouvard and Pécuchet* compliments and points up the characters of his two old dafties, especially their hopes for an idyllic end to their days and the realities of their lives. One day the two take a gentle stroll through the countryside:

Little clouds flecked the sky; the tops of the cornfields swayed in the wind; alongside a meadow a little stream was murmuring, when suddenly a revolting pong stopped them in their tracks and they saw the putrifying carcase of a dead dog lying between some brambles on a heap of stones. 'One day we'll be like that,' commented Pécuchet stoically.

Thus nature symbolizes the whole comically sad tale.

So nothing goes right for the two lovable, pathetic loonies on their farm in the valley of the Orne. Their seed-crops are pitiable; a girl farmhand becomes pregnant; the artichokes perish; too much dung spoils the strawberries; too little dung ruins the tomatoes. Everyone swindles them, complaining while they do so at having to work so hard for the Parisians. Pécuchet grows to adore his orchard and hotbed, with its bowls of geraniums and sunflowers. 'But the hotbed swarmed with grubs,' wrote Flaubert. 'The cuttings failed to take; grafts broke away; the runners dried up for lack of sap; roots of trees rotted; the playful wind blew down the beans; and broccoli, aubergines and turnips all died.' Instead of offering their workers cider, Bouvard made them beer. 'The result was stomach-aches, with children crying, women groaning and the menfolk furiously threatening to quit.' Only a giant cabbage consoled the two would-be Norman farmers, and it ended up so huge as to be quite inedible.

As educated gentlemen Bouvard and Pécuchet read all they could find about farming. Everything misled them. 'The barometer deceived them and they learned nothing from the thermometer.' Then they read that a priest of Touraine in the time of Louis XV had discovered that a leech placed in a glass jar would climb up the side when it was about to rain, sit at the bottom when fine weather was promised and move agitatedly when a storm threatened. Bouvard and Pécuchet put such a leech in a glass jar. Since its every movement was contradicted by the weather, they added another three leeches. All four behaved differently.

Above all they, like Flaubert, loved Normandy manure heaps. Bouvard, encouraged by Pécuchet, had a frenzy for them.

Into the compost heap he threw together tree-branches, blood, chicken feathers, everything he could lay his hands on. He bought Belgian chemicals, Swiss fertilizers, lye, pickled herrings, seaweed and rags. He ordered guano dung and even tried to manufacture it himself. His extreme principles forced him not to waste a drop of urine. The farm privies were suppressed. The fragmented carcase of any dead animal was brought into the yard where his dungheap festered. In the midst of the stench Bouvard smiled.

As this manure, now turned liquid, was sprayed over his crops he upbraided those who held their noses, with the cry, 'It's gold; it's gold!' He regretted that he did not possess yet more heaps of manure. In Flaubert's words – words that reveal his insight into Norman farming – 'Happy is the land whose natural caves are filled with the droppings of birds!'

Part of Flaubert's *Madame Bovary* is set where Normandy, Picardy and the Île-de-France come together. Although he describes it as a bastard region, whose speech is as characterless as its landscape, Flaubert's own magical descriptions of the area delightfully contradict this. Take, for example, this passage of magnificent evocation:

The river flowing through this valley divides it into two quite different regions. On the left bank everything you can see is pastureland; from the right bank stretch ploughed fields. The pastures extend along a low chain of hills until they reach the grassy land of the Bray country. The gentle slopes of the plain by contrast widen as they spread to the east, their golden fields of grain extending as far as anyone can see. Along the edge of the grass the white line of a stream divides the meadow's colour from that of the cultivated land, and so the countryside resembles a huge velvet cloak, spread out and boasting the colours of green edged with silver braid.

Flaubert relished the grand houses of Normandy, white manors viewed through an iron fence, their round lawns decorated with a couple of cast-iron urns and a cupid holding his finger to his lips; but he also loved the plastered Normandy farms where he set his *Madame Bovary*, reached by roads lined with aspen trees, enclosed by hedges, emaciated pear trees clambering up their walls, their courtyards surrounded by straggling outbuildings, the main farm embellished with black diagonal timbers. He described their thatched roofs which covered the upper third or so of the low windows as 'fur hats pulled down over eyes'. Among thickly growing trees, against which were propped ladders and on whose branches hung a lazy scythe, stood cider presses, distilleries of *eau de vie* and cart sheds. As he noted, the farmers would soak dry brown bread in their cider and then feed it to their young chickens.

A century later little had changed. Mrs Robert Henry, who bought a Normandy farm in the pays d'Auge in 1937, discovered that most of the neighbouring farms were family affairs, though not always owned by those who farmed them. 'Every farmer kept a kitchen garden in which he grew his soft fruit and vegetables, and as in many Scottish gardens, flowers bordered the vegetables.' Land, she found, was jealously guarded, though when a farmer died the Napoleonic law, which called for a division of his property between the widow and their children, meant that parcels did come on to the market. Then the price would be reasonable. She spotted that the Norman people liked to own land but did not gamble with it. 'They tended to collect it as they collected sovereigns and the Louis d'or hidden away in an old stocking – because it made them feel good to have a bit of land available and a bit of gold.'

This was the so-called Norman peasant, a man who, when Mrs Robert Henry first came here, was precisely:

as Guy de Maupassant described him in a previous century – suspicious, crafty, never committing himself, a lover of devious ways and ghostly secrets, a firm believer in sorcery and an imbiber and worshipper of his own brew of cider and applejack. That he was seldom sober and that when on the eve of tragedy he was apt to hang himself from a rafter in his cider press was undeniable. But as a grafter of apple trees, as a woodcutter, as a fashioner of faggots and six-foot tall walls of logs, as an artist with the scythe and as a lover of woods and pasturage and country lore he was a joy to watch and to emulate.

Guy de Maupassant loved these peasants. He was born in 1850 near Fécamp, with its lovely medieval church and splendid harbour. Flaubert introduced him into literary circles. Soon he had become a disciple of Zola. Many of his 250 or so magical short stories are set in his native province, and his insight into the psychology of the local peasant gives them a flavour quite distinct from the Normandy tales of his mentors. *A Normandy Joke*, for instance, tells of the wedding night of Jean Patu, the richest farmer in the neighbourhood, and his bride Rosalie Roussel – courted by virtually every eligible young man of the district and, as Maupassant put it, choosing Jean 'partly, maybe, because she fancied him more than the others, but yet more because as a careful Normandy girl she spotted that he possessed more Louis d'or than they had'.

Patu was an ardent sportsman, with many expensive guns, dogs, keepers and ferrets, as well as a burning hatred of poachers. Even as the wedding feast was beginning he heard what appeared to be poachers' guns in the distance and ran off to try to catch them. Returning, he joined his guests and bride at a formidable Normandy feast. More than a hundred people could be seated in the massive farmhouse, and others fed outside. From time to time the farmers, sated with food and drink, would go outside to relieve themselves, their scarlet-faced womenfolk with bursting corsets soon following their example. Dubious jokes were exchanged. As Maupassant observed, 'For the past hundred years these same vulgar jokes had been told on similar occasions, but though everyone knew them, everyone roared with laughter.' The bride, as was correct, blushed.

Some of the young men now began to taunt Patu with the thought that poachers would profit from his wedding by stealing his game while he was in bed with Rosalie. 'Just let them come!' replied Jean angrily; but one of his taunters answered, 'They surely won't make you neglect your duty.' Then Maupassant deliciously describes the way the bride and groom undress for each other, shyly yet trembling with expectation. Meanwhile some of Patu's guests are setting him up, feigning to be poachers themselves, firing off shots outside the farmhouse. 'Leave them alone,' cries Rosalie to her new husband. 'It's no concern of yours. Come to bed.' But Jean, flying into a rage at the thought of being robbed of a few game, puts on his clothes, takes down his gun and jumps through the window into the farmyard, promising to be back in a few minutes.

Rosalie waits an hour, two hours and all night. The following morning she agitatedly sends the servants to look for her spouse. They find him a couple of leagues away, trussed hand and foot, his trousers turned inside-out, three dead hares hanging round his neck, his gun broken, himself in a total rage and a placard on his chest reading, 'Whoever goes on a chase loses his place.' In later days, his anger cooled, Jean himself would ruefully tell how his friends had caught him in a snare like a rabbit. And Maupassant ends his tale, 'This is how they entertain themselves in Normandy at a wedding.'

Guy de Maupassant's superb novel *Bel-Ami* is set in a village named

Canteleu overlooking Rouen, where Georges Duroy and his wife Madeleine spend their honeymoon. Here, as ever, Maupassant can transform the most trivial events into quivering eroticism. The two are in the train on the way from Paris to Canteleu, planning to spend their first married night together at Rouen. The train passes through the long station of Batignolles and then crosses 'the mangy-looking plain that extends from the fortifications to the Seine'. They rumble over the bridge at Asnières, delighted by the sight of boats, fishermen and rowers on the river. Duroy begins to kiss his new wife, professing his joy that he has at last won her. In a low voice she replies, 'That is very nice', looking him straight in the face and smiling. Duroy thinks to himself, 'I'm too cold, or maybe too stupid. I ought to be progressing faster than this', so he pulls her to him, eagerly kissing her, his lips quivering. Instead of responding she pulls away, stands up quickly and admonishes him with the words, 'Now, Georges. Stop it. We aren't children. We can easily wait till we reach Rouen . . . Kisses in a railway train aren't worth anything,' says Madeleine, in schoolmistress manner. 'Trust my experience. All they do is upset you.' Then she relents, and blushingly adds, 'You know you should never cut green wheat.' So Georges and Madeleine sit cheek to cheek almost motionless, 'happy to feel themselves so close together, their eyes peering through the carriage window and from time to time glimpsing through the darkness the lights of houses. Then comes one of Guy de Maupassant's brilliant strokes. They arrive at Rouen and he describes their night in one laconic sentence. 'They put up at a hotel overlooking the quay.'

In his short story *Our Hearts* the novelist also used the device of a train journey from Paris to describe the richness of the Normandy landscape in late July: 'undulating countryside, with fertile valleys with the peasants' dwellings, their pastures and orchards, all enclosed by rows of massive trees whose heads shone tufted in the rays of the sun' – a country of cider-orchards and oxen. He noted the enormous cows that you can still see today, whose 'glaring patches of white make bizarre designs on their flanks', as well as ruddy bulls with huge curly foreheads. 'Here and there a river appeared, winding along the foot of poplar trees, while under a thin gauze of weeping willows a grassy stream would occasionally flash.'

Climbing into Avranches I have experienced the same *frisson* of delight as Guy de Maupassant attributed to André Mariolle, the hero of *Our Hearts*. It is a city that seems, he wrote, 'from a distance much like a fortress but as you draw nearer is perceived for what it is, an ancient pretty, countryside Norman town.' Avranches still preserves its botanical garden, once tended by medieval monks and transformed in the eighteenth century by a professor of natural history named Perrin into a botanists' paradise.

Longing to meet his beloved, Michèle de Burne, André makes directly for this garden once he has deposited his baggage at a hotel. This Jardin des Plantes at Avranches enjoys a stupendous view of the bay of le Mont-Saint-Michel, and Guy de Maupassant here exults in it: 'an apparently unending plain of sand merging in the distance into the sea and sky, with a river meandering through it and from time to time pools of water glistening in the sand like plates of burnished metal'. In the middle of this seemingly interminable stretch of sand rises the monumental crag on which is built the abbey of le Mont-Saint-Michel. Further on André makes out the peaks of half-submerged rocks, and to the right an apparently limitless green forest. 'At one glance the scene revealed on the one hand the grandeur and the sublimity of nature and on the other its freshness and grace.'

As Guy de Maupassant inevitably perceived, a hotel on le Mont-Saint-Michel is a magical place (though fairly expensive) for lovers. Since I do not understand why he has gained the reputation of being a lubricious author, let me offer two entrancingly delicate descriptions of how in *Our Hearts* André Mariolle and Michèle de Burne achieve ecstasy. On his first stay on the mount, André remains leaning out of his hotel window in the town's sole winding street, as gradually every sound dies away and the silver high tide rises. He has 'a presentiment of some inexplicable marvellous fortune'. Suddenly a hand touches the handle of his door. A woman enters, 'wearing one of those *robes-de-chambre* that seem made from snow as well as silk and lace', carefully closing the door behind her. 'Then,' continues Maupassant, 'as though she had not even seen him standing framed by the window and overwhelmed with happiness, she walked directly to the mantelpiece and blew out the two candles'.

Later in *Our Hearts* Maupassant is even more laconically seductive. André Mariolle and Michèle de Burne 'clasped each other in one of those embraces that give the strange double sensation of bliss and unconsciousness'. And all this takes place, almost sacrilegiously, on le Mont-Saint-Michel.

Yet alongside these delicious moments what remains in my mind from his works is a luscious appreciation of the Norman countryside and the patient farmers who care for it. Guy de Maupassant's landscapes gleam and burn with colour, save where the rich trees of Normandy bring shade. His *Le Crime du Père Boniface* is set in June, 'that green and flowery month when the plains are at their best. A man, dressed in a blue shirt with a red-braided black kepi on his head, was crossing the fields of rape, oats and wheat, the harvest reaching as far as his shoulders, his head appearing above the ears of corn and seeming to float on a calm and verdant sea whose gentle waves were stirred by the light breeze.'

This landscape and seascape is used to remarkable psychological effect in one of the stories that make up Marcel Proust's *À la recherche du temps perdu*. As everyone knows, there is a markedly autobiographical element in these stories; and this element applies to their settings too. As a child Proust would spend part of each summer with his grandmother at one of the Normandy Channel resorts: Trouville, Dieppe or Cabourg. Cabourg was also the scene of a holiday with his mother in 1880. The boy loved these holidays. In Madame Proust's diary are found the words, 'Letter from my darling Marcel, Cabourg, 9 September 1891. "How different from those years at the seaside when grandmother and I, battling together against the wind, used to talk – so perfectly at one with each other."' Madame Proust added, 'At one! Never was a child so perfectly at one within a family and so dearly loved.'

As a young man Proust made further sorties into Normandy, to the home of Madame Lemaire at Dieppe, for example, along with his cousin Reynaldo Hahn. After his mother's death in 1905, Proust suffered a deep depression which lasted for two years and can be discerned in an article of 1907 in *Le Figaro* which speaks of 'the slow work of destruction in the body we love, with fading eyes, hardening arteries and hair slowly turning white'.

Proust at last managed to throw off the lassitude caused by his loss, and now he returned annually to Cabourg, from 1907 to 1914. He stayed in the Grand Hotel, which with its casino had been built in the 1860s, rebuilt in the 1880s and reconstructed in the year his annual visits began. Proust deplored the vulgarity of the other guests. To exclude the sound of noisy neighbours he needed three rooms in the hotel, either living on the top floor or renting the room above his own so as to avoid hearing footsteps overhead. One room he reserved for his cook Félicie. 'Am I being slightly ridiculous perhaps to bring along my ancient cook to a hotel?' he would ask.

Thus closeted, he would work throughout the day, living in the smallest of his rooms, his valet in the largest, disturbed only by servants whom he had taught to bring gossip and appetizing snatches of information about the other guests. Then, at dusk, he might go out with a parasol or at least stand on the doorstep of the hotel, pleased that the sun had set and that his asthma was thus at bay, before settling at a large table in the dining room and entertaining with champagne anyone who was willing to sit with him.

Sometimes he would gamble by proxy. During one season the invalid surprised everyone by dancing every other night. And of course he wrote, once confessing that he had not turned off the light for a stretch of sixty hours. He believed that death was not far away, and would frequently quote the Gospel of St John (filtered to him through a remark of John Ruskin): 'Work while you still have the light.'

When his health was stronger Proust toured Normandy in a taxi, driven by a nineteen-year-old chauffeur called Agostinelli and living mostly off *café au lait*. On these journeys he exulted, for instance, in the stained-glass windows at Évreux cathedral which, he wrote 'had miraculously managed somehow to snatch jewels of light out of a rainy sky'. But Cabourg he loved most of all, drawing on its ambience for the imaginary summer resort of Balbec in his exquisite *À l'Ombre des jeunes filles en fleurs*, the story which won the Prix Goncourt in 1919 (and was translated into English by C. K. Scott Moncrieff as *Within a Budding Grove*).

Here Proust's adolescent hero Swann imagines himself in love with not just one but a whole gaggle of girls, among whom is the reticent Albertine. Here too he meets the blond Robert de Saint-Loup and his strange uncle Baron de Charlus. On a second visit to Balbec Swann realizes that he really is in love with Albertine, at which point the sexual ambiguities of Proust's own self and of his novel burst out through two virtually accidental discoveries: that Baron de Charlus is homosexual and that Albertine is intimate with a young woman named Vinteuil, whom Swann had once glimpsed through a window with a known lesbian.

Proust's analysis of human emotion is at its most masterly in *À l'Ombre des jeunes filles en fleurs*. Swann arrives at Balbec having more or less successfully recovered from a desperate infatuation with a girl named Gilberte, and through him Proust broods on the irrationality of passion. On the way from Paris, Swann had already experienced a fugitive desire for a fisherwoman. As he arrives at Balbec/Cabourg Proust's hero muses:

When I went with my grandmother to Balbec I had reached a state of almost total indifference to Gilberte. When I fell under the spell of a new strange face, when I began to plan discovering Gothic cathedrals and Italy's palaces and gardens with some different woman, I told myself sadly that our love in so far as it attaches itself to one person in particular is perhaps not very real, for if pleasant or unpleasant trains of thought can for a time so much associate themselves to one woman as to make us believe she actually inspired them, yet the moment we detach ourselves, either deliberately or subconsciously, from these associations, this love for one woman will spring up again and attach itself to another as if it came entirely from within ourselves and not from them at all.

Yet we know that soon he will be tormented at the thought that he cannot totally control every single movement or thought of Albertine.

The emotional ambiguities of Proust's novel are relieved by a delicious insight into the mores of the Normandy he knew. The petty snobberies of fashionable Cabourg had tuned his powers of description, and at Balbec itself the novelist delighted, first in Swann's terror at seeing the monumental mock-marble staircase, and then in his amazement at the manager with whom his grandmother was discussing terms. This 'mandarin', both his face and voice scarred – the one with pustules, the other with a bizarre half-genteel pattern of malapropisms – would classify the guests as either gentry or crooks, managing to work out by some arcane method what he decided was their financial and social status. In Balbec, too, Marcel Proust deftly describes the inhabitants of, and visitors to, these fashionable Normandy seaside resorts at the turn of the century: lawn-tennis players sporting white hats; the stationmaster among his tamarisks and rose trees; a lady in a straw boater on the way to her bungalow, calling to her little dog which has stopped to examine something in the road. At Cabourg there is an elegant, long promenade between the casino and the sea. In Proust's day it was called the promenade des Anglais; today it is rightly known as promenade Marcel-Proust.

Proust, Flaubert, Maupassant, Zola: what is it about Normandy that gives these brilliant novelists their fascination with affairs of the heart and a powerful feeling for eroticism? Proust, at least, was clear that it must have something to do with the lush fields and wild seascape of his favourite region.

In a revealing sentence he once wrote that 'Literature can only depict a woman as if she were a mirror reflecting the colours of the tree or the river alongside which our custom is to draw her.' The very Normandy countryside was, for Marcel Proust, erotic, crammed with sensuality. 'Desire for a woman seemed to me to add something utterly exultant to the charms of nature, and nature in return enlarged what in women had been till then too much restrained.' Women, whether illuminated by the headlamps of his taxis or spotted walking along the dykes holding back the sea, seemed to him like arbours of roses enhancing a garden on the cliffs. And, of course, Normandy rain and sun creates stunning roses.

As for the sea itself, its colours in Proust are reflected in the eyes of seductive girls and above all in those of the elusive Albertine. To describe her sullen moments he drew on the myriad colours of the waves. 'On some meagre days, when her face was grey and her aspect gloomy, a violet transparency appeared to cloud her eyes, seemingly seeping in from the sea.'

So the sea insistently flows through Norman literature. Descended from the Vikings, the Normans also happen to be a race whose navigators in the sixteenth century sailed uncharted seas to reach America, Madagascar, Sumatra and Florida. Normandy-bred Samuel Champlain, who sailed from Le Havre in 1608, founded Quebec the following year. Not surprisingly these same Normans produced an author who created the genre known as 'voyage literature'. Jacques Henri Bernardin de Saint-Pierre was born in 1737 at Le Havre and soon developed a remarkable enthusiasm for travelling the world. His uncle Godebout was a ship's captain and he took the young Bernardin de Saint-Pierre on a trip to Martinique when the boy was only twelve. After studying at Rouen and training as an engineer the young man was soon off on his travels again – to Holland and Germany, Malta, Russia and Poland, whence he travelled in the company of a Polish princess to Vienna, Dresden and Berlin.

The only place he seemed not to like was the Île-de-France. When his father died, leaving him penniless, Bernard de Saint-Pierre was unhappily obliged to resort to Paris to try to earn a living. The post of captain-engineer to the king enabled him to escape on a journey to Madagascar to work for the dauphin there.

His return to France in 1771 marked a major turning point in his life, for now he became an *habitué* of Parisian philosophers and a lifelong disciple, as well as a personal friend, of Jean-Jacques Rousseau. Rousseau's views on the harmful influence of modern society, which corrupts unfallen human nature, reinforced Bernardin de Saint-Pierre's personal dislike of Parisian life. He also enthused over his master's notions of education, particularly as expounded in Rousseau's novel *Émile*, which again stressed the perfection of a life unsullied by the inequalities brought about by so-called civilization, by property, commerce and science.

Bernardin de Saint-Pierre developed a desire to emulate his master as a writer, and in 1773 published his two-volume *Voyage à l'Île-de-France*. It met with little success, but the would-be author persisted. His *Études de la Nature*, which appeared in 1784 six years after Rousseau's death and avidly pursued the lifelong themes of the great philosopher, marked the beginnings of Bernardin de Saint-Pierre's popular success. It had reached a third edition by 1788, and in that edition appeared his masterpiece, *Paul et Virginie*.

Paul et Virginie is a romantic, delightfully written and sentimental tale set on the island of Mauritius, far from the corruptions of society. This idyllic love story begins with a couple of children born into families so harmoniously at one with each other and the state of nature that Paul's mother likes nothing better than to breast-feed Virginie while her own son is being breast-fed by Virginie's mother. Brought up in this state of nature, the children dream of marrying from their earliest moments of consciousness. Their idyll expounds a sinless world where man and nature are at harmony with each other under the blessing of a bountiful God. If such exotic utopianism has taken a critical bashing since his time, Bernardin de Saint-Pierre's *Paul et Virginie* was a major success in his day and made his fortune.

He continued to preach the same themes for the rest of his life, publishing his *Voeux d'un Solitaire* in 1789, then an exotic, unbelievable account of life in an Indian cottage the following year and in 1812 his last work, appropriately entitled *Harmonies de la Nature*. In my view not one of these works, nor his *Voyage à l'Île-de-France*, is remotely readable in the way that *Paul et Virginie* magically remains so.

Bernardin de Saint-Pierre managed to keep in favour with every French government, whether royalist or revolutionary, and in 1807 was chosen to eulogize Napoleon Bonaparte and became president of the Académie Française. It is pleasing to relate that when his beloved first wife died in 1799 and the sixty-seven-year-old author married a beautiful young girl aged twenty, their marriage succeeded splendidly until his death at Eragny-sur-Oise in 1814.

How does one explain such literary fecundity? What has made Normandy so prolific in native writers and other literary geniuses so keen to exploit its unique character in their works? Part of the answer must lie in the ready accessibility of Paris, with its literary salons and its publishing houses. From Normandy native-born writers could easily penetrate France's major cultural centre. Flaubert, for example, has often been described as 'the great Normandy barbarian', but his first masterpiece, *Madame Bovary*, made its initial appearance in *la Revue de Paris*.

Similarly Lucie Delarue-Mardrus, who was born at Honfleur in 1874 and spent much of her youth there at Le Breuil, entered the Institut Normal Catholique in Paris at the age of eighteen, where although her unrequited passion for one of her women teachers brought out her latent lesbianism, she married the Egyptian who had made the definitive French translation of *A Thousand and One Nights*. He enabled her to enter the circles of such congenial geniuses as André Gide, Sarah Bernhardt, Alfred Jarry, Colette, Rodin, Gabriele d'Annunzio, Maurice Maeterlinck and Anne de Noailles – not to mention Claude Debussy, Octave Mirbeau and Paul Valéry. A formidable group if ever there was one, they helped her to write and get published in numerous Parisian journals. They also relished the *succès de scandales* of her *Deux amants, Le roman de six petites filles, Toutone et son amour, L'ange et les pervers, Une femme libre et l'amour*, as well as encouraging her gift for painting and sculpture.

Literary traffic also flowed the other way, from Paris into Normandy. Established Parisian novelists and poets could make forays north for exotic or symbolic copy – an explanation in part confirmed by the numerous Parisian protagonists of their literary creations, even when these are set on the banks of the Seine. The delicious land and seascape proved irresistible.

The romance of Normandy was certainly discovered well before the nineteenth century. Le Mont-Saint-Michel, for example, is stunningly illustrated in a miniature of the famous *Très riches heures du duc de Berry*, with a glamorous St Michael flying above it and about to plunge his sword into a faltering winged devil. Again, in 1580 a celebrated traveller named Jacques-August Thou marvelled at the conical rock from which the abbey of le Mont-Saint-Michel sublimely rises. He described even then its little boutiques, its pilgrims and shrines, the devotional images and jewels sold to its thronging tourists. Yet although Normandy had excited the imagination of men and women for centuries, the Romantic age brought a fresh upsurge of exultation in its rich, variegated nature, its Gothic cathedrals and the strange ancient monastery on its rocky perch surrounded by sea.

As the Romantic movement was beginning, this region and its remarkable abbey thrilled the pioneer of Romanticism, René de Chateaubriand, with exceptional passion. Born at nearby Saint-Malo in 1768, he came to adore the seashore, the exciting storms and the wild waves of the sea between his birthplace and the monastery of le Mont-Saint-Michel. This coastline undoubtedly inspired one of his most famous passages – one in which Chateaubriand's response to the frequently tormented Normandy seascape induced him to invest it with human characteristics.

Between the sea and the land spread Pelagian frontiers, indecisive landscapes which cannot make up their minds where they stand. The lark of the countryside flies alongside the lark of the sea. The plough and the fishing smack each shear their way through the earth and the sea. The sailor and the shepherd borrow each other's language. One speaks of 'fleecy' [*moutonnant*] waves, the other of 'flocks' [*flottes*] of sheep.

Gothic, gloomy, green, lashed by the sea, Normandy lent itself perfectly to Romanticism. Among the Parisian giants who now explored the region with relish was Victor Hugo (who had befriended the young Flaubert in the literary salons of Paris); and Hugo inherited from Chateaubriand both a passion for the sea off the Normandy coast and the same fallacy that these waters mirrored his own feelings. A section of his poem 'Les quatres vents de l'esprit' is dedicated to the environs of Avranches which overlook the Normandy coast. Hugo's poem here imagines that the deep waters share his own cosmic gloom:

> Sick unto death, I contemplate the world;
> Ah! how vast is the sea and how heavy is my heart!

In June 1836, having crossed from Brittany by way of Pontorson (whose twelfth-century Norman church of Our Lady and extremely pretty arcaded sixteenth-century hôtel Guiscard de la Ménardière should delay any discerning traveller), Hugo and his actress friend Juliette Drouet reached le Mont-Saint-Michel, playfully dubbing each other Totor and Juju. The Norman countryside, which the celebrated poet had seen for the first time on a short visit three years previously, had already overwhelmed his soul: 'ineffable, immense, formidable and charming', as he described the land.

As well as caring for Juliette Drouet, in 1836 he frequently thought of another cherished lady friend, Louise Bertin, who at that time was living in Bièvre. As soon as Victor Hugo had arrived at le Mont-Saint-Michel in June 1836, he wrote to tell her that this was 'truly the most beautiful spot in the world – apart from Bièvre of course'. In words recalling his former eulogy of Normandy he continued, 'It is difficult to write about a place at once more terrible and charming than you and I have ever visited.' The blue expanse of sea, the green expanse of countryside, the mists, the clarity of the air, birds taking wing, ships taking sail, and suddenly the pale face of a miserable prisoner in the jail of le Mont-Saint-Michel – all this brought to him more forcefully than ever before 'the cruel antitheses so often found between human beings and nature'.

Although the monastery on le Mont-Saint-Michel was in sad condition in his day (its superb knights' hall turned into a workshop, its golden statue of St Michael replaced by four black poles used for the newly invented telegraph system, and its Romanesque nave used as a filthy refectory), Victor Hugo was profoundly impressed.

> Saint-Michel rises sheer above the wild waves,
> Cheops of the west, pyramid of the seas.

His mistress wantonly carved her initials, J.D., on a stone in the cloisters, and the date 1836, an act of vandalism sadly obliterated when the monastery was being restored in 1872.

The romance of the Normandy coast next entranced the novelist Henri-Marie Beyle, who wrote under the pseudonym Stendhal. 'If I ever were condemned to live in the provinces anywhere close to Paris I would stay at Avranches or Granville,' he declared in 1838. He admitted that his first temptation would be to take an apartment in Tours or Angers, for the soft winters of the Loire valley are far removed from the rigours of the Normandy climate during that season. What clinched his decision, though, was the character of the Normandy fisherman. 'Your neighbour at Tours or Angers displays provincial pettiness and intrusive curiosity a hundredfold meaner than you find at Granville or Angers. The answer is found in this rule: "Closeness to the sea overcomes trivial nastiness."'

Curiously enough, Stendhal did not warm to the architecture of Granville. Perched on a schistose cliff advancing into the sea, Granville is crammed with picturesque houses, many of them built in the sixteenth and seventeenth centuries out of local granite. It also boasts a splendid church dating from the same eras (apart from its baroque façade). Among the oldest of the houses is the sixteenth-century granite house standing at no. 14 bis, rue Notre-Dame, with its pretty gable. Among the finest is the late seventeenth-century hôtel de Ganne-Destouches at no. 45, rue Saint-

(Above) *The stunning ensemble of the Abbaye-aux-Hommes, Caen, consists of the Romanesque church of Saint-Étienne and the eighteenth-century classical convent, now the town hall.*

(Previous page) *The former cathedral of Saint-Pierre at Lisieux is often unjustly neglected because of the rival attractions of the twentieth-century basilica of St Thérèse.*

(Opposite above) *The fish market at Grand-Camp.*

(Opposite below) *Dieppe, with its tranquil harbour, is dominated by the Romanesque dome of the church of Saint-Remy and the flamboyant Gothic belfry of the church of Saint-Jacques.*

Looking down from Château-Gaillard over a great loop of the River Seine and the twin villages of Les Andelys.

(Left) Some of the half-timbered houses of Pont-Audemer, washed by one of the many streams of the River Risle which meanders through the town.

The exquisitely restored Japanese bridge which Claude Monet built in 1895 for his garden at Giverny spans his water-lily pond.

(Above) *The pepperpot towers and chimneys of the Renaissance Château d'O near Mortrée, set in an artificial lake.*

(Opposite) *Cliffs near Arromanches overlooking the remains of ferro-concrete boxes towed here in 1944 to make an artificial harbour for the invading British.*

(Overleaf) *This flamboyant Gothic staircase in the left transept of Rouen cathedral was created by Guillaume Pontifs in 1480.*

Jean. Just forty years before Stendhal's visit the royalist Chevalier Destouches had been arrested by the republicans at this house and delivered to the Avranches jail to await execution by the guillotine.

Five years previously the royalist Vendéens had besieged Granville and had been repulsed only after a bloody struggle, during which the defenders of the town had burned down a whole street to prevent its capture by their enemies. The Convention in Paris was so delighted by this heroic resistance that they granted Granville the privilege of dubbing itself Granville-la-Victoire. To this day you can see the cannons and batteries which remain from this heroic episode.

Neither the elegant houses nor the cannonry impressed Stendhal. He climbed up to the town only to judge its houses 'black and dreary, very much alike and greatly resembling those of the small towns of England'. Walking out to the meadow that juts out into the sea, he heard a village child say to her companions, 'How often you have heard about the end of the world. Well, this is it.' Stendhal commented, 'How appropriate!' He spotted an iron twelve-pounder and the remains of a battery abandoned in this meadow, but was more taken by what he described as some unhappy sheep buffeted by the wind. Then he returned to the town and its magical parish church, which Stendhal judged 'a remarkably depressing building'. Admittedly at that moment some twenty young girls were about to bury one of their friends. Stendhal recalled the scene, which perfectly complemented his mood. 'Apart from myself as spectator the only men present were the beadle who seemed drunk, and the old priest who was frozen and in a hurry.' Such obsequies, he decided, were better performed in Florence, where they always took place at night.

Stendhal regretted his judgment. He returned to Civitavecchia and much appreciated its Italian beauty, but its eternal sun was intensely monotonous to him. He longed for the rain of 'la belle et verte Normandie d'Avranches', and the new novel he began in October 1839 he determined would be called *A Voyage in Normandy*. (In the end he entitled it *Lucien Leuwen*.)

Stendhal clearly loved Normandy; yet I have to confess that Victor Hugo's response to this entrancing region seems to me yet more romantic, combining nostalgic memories of living there in the company of elegant women with a rich evocation of the countryside, the fields, the trees, the sea and the sky:

> *Ami, vous souvient-il, quand nos quittions Avranches?*
> *Un beau soleil couchant rayonnait dans les branches;*
> *Notre voie, en passant, froissait les buissons verts;*
> *Nous regardions, tous trois, les champs, les cieux, les mers;*
> *Et l'extase, un moment, fit nos bouches muettes,*
> *Car elle, vous et moi, nous étions trois poètes.*

(Friend, do you remember when we were leaving Avranches?
A gorgeous setting sun was shining through the branches;
As we journeyed, our route rustled the green bushes;
So we admired the fields, the sea and the sky, all three,
And for a moment the ecstacy made us dumb,
For the landscape, you and I, the three of us were poets.)

Enthusiastic romanticism soon turns to excess, and this too happened in Normandy. If over-the-top eroticism seems an odd contrast with the apparently phlegmatic character of today's Normandy peasant, I must ask you to read the immoderate works of Octave Mirbeau, who was born at Trévières in the Calvados in 1848 and died a professed anarchist sixty-nine years later. Take his novel *L'abbé Jule*, which appeared in 1888. The scene where the abbé seduces a stupid peasant girl still scandalizes one's bourgeois or Christian morality. '"Come here,"' the abbé ordered. The girl did not move. '"Come here instantly," the abbé repeated, his voice growing harsher and his breathing more and more rapid, a strange passionate fury forcing his arms in front of him, twisting his hands, precipitating his whole flesh towards some scarcely imaginable, absurd and deadly crime . . .'

Again he cries 'Come here', but the stupid, numb girl simply stares at him, this hideous priest, this black devil.

Then, brusquely, like a beast attacking its prey, he rushed at her. Caring not whether he might strangle the girl, he took her neck with one arm and with his free hand seized her breasts, which he proceeded to slash, to torture, to crush savagely, atrociously. In a second he felt his claws grasping religious objects: a scapular, crosses, lockets that had been blessed and now were hung on a steel chain against the flesh of the miserable girl. To twist and break and stick them into the flesh of this woman, to mingle them with the profane caresses with which he was bruising her body brought him an excruciatingly horrible pleasure. And all the time he exuded filthy, dreadful words, unutterable words, blasphemies interspersed with hiccoughs and gasps for breath.

Goodness! But no account of Normandy is complete without a *morceau* of Octave Mirbeau.

Yet I have a strong impression that a good number of the nineteenth-century Normandy Romantics were re-creating a homeland more mythical than real. Take the mostly reprehensible and wildly ultra-royalist Barbey d'Aurevilly, who was born at Saint-Sauveur-le-Vicomte in 1808 into an old Normandy family from Caen, where he studied law. Dandy and drunkard, utterly indisciplined in his youth save as a fearless, almost foolhardy army officer, he spent most of his life in Paris with frequent excursions to Caen. Around 1830 he became the lover of Louise de Costils, who happened to be the wife of his cousin.

Jules Amédée Barbey d'Aurevilly's unmistakable literary excesses are instantly revealed in the titles of his works: *L'Amour impossible, Du Dandyisme et du Georges Brummel, Un Prêtre marié, Une Vieille Maitresse.* Violence, infidelity, excessive passion and swagger abound. In 1851 under the influence of a Mme de Bouglon he stopped drinking, but the abandon and utter lack of caution in his writings continued and he started drinking again in 1860. In 1874 he published a series of stories under the title *Les Diaboliques*. In one of them a doctor and a friend are walking in a botanical garden when they come upon a strangely menacing couple, a fascinatingly exotic woman of forty in the arms of a forty-seven-year-old dandy. The doctor explains that they are the count and countess of Savigny. She was born Hauteclaire Stassin and had become an adventuress and swindler. None the less the count had fallen deeply in love with her. In spite of having reluctantly to marry a young woman of noble birth, he remained hopelessly entranced by Hauteclaire, who had moved into his household as a chambermaid. The count's wife shortly died of a mysterious malady, and the doctor became convinced that the lovers had poisoned her. Two years later the lovers married without the slightest remorse.

Les Diaboliques so much offended the public morality of the Third Republic that the first edition was seized by the public prosecutor's office and Barbey d'Aurevilly would have been put on trial, had not the moderate and influential republican politician Léon Gambetta intervened on his behalf.

Such a spirited writer naturally enough warmed to the violence, as well as the ardour and courage, of his Norman ancestors. His novel *Le Chevalier des Touches*, published in 1864, expounds on the notion that these Norman attributes still abound in contemporary Normandy. 'One isn't a Norman just for plums,' one inhabitant tells Baron de Fierdrap; 'you must realize, as I do, that the blood of these pirates from the North still runs in the veins of the weakest sabot-shod Normandy peasant.'

I tentatively offer the close proximity of Paris, Normandy's own glamour and the wildness of some of her native writers as some explanation of a literary crop as rich as that of her lush fields and orchards. But another reason for such a wealth of literary achievement must also be the 100-year-old tradition of Norman cultural sublimity. As you read Guy de Maupassant or Marcel Proust in front of your fire after dinner, you can easily forget the ancient patrimony of Normandy.

Reading their works as you sit beside the magical, often ruined monasteries of this region you cannot fail to spot that this is the land of Lanfranc and Orderic Vitalis. The so-called father of English literature, Geoffrey Chaucer, lived in the second half of the fifteenth century. Four centuries earlier a Normandy poet named either Turold or Théroulde wrote the oldest epic poem in the French language, the *Chanson de Roland*. Scholars surmise that the poet was born in Avranches and may even have taken part in the Norman conquest of England, becoming Abbot of Peterborough after the English defeat. His pupil, the troubadour Taillefer, is said to have declaimed stanzas of the *Chanson* to rouse the ardour of William the Bastard's soldiers before the battle of Hastings. At this time the epic was preserved only in memory, written down later, around 1080, in a manuscript preserved at Oxford. Two other copies of the *Chanson de Roland* have been discovered, both at Peterborough. The *Chanson de Roland* begins with a eulogy of le Mont-Saint-Michel:

> *Molz pelerins qui vunt al Munt*
> *Enquierent molt e grant dreit unt*
> *Comment l'igliese fut fundee*
> *Premerement et estoree.*
> *Cil qui lor dient de l'estoire*
> *Que cil demandent en memoire*
> *Ne l'unt pas bien ainz vunt faillant*
> *En plusors leus e mespernant.*
> *Por faire la apertement*
> *Entendre a cels qui escient*
> *N'unt de clerzie l'a tornee*
> *De latin tote et ordenee*
> *Pars veirs romeius novelement*
> *Molt en segrei por son convent*
> *Un jovencels moine est del Munt*
> *Deus en son reigne part li dunt.*

> (Most pilgrims who come to the Mount
> Enquire much – and quite rightly so –
> How the church was first
> Founded and sustained.
> Those who tell them the tale
> Which they ask for do not remember
> It well, but tumble into error
> And misapprehension in many places.
> So as to make it clear
> And intelligible to those who possess
> No literary skills, it has here been rendered
> From the Latin, and totally transcribed
> Into a new Romanesque version,
> Done in secret by a young man
> On behalf of this Mount, his own convent.)

Then enfolds the heroic tale of the last, futile stand of Charlemagne's knights in 778 at the pass of Roncesvalles in the Pyrenees.

Small wonder that the age of William the Bastard produced Norman poets dedicated to praising heroism and adventure. Around 1020 a poet named Guillaume was born at Préaux, near Pont-Audemer. He studied at Poitiers, hence his name Guillaume de Poitiers, and served as William's chaplain during the conquest of England. His memoir of these stirring times survives, entitled *Gesta Guillelmi II, ducis Normanorum Anglorum*. And another contemporary Norman historian, Raoul de Caen, has left us an account of the first crusade.

Theologians in Normandy were now writing abstruse monologues about the philosophy of being, and such like. Étienne de Rouen, a monk from le Bec-Hellouin who died in 1149, wrote a subtle commentary on the works of Aristotle. But the next greatest Norman writer after the author of the *Chanson de Roland* was Robert Wace, born in Jersey around the turn of the thirteenth century. Henry II made him prebendary of Bayeux cathedral. In gratitude Wace wrote epic works celebrating the Norman dynasty. He was a prolific author, but his masterpiece is unquestionably the *Roman de Rou*, which he wrote at Caen around the year 1160. And his language moved significantly from Latin towards medieval French. As Victor Hugo put it, in the works of Wace 'the barbarian princes now heard someone singing another rhythm than that of the Caesars'.

Listen to Wace in the *Roman de Rou*, not merely celebrating the legendary strength of William Longue-Épée but also exulting in his physical beauty:

Williame Lunge Épée fu de haute estature.
Gros fu par li espaules, greile par la cheinture,
Games out lunges dreites, large la forchure,
Nestoit mie sa chair, embrunie ne obscure.
Litez porta hault, lung out la chevelure,
Oils dreits et a-persout, et dulce regardeure,
Mes a ses ennemiz sem la mult fiere e dure,
Bel nez e bele bouche, et bele parleure,
Fors fu comme dehanz et hardie sans mesure
Ki son colp atendi, de sa vie nout cure.

(William Longue-Épée was tall in stature.
His broad shoulders were pockmarked from his chain mail,
Straight, long and strong were his legs,
And his flesh was clean – not cloudy or dark.
He carried himself high, and his hair was long.
His eyes were straight and piercing, withal with a gentle look,
Though to his enemies they were fierce and hard.
He had a beautiful nose, beautiful mouth and was beautifully spoken.
Unusually strong and immeasurably hardy,
He was anxious neither for his own self nor his life.)

Wace also searched out the legends of ancient times, seeking to enrich Norman literature with the stories of the Anglo-Saxons. He wrote about King Arthur, the Knights of the Round Table, Merlin, the Holy Grail and Tristan and Iseult. One of his successors, an Anglo-Norman poet named Béroul, composed a yet more heroic version of *Tristan et Yseult* maybe twenty years later. Norman clerics, secure in their monastic libraries, now poured out bestiaries, legendary tales, lists of ecclesiastical heroes, chronicles, fables, histories of the crusades, even an imitation of the *Consolation of Philosophy* by Boëthius, this last by Simon Dufresne who lived in lower Normandy in the second half of the twelfth century.

Medieval Normandy soon seemed to dominate the literary life of France, just as Normandy would again do so in the seventeenth and nineteenth centuries. Guillaume de Jumièges occupies the first rank among eleventh-century historians, a writer whose learning takes medieval chronicles out of the realm of legend into a sifting of the historical truth. In the next century the prolific Alexandre de Bernay invented the verse form known as the Alexandrine. The first woman to write French poetry was Marie de France, who was born around 1180 and set her famous *Legend of two lovers* in the Eure. Another celebrated French troubadour was the Norman Jean Renaud, who was born at Bayeux and died in 1201.

The great monastic libraries of Normandy inevitably inspired some of its native men of God to brilliant, and therefore almost heretical, speculations. Let me mention only one such quasi-heretic. Richard Simon was born in Dieppe on 13 May 1638, dying there seventy-four years later in some disgrace, not for any misbehaviour but because his genius was too far advanced for the orthodoxy of his time. Fascinated by Eastern Christianity and by Judaism, he published in 1678 a *Critical History of the Old Testament*, which for the first time set about the difficult task of solving who wrote the first five books of the Bible (which tradition erroneously attributed to Moses). Both Catholics and Protestants were outraged that he should question a received truth. Richard Simon was expelled from the Parisian oratory where he had lodgings, and he retired to his native Normandy to the pretty hamlet of Bolleville not far from Lillebonne. There he worshipped in the charming thirteenth-century parish church which had just been enriched with a new nave, writing incisive works of biblical criticism and ecclesiastical history, which were mostly published abroad and almost completely ignored.

If the brilliant Richard Simon has never gained his due reward, two of his Normandy contemporaries in the seventeenth century, François de Malherbe and Pierre Corneille, remain acknowledged masters of French literature. Born at Caen in 1555, Malherbe profited from his noble home to enter the court of the Duke of Angoulême, Henri II's illegitimate son.

Angoulême's household was based in Provence, and after his death in 1586 Malherbe continued to live either in Provence or in Normandy, producing poems which received but little attention, until in 1600 and 1605 he pulled off two stunning pieces of obsequiousness.

First he wrote a poem saluting the entrance of Marie de Medici into Aix. This 'Ode à la Reine pour sa bienvenue en France' was followed five years later by another commissioned by Henri IV to celebrate one of the king's successful campaigns. Malherbe's lyrically entrancing 'Prieure pour le Roi Henri le Grand alland en Limousin' so delighted the king that he determined to give the poet a permanent place at his court.

Soon Malherbe was universally admired, with schools of poets waiting on his words (though his last years were darkened by the murder of his son in a duel). He reformed the whole practice of French poetry, forbidding the remotest ambiguity, insisting on the precise use of the Alexandrian metre, a reform which set the pattern of verse in France for over two centuries. Some said that he had grievously limited the scope of poetry, but his own limpid verses gave the lie to this.

Thenceforth flowed prolific official verses, occasioned by any royal event or public act. They are fluent, even exquisite. In 1624, for example, he lauded King Louis XIII for destroying the Protestant revolutionaries in the Midi whose aspirations had threatened the unity of France, brilliantly combining this with the most outrageous self-praise in a fashion that no fellow writer can fail to admire:

> Nothing approaches your value,
> Upon which our well-being so depends.
> Your courage, ripening in its green season,
> Has given us peace on land and sea.
>
> Poisonous years are gone; you have utterly killed
> The hydra of France as it powerfully revolted.
> Truly, to place upon your forehead the world's wreathe
> Is justly and with reason merited by our happiness.
>
> But know this, my king, you have me as witness
> To your most beautiful action: to obey you
> Is for us the highest of duties.
>
> Everything we loan to you; but not in equal portion.
> Common works last but a few years,
> But what Malherbe writes lives for ever.

Malherbe's yet more remarkable contemporary, Pierre Corneille, was born in 1606 at Petit-Couronne, eight kilometres south-west of Rouen. You can still visit the home in which he was brought up, a half-timbered house bought by his father two years after the prodigy's birth. Corneille was taught by the Jesuits of Rouen and set out on a career as a barrister, but in 1629 he confided to a passing troupe of players the manuscript of a comedy, *Mélite*, which they performed in Paris the following year. Its success persuaded Corneille to renounce the law and take up the profession of dramatist.

The decision transformed French theatre. Comedies, fantasies, a baroque feel for dramatic illusion, as well as the ability to reflect contemporary manners with ice-cold accuracy, endow Corneille's plays with a unique magic. His four superb tragedies, *Le Cid*, *Horace*, *Cinna* and *Polyeucte* appeared between 1637 and 1642, each commenting obliquely on the political traumas of the age of absolutism. At the same time he was emulating Malherbe, by developing rules which dominated French theatre for generations: the notions of unity of action and time, with no violence appearing before the spectators' eyes, seem only to have intensified the impact of his drama.

And Corneille proved equally fecund at writing comedies, above all *Le Menteur*, which was first performed in 1643 and profoundly influenced Molière. Unfortunately for Corneille, audiences began to prefer Racine and as a result the old age of the Norman dramatist was considerably embittered.

As true Normans, both Malherbe and Corneille also wrote love poems (which the former cunningly published as *Psalms*). What all these great Normandy poets and novelists had in common (as did Gustave Flaubert, Guy de Maupassant and Émile Zola among those we have already seen) was the superb ability to evoke love. In addition, François de Malherbe's famous poem beginning 'Beauté, mon beau souci, de qui l'âme incertaine' is frequently said to have introduced a new morality into the love affair. I am not so sure that he did:

> Beauty, my beautiful dream, whose uncertain spirit
> Like the ocean has its ebbs and flows,
> Think how you may ease my sorrow,
> Or I shall decide to suffer it no more.
>
> Your eyes have charms that I love and value
> Even more than my own freedom;
> But to hold on to me, if they understand my condition,
> They will need quite as much love as beauty.
>
> Just when I suppose I have achieved my heart's desire,
> Some excuse or other always gets in the way.
> This is the never-ending shroud of Ulysses's wife,
> Whose night's work was unravelled again each morning.
>
> Madame, I warn you, you are losing your glory.
> Having promised yourself to me, you laugh at me.

If you cannot remember this, your memory is fallible,
And if you do remember it, you are faithless.

Always as I reckon I have loved the best,
Allowing only death to come between us;
So if it comes about through any other cause, you are to blame
For making vows but not practising what you preach.

Are the tones of this love poem by Malherbe resonant in the verses which Pierre Corneille addressed in 1658 to the lovely, young and utterly uninterested Marquise du Parc, whom both he and Racine fruitlessly adored? There are other resonances too, a pleasing acerbity over some pretty coquette to whom time will soon bring her comeuppance, as well as the proper pride of an ageing lover who knows that his wrinkled brows do not mean that he is to be despised. Corneille wrote:

Marquise, if my countenance
Has a few elderly traces,
Remember that at my age
You won't look much better.

Time pleases itself by affronting
The most beautiful things;
It will make your roses fade
Just as it has wrinkled my forehead.

The same course of the planets
Rules your days as it rules mine:
Once I was like you;
You shall be as I am.

Even so, I still possess a few charms,
And fairly striking they are too,
So I'm not too alarmed
At the ravages of time.

Many people adore you;
But those you at present scorn
Will still be around
When the others are used up.

These shall be able to enjoy the glory
Of eyes which seem sweet to me
And a thousand years on make people understand
What pleases me in you.

In this new race
Where my reputation will be safe,
You will be beautiful
Only if I have said so.

> Think about it, beautiful Marquise,
> Though an old grey fellow fills you with dread,
> You would be well advised to flatter him
> If he is made like me.

May I now leap a couple of hundred years or more to draw my readers' attention to the persisting skills of the Normandy poets at writing such unsurpassed love poems. My excuse is that Rémy de Gourmont, who in 1858 was born in the château de La Motte (which you can still see at Bazouches-au-Houlme in la Suisse normande) was descended through his mother's line directly from Malherbe. Educated at Coutances and Rouen, like many other Normandy writers he took advantage of the closeness of the capital of France to advance his literary career. In Paris he was one of the founders of the journal *Mercure de France*. He loved to celebrate travel in exotic climes, publishing at the turn of the century such works as 'Heures d'Afrique' and 'Heures de Corse'. Dying in 1915, he lies today in the cemetery of Père-Lachaise. He was also a pagan, a sensualist and a nonconformist. The poem which I most warm to is his 'Léda', a lusciously erotic account of the seduction of the wife of Tyndareus, King of Sparta, by the god Zeus, who appeared to her in the form of a swan:

> The innocent Leda was washing her naked limbs,
> The grace of her body enchanting the waters of the stream,
> And the reeds, in the grip of unrecognizable troubles,
> Were singing a song as old as it was new,
>
> When the swan appeared, a white ship on the river.
>
> When the swan appeared, a white ship with a golden prow
> Leda was thrilled and sat pensive,
> Then slowly, silently, approached the bank
> And lay on the grass in the shadow of a tree.
>
> The bird advanced, beautiful, ardent and dreamy.
>
> The bird advanced, beautiful, ardent and with an air
> So royal, so masculine, that Leda was so much entranced
> As to regret that in the error of her flesh
> She was not a swan to whom he might make love.
>
> Between the shade and the soft charmed grass.
>
> Between the shade and the soft grass and the lilies
> Leda sagged under the weight of the distinguished bird,
> Completely dripping the Simoïs waters,
> And her astonished body shuddered and gave in.
>
> Just to stroke the plumage of a swan.

Let me continue this account of the scribblers of Normandy with another love poem, this time written by a husband to his wife. André

Breton was born in 1896 at Timchebray in the *département* of the Orne. In one of her (rare) lapses, that amateuse of Normandy, Miss Nesta Roberts, comments that the little town 'specializes in the manufacture of gardening tools, which makes it an unexpected birthplace for ... one of the leaders of the Surrealist movement'. Quite the contrary, surrealism specializes in juxtaposing the most unlikely implements; to contemplate gardening tools makes for fine love poetry, as André Breton's verses to his wife reveal. My daughter Emma-Jane, who translated these fearfully difficult stanzas for me, commented as she did so that if any husband of hers had written such a poem, she would both have loved him and beaten him up. Breton's poem reads:

> My wife has hair like a forest-fire
> Her thoughts are flashes of scorching heat
> Her figure is like an hour-glass
> Like an otter between the teeth of a tiger
> My wife has a mouth like a rosette
>   – a bouquet of the finest stars
> Her teeth resemble the footprints of a white mouse
>   on the white earth
> Her tongue is like smooth amber and polished glass
> My wife has the tongue of a knifed sacrificial victim
> The tongue of a doll that can open and close its eyes
> A tongue of incredible stone
> My wife's eyelashes seem to have been drawn by a child
> Her eyelids mirror the rim of a swallow's nest
> My wife's temples look like the tiles of a greenhouse
> With steaming windows
> Her shoulders are made of champagne
> Resembling the fountains made by dolphins' heads
>   as they break through the ice
> My wife's wrists are like matchsticks
> Her fingers are aimless, looking like the ace of hearts
> As well as cut hay
> Her armpits are like sable
>   and match the streaks of the night on St John's feastday
> Burgeoning like privet hedges and wild birds' nests
> Her arms are like sluices and the froth of the sea
> A mixture of corn and flour
> My wife's legs are rockets
> She moves like a despairing clock
> My wife has calves like the core of elder trees
> She has initialled feet.

With a Normandy wife whose armpits are like privet hedges and who moves like a despairing clock, we have reached the alarming twentieth-century and another extraordinary outburst of Norman creativity.

Yet from the surrealism of André Breton to the unrestrained lunacy of Raymond Queneau is a largish step. Queneau is virtually untranslatable into English, though some (including himself) have made valiant efforts to do so. Born at Le Havre in 1903, he studied at the local lycée, a mediocre scholar except in philosophy, which he continued to study at the Sorbonne. The taste for the low life, which appears in his novels must have developed here, for Queneau combined his Sorbonne studies with many happy hours spent in billiard halls.

He also loved the cinema, and later collaborated with the Spanish surrealist Luis Buñuel on the script of *La Mort en ce jardin*. By 1924 he was a member of le Groupe Surréaliste and writing for its journal. His own novel *Zazie dans le métro*, which won a prize for black humour (only the French could invent such a prize), was turned into a celebrated film; yet I like better the tale of a wandering fairground worker, *Pierrot mon ami*, which Queneau wrote in 1942, if only for the joy of reading about a hero who manages to avoid not only all responsibility but even a large inheritance which is rightfully his.

The thirst for novelty and the brilliant, sometimes bizarre innovation seen in André Breton and Raymond Queneau spilled over into Norman composers as well as writers. No fewer than four of them made remarkable and diverse impacts on the development of twentieth-century music. The work of Erik Satie, for instance, as well as being fascinating in its own right, significantly influenced composers of the calibre of Poulenc, Debussy, Milhaud and Ravel. In 1919 Igor Stravinsky went so far as to say that 'French music consists of Bizet, Chabrier and Satie'.

Satie, whose musical witticisms, as well as his low life in Paris, Queneau would have relished, was born at Honfleur in 1866 to the Scottish wife of a Normandy ship broker. The family moved to Paris after the Franco-Prussian War; but when his mother died Erik was shipped back to Normandy to live with his grandparents. Back in Paris after the remarriage of his father, the boy hated his stepmother. Already he was showing the characteristics that would later make his music so enterprisingly new and his life so extreme. He entered the Paris Conservatoire, but since he rarely turned up for classes was expelled in 1882 as being not up to standard.

He was helped into print by the music-publishing firm now set up by his father, who brought out some of his songs and the three Sarabandes of 1887 – notorious for their unresolved ninths – which deeply impressed and influenced Debussy.

Two apparently contrasting preoccupations now inspired Satie: the hedonistic life of the café Chat Noir on Montmartre, and Gregorian chant with its accompanying mystical medieval religion. Naturally his bourgeois parents disapproved of the former. Satie's money soon ran out, but his friendships remained, especially a deep attachment to Debussy. His love affair with the artist Suzanne Valadon, whose illegitimate son was Maurice Utrillo, was stormy. He attacked in print Colette and her husband Willy, who was so incensed as to try to beat up Satie when they met at a concert.

A sizeable legacy now enabled Satie to indulge his taste for exhibitionism by purchasing twelve identical grey velvet suits. Yet all the time he was turning out intricately orchestrated works, some of them in collaboration with Debussy himself, many of them embodying the same buffoonery he liked to display in his daily behaviour. Alas, his extravagant life and, it must be added, his generosity soon impoverished him. The innovative Satie was forced to spend fifteen miserable years earning a living by playing the piano in cafés and by writing songs for the music halls. Then in 1911 Ravel came to his rescue by playing one of his Sarabandes at a concert; the musical public remembered Satie, and his works were once more in demand. Debussy also conducted some of his works – but was disconcerted that the public welcomed the music of his underling so enthusiastically. Most important of all, in 1915 the young Jean Cocteau heard and was impressed by the music of the wayward Norman. Cocteau began to promote Satie among his influential friends and in his writings. And in May 1917 there opened *Parade*, a collaboration between Cocteau, Diaghilev, Massine, Picasso and Erik Satie, with the composer's music perfectly matching the Cubist designs of Picasso.

France was scandalized. One critic so annoyed Satie that the composer sent him a deeply offensive postcard – resulting in a heavy fine and an eight-day suspended prison sentence. But the scandal made Satie famous, and he became the hero of the group of young composers who called themselves the 'nouveaux jeunes' but who, along with Satie, have gone down in musical history as 'les six'.

Satie was now composing some of his finest music – including the cantata *Socrate*, based on Plato's *Dialogues*. Two other pieces confirmed his reputation for scandal. In both these works he collaborated with some of the most remarkable innovators of the century. His 1924 ballet score *Mercure* was written for Massine and the designs were by Picasso. *Relâche*, which appeared in the same year, incorporated a brief film by René Clair and was designed by the surrealist Francis Picabia.

Sadly the years of excess were now taking their toll on Satie's health, and the following year the composer died in hospital of sclerosis of the liver.

During Satie's brief period as a student at the Schola Cantorum in Paris one of his fellows was a would-be composer three years his junior. Albert

Roussel had been a naval cadet, a midshipman and then a commissioned officer, but in 1894 he gave up a seafaring career to devote himself entirely to music. Though no rake in the Satie fashion, his life was far from sedentary, and his wide travels influenced his sometimes quite esoteric music. His naval career had taken him to French Indo-China; in 1909 he and his wife made a long visit to Asia; and in 1915 he enlisted in the French artillery, serving till January 1918 as a transport officer. Four years later he bought a home at Vasterival on the Normandy coast (hence his appearance in my book), and when he died of a heart attack in 1937 his body was, by his own wish, interred in the local cemetery there.

If the exoticism developed by Satie and his allies was remarkable, Roussel's own innovations were yet more so. They include an attempt to assimilate what he surmised to be Hindu savagery into a balletic opera called *Padmâvati*, which he composed on the Brittany coast after being invalided out of the army. Roussel adapted the forms of Hindu scales both here and in a work of 1924 named *Krishna* after the god. Roussel's symphonies, too (especially his Second Symphony) incorporate some of the Hindu elements found in his *Padmâvati*. But he also could respond sympathetically to western legends (particularly brilliantly in his ballets *Aenéas* and *Bacchus et Ariane*), to Chinese poetry and to the Jewish psalms.

While Albert Roussel squeezes into this book only by his brief contact with Satie and by choosing to live and be buried overlooking the Normandy sea, André Caplet appears here as a full-blooded Normandy composer and conductor. Born at Le Havre in 1878, by the time he was fourteen his gifts had made him a violinist in the Grand Theatre of his home town. Two years later he was a student at the Paris Conservatoire, and unlike Satie was phenomenally successful there. In his first year he took the place of his teacher Leroux as a substitute conductor at the Théatre de la Porte-Saint-Martin. By 1899 he was director of music at the Odéon.

A distinguished career as an international conductor seemed assured when Caplet was appointed conductor of the Boston Opera in 1910, but four years later he volunteered to defend his country against Germany. Severely gassed during the war, his ill-health subsequently persuaded him to take up the life of a composer. What I find remarkable is how his works, individual though they are, reflect the same desire for innovation and exoticism shown by his fellow Normans. Caplet used even wider intervals than Satie; he expected singers to learn new techniques; and, like Satie, he was imbued with Christian mysticism – expressed most famously in his choral work *Le miroir de Jésus*.

One member of 'the six' who gathered around Satie actively disliked his supposed leader's music, infinitely preferred Caplet, and went on to write innovatory music of his own. Arthur Honegger was born at Le

Havre in 1892. Le Havre possessed a large Protestant community which for many years was not allowed its own 'temple', but in the mid-nineteenth century prejudice relented. The Protestant church became a centre of culture as well as religion, its Strasbourg-trained pastors bringing an unusual German influence into this part of northern France.

So almost by chance Arthur Honegger's birthplace was greatly to influence his subsequent career. At the age of fifteen he sat in the Protestant church there and heard André Caplet conduct Bach cantatas. In this same church he also listened and warmed to the singing of Bach chorales – music whose polyphonal influence regularly appears in many of his major works, alongside elements that Honegger drew from Debussy and the Parisian impressionists.

Others in Satie's circle influenced the composer. Jean Cocteau was the librettist for his *Antigone*. But the Norman trait of innovation is ultimately what characterizes Honegger. Alongside the Gregorian chant which had been utilized both by Satie and Caplet, alongside Protestant cantatas, Arthur Honegger's music deploys his celebrated twelve-note techniques, jazz rhythms, dissonance and even (for instance in his extremely popular *Pacific 231*) the rhythms of a railway locomotive. In his own delightful fashion, Honegger proved quite as exotic as his fellow Normans André Breton and Raymond Queneau.

Am I fanciful in affecting to hear, in the extended chords of these innovators, the plaintive Normandy sea, those same waters which so entranced the great Normandy writers? Bizarreness, mysticism, eroticism and exoticism again and again combine in these geniuses, with more than a hint of excess, along with a taste for passionate love and for the low life. And, like Antaeus, these Normandy masters seem to derive their enormous strengths from the luscious earth which bore and upheld them.

A violent splash of colour

Nowhere offers the tourist the pleasure of appreciating great art *in situ*, so to speak, more than Normandy – by *in situ* I mean hung in humble or great galleries set amid the scenes that originally inspired the artists to set up their easels.

If the landscape, seascape and inhabitants of Normandy have inspired and taxed the descriptive powers of the greatest of French novelists and poets, they have likewise attracted and entranced some of France's finest painters. Not surprisingly one can often trace a fruitful connection between the writers and painters, since both drew their strength from the same luscious region. The nineteenth-century poet Rémy de Gourmont, for instance, (who was also an essayist, novelist, dramatist and pro-digious eater) was descended from a family of painters and typographers which had flourished in Normandy from the end of the fifteenth century. Again, in the musée Thomas-Henry at Cherbourg, among other riches, are some fascinating engravings by Buhot, who happened also to be the illustrator of Barbey d'Aurevilly's *Les Diaboliques*. And, as we shall shortly see, the poet and critic Charles Baudelaire, who loved to visit Normandy, was instrumental in lifting one of the region's greatest painters out of a deep financial and spiritual depression back to triumphant creativity.

Great Normandy artists go back, however, far earlier than the nineteenth century, and certainly as far back as Nicolas Poussin – if not France's greatest painter, certainly one of her most influential. The received theory about the sublime, allegorical landscapes of Poussin (who was born near Les Andelys in the 1590s) is that instead of truly reflecting nature they are in fact highly formalized paintings, corresponding to the theories of 'ideal landscapes' set out by the Bolognese artist Annibale Carracci. Certainly Poussin spent much of his working life in Italy and was undoubtedly influenced by Carracci; but I find it interesting that his deep interest in landscape did not develop until after he had returned to France for a short time, to live in Paris under the wing of his fellow Norman Pierre Corneille. Is it not conceivable that despite the almost mathematical care with which they are worked out, the rich trees and limpid waters that he depicts owe much to the memory of his own fecund province, as well as to the Roman *campagna*? In Normandy we can decide for ourselves by visiting the rich collection of Poussins on display in the musée des Beaux-Arts, Rouen.

Another Norman genius, Théodore Géricault who was born in Rouen in 1791, resembled Poussin in spending much of his short working life outside Normandy. But two elements in his work surely derive in part at least from his Norman background. Géricault painted magnificent, spirited horses (many of them now hang in the musée des Beaux-Arts, Rouen). And his own passion for riding (and his death, aged thirty-three, from a riding accident) reminds one that in 1665 Colbert had founded in Normandy the Haras-du-Pin, that superb stud-farm which remains unrivalled throughout the world. His first major work, the 'Charging Chasseur' of 1812, which now hangs in the Louvre, depicts a rearing horse on a smoking battlefield, a beast that far outshines the wild, handsome officer who rides him. When Géricault went to Rome, his unachieved ambition was to create a frieze of entirely riderless racing horses.

Again, although Géricault's 'Raft of the Medusa' derived its *succès de scandale* chiefly from the fact that the shipwreck it depicts was rumoured to have been the result of governmental folly, does its fearsome sea not also derive from the wild Normandy coast? When Géricault escaped public disapproval by spending two years in England, his chosen subjects were his beloved horses and their jockeys.

If Guy de Maupassant portrays the rustic Norman as a cunning, even shifty peasant, Jean-François Millet offers a different and unjustly maligned view. Though he worked for many years in a studio in Paris, he was born in 1815 in the hamlet of Gréville not far from Cherbourg (whose musée Thomas-Henry displays a fascinating collection containing some thirty of his works). Because of his pious, some would say sickly 'Angelus' Millet today has the reputation of portraying an oversentimental version of de Maupassant's far from naïve peasant. The truth is that most of his rustic paintings utterly belie that judgment.

Once installed in Paris, Millet initially displayed a facility for copying the sensuous nudes of Fragonard. Soon, however, he turned to depicting the world of the French peasant in a far from lachrymosely tender way, revealing the hardship and occasional misery of his life in the Normandy countryside as well as the peasants' essential seriousness, even melancholy. In his own day Millet was, in consequence, accused of painting not sentimental country scenes but subversive, not to say socialist, art.

Not all is gloom in Millet. His sole long stay in Normandy after setting up his Paris studio was while taking refuge at Cherbourg during the Franco-Prussian War, yet one of his masterpieces glowingly depicts the Normandy apple-harvest, and shortly before his death in 1875 he completed a lovely evocation of the church of his humble birthplace.

Millet died in the same year as a friend and fellow artist, J.-B. Corot – though, before his own death, Corot managed to set up a handsome endowment for Millet's widow. He and Millet had both settled at the small village of Barbizon in the Fontainebleau forest, among a group of nineteenth-century artists seriously preoccupied with landscape painting. And just as Normandy not only produced its own native novelists but also attracted, by the quality of its landscape, other great writers, so the Paris-born Corot who quested for satisfying landscapes in England, Switzerland, the Low Countries and Italy also found Normandy highly congenial. The result is that the musée du Bocage in the town hall at Flers displays among its unexpectedly fine collection of Barbizon paintings some superb Corots.

Among the works by other Barbizon artists hanging in this little gallery are paintings by Charles-François Daubigny. Daubigny had the habit of painting from a specially constructed studio boat, and his love of depicting the evanescent rivers gives his work a delightful link with a generation of artists who were to find in Normandy so powerful an inspiration that they revolutionized French painting in the second half of the nineteenth century.

Daubigny enormously inspired a friend who was an incomparably greater painter, Eugène Boudin. To use Boudin's own words, Daubigny imbued him with the desire 'to steep myself in the sky, to capture the tender clouds and to let their mass float in the background, far away in the grey mist, whilst the blue blazes forth'.

Eugène Boudin was born the son of a sailor at Honfleur in 1825 in a house that still stands (no. 27, rue Bourdet). He died at Deauville in 1898. 'Perhaps it is due to the small size of the harbour that Honfleur has escaped the ravages of time, the devastation and rebuilding which, in the aftermath of war, have disfigured the majority of large European seaports,' writes Boudin's biographer Jean Selz.

Passing in front of the monumental door of the harbour master's office, surmounted by a Virgin and Child between two slate-capped turrets, or walking around the docks, along the Sainte-Catherine wharf with its narrow gray or brown houses, or down to the Saint-Etienne wharf where the former chapel today houses the Vieux Honfleur Museum, the traveller is struck by the contrast between the age-old stones and the ever-changing sky, with clouds constantly scudding before the Seine estuary wind.

Jean Selz finely adds, 'It is this breath of the past mingling with the fresh sea breezes that seems to whisper in the ear a name that still haunts the entire Normandy coast: Eugène Boudin.'

Charles-Théophile Féret, that proud, now alas virtually forgotten Normandy patriot, whose stories about Quilleboeuf and the Rouen region (*Contes de Quilleboeuf et du Roumois*) were avidly devoured in the earlier part of this century, wrote a series of poems published in 1902 as *La Normandie exaltée*, glorifying the province he loved. His verses on Honfleur seem to me to sum up perfectly the effect the town must also have had on Boudin:

> The shadow of a great cloud rests on the water like an island.
> The estuary is more beautiful than any novelist could have invented.
>> The ancient waterway
>> Spreads its wings through the town.
>
> Beyond the dirty old roofs the great hayfields open out,
> And there in the blue pastures are the farms.
>> From afar wafts the scent of apples,
>> Mingling with that of the tarry ropes.
>
> I haven't yet ended my ecstasy,
> Honfleur where I was born, with your roofs of slate,
>> Oh richly-endowed town,
> Diverse, well-seasoned.
> Are those your antiquated remarkably sagging roofs?
> Is that your little marina and beyond your green countryside?
>> These I love, as well as your port
>> Which leaves you always half-open.
>
> In this town you find only goodness and purity.
> As for me, devoted for ever to my utopia,
>> I simply love it, just as one loves
>> One's father and one's mother.

In Boudin's day only the new eastern dock at Honfleur had been constructed. Then, as now, the quai Saint-Étienne was its unbelievably quaint self, the ancient governor's house retained its portcullis, and the heart of the minuscule town, the 'Enclos', led picturesquely down to the old dock.

Honfleur has yet more to commend it, above all a unique church, dedicated to St Catherine and built entirely out of wood by mariners and shipwrights at the close of the fifteenth century. Some conjecture that this unique matelot's church was planned as a mere temporary expedient, the citizens of Honfleur waiting for a time when they could afford a proper stone church. In my view this is far from likely, for when the port began to prosper again and the church proved too small for the faithful, rather than pull it down and build afresh in stone, the Christians of Honfleur simply added to their church a second nave, just like its first one, resembling nothing less than the keel of an upturned ship.

In this environment the young Eugène Boudin imbibed the Normandy sea. In 1835 the Boudin family moved to Le Havre, for Eugène's father took a job with a shipping company plying its trade between Hamburg and Le Havre. The young Eugène left school aged twelve and worked first as a printer's clerk and then in a stationer's shop. Three years later his father changed his job again, enlisting as a seaman and remaining a mariner for the next twenty-four years. Without rejecting this heritage, the young Boudin preferred art. The stationer's shop where he worked also did some business framing pictures. Eugène was able to examine them close at hand, and his first attempts at painting were even improved by the advice of an artist-visitor to Le Havre, Jean-François Millet no less. Soon a few local patrons were buying his early seascapes.

The embryo artist struggled and saved enough to go and live in Paris, where he pored over the masterpieces in the Louvre and made a little money by copying classical paintings for rich patrons. One of these copies, of Ruisdaël's 'The Stream', he sent back to Le Havre (where it hangs today in the municipal museum), for the municipality had made him a three-year grant, provided that he sent back a couple of pictures each year for the town collection.

On his return to Le Havre in 1854, Boudin noted in his diary, 'Nature remains far richer than I can paint her.' In that year he spent three months living just outside Honfleur at the famous 'Ferme Siméon', an inn beloved of artists such as Corot and Daubigny, who had come to paint the Normandy coast. The Ferme Siméon is now a celebrated hotel and restaurant, and you can still walk the ten minutes or so to the Côte de Grâce and there sit on a bench and overlook their favourite view of the estuary of the Seine.

Should I urge you to sample the ambience, the quaint but well-kitted-out bedrooms, and the food of the restaurant and hotel of la Ferme Saint-Siméon in the rue Adolphe-Marais at Honfleur? Needless to say, Mother Toutain, who looked after Boudin and Monet and countless other artists, is no longer in charge. The cost of the menu, alas, rises far beyond the pocket of all but the most successful painters. Only the old farmhouse remains from those heady days 150 years ago, though pseudo-ancient buildings have been added to accommodate the twentieth-century traveller. My answer is yes: if you can afford a four-star hotel redolent with the ghosts of nineteenth-century artists, try la Ferme Saint-Siméon. When I was last there the patron's wife reinforced Normandy's ancient connection with England by having been born across the Channel. The kitchen at la Ferme Saint-Siméon proudly boasts of its succulently cooked lobsters, the tenderness of its saddle of young hare and, above all, its Normandy apples served in puff pastry – and rightly so. I should add that in my view a meal at la Ferme Saint-Siméon is also worth paying for simply to sip a Calvados after dinner and meditate on the remarkable influence of this sweet Normandy *auberge* on late nineteenth- and early twentieth-century art.

To return to its *habitué* Boudin, slowly his work developed and connoisseurs began to appreciate and patronize him. Courbet, by now a successful artist, used to stay with him at the Ferme Siméon and, warming to Boudin, introduced his work to Charles Baudelaire. When Boudin sent his first large picture to the salon des artistes français, Baudelaire shrewdly described it in a public review as 'very good and painstaking'. In Normandy today one can judge whether or not both epithets are fair by scrutinizing Boudin's 'Pilgrimage at Sainte-Anne-la-Palud', for it now hangs in the musée des Beaux-Arts André Malraux at Le Havre.

This picture was painted in 1858. In the same museum is another lovely picture, done eleven years later: Boudin's 'Lady on the beach at Trouville'. By this time he had made friends with a remarkable, alcoholic Dutch watercolourist named Johann Barthold Jongkind, and together they painted at Trouville in 1862. Jongkind's style was so fluid that many described it as incompetent, but he decisively influenced Boudin towards a much greater freedom of expression. The sky and the seaside now increasingly fascinated Boudin. Repeatedly the beach at Trouville inspired sketches and paintings, even though he regarded its fashionable sunbathers as gilded parasites. The pretty lady with a parasol whom he painted sitting on the beach in 1880 (which you can now see in the musée Boudin at Honfleur) was there not because Boudin admired her, but because the stunning red of her parasol so magically complimented the sea and the sky.

Recognition came late. Such masterpieces as the 1880 'Regatta at Antwerp', which today also hangs in the musée Boudin at Honfleur, were painted while the artist was still struggling for a living. Three years later he was at last on the brink of success. An art dealer and generous supporter of the Barbizon school, named Paul Durand-Ruel, opened his new gallery on the boulevard de la Madeleine, Paris, with a sizeable exhibition of Boudin's sketches and paintings. Boudin was astonished by

the critical acclaim his canvases evoked. The subsequent financial
security enabled him to build his own home at Deauville. And at the age
of sixty-seven he could visit Italy for the first time. Yet although Boudin
now relished the Mediterranean coast and Venice, Normandy remained
his first love. The last pictures he ever sent to the Paris salon were eight
sketches of Venice, two seascapes and two views of Deauville. The
following year, on 8 August 1898, he died at his Deauville home.

'At times I walk around utterly depressed,' wrote Boudin, 'looking at
the light which bathes the ground and shimmers reflected in the water as
well as playing over people's clothing. I feel completely weak when I
think how much skill is required to overcome the problems of painting it.'

Those problems were superbly overcome by Claude Monet. As Monet
himself expressed it at the end of his life, 'my only virtue has been to have
painted directly from nature, attempting to depict the impression made
on me by the most fleeting effects'.

Monet was by birth a Parisian, but around 1845 when he was only five
his family moved to Le Havre, where his father became an assistant to a
wholesale grocer. Thus the artist came to know and love the Seine, which
remained close at hand throughout almost his entire working life.
Initially, however, he proved his artistic facility as a teenager by selling
the citizens of Le Havre comical caricatures of themselves. One day, in
1857, when the impoverished Boudin was painting in Le Havre, he took
the seventeen-year-old out into the countryside. Monet watched the
older man paint and, in his own words, felt a veil torn from his eyes. For
the first time, he confessed, 'I understood what painting might be.'

Although Monet's father generously insisted that his son train in a
Paris studio, all the artist's real influences came from meeting kindred
spirits in Normandy itself, including the mercurial Dutchman Jongkind,
on whose work Monet's first seascapes were patterned. Two fellow
pupils in Paris, Pierre-August Renoir and Alfred Sisley, became firm
friends; and Monet displayed his singular originality by deriving unexpected inspiration from Japanese colour prints with their immense *élan*
and apparent freedom of style.

For anyone who has seen and admired Monet's work, parts of the
Normandy coastline often seem to have been modelled on his paintings,
and not vice versa. I saw his 'Stormy sea at Étretat' in the Jeu de Paume,
Paris, long before I visited that curiously gnawed-out cliffside, and still
remember the painting quite as much as the actual scene, remarkable
though that is.

Domiciled at Argenteuil on the Seine north of Paris after 1871, Monet
followed Jongkind's example and converted a boat into a studio. A year
later he painted a celebrated scene of Le Havre in the mist, which gave the
name to a whole movement of modern art and now hangs in the musée

Marmottan in Paris. Painted with extreme rapidity and very broad strokes, the picture is remarkable for the violent red of its sun and the streak of red that runs down the canvas where the sun is reflected in the sea. Not believing that he could truly call such a rapid, though astonishing sketch a portrait of Le Havre, Monet entitled it 'Impression, sunrise' ('Impression, soleil levant'), and the critic Louis Leroy picked up the word to dub all Monet's group 'Impressionists'.

Monet was still relatively poor. He grew poorer still when not only did his friend and benefactor Paul Durand-Ruel find himself in financial trouble, but another patron named Ernest Hoschedé went bankrupt and fled from his creditors to Belgium. In 1878 Monet, his ailing wife and his family were forced to leave Argenteuil for a cheaper home in the village of Vétheuil, further down the Seine. They took with them the wife and children of Hoschedé. Although Monet's own wife died the following year and he lived with Alice Hoschedé for the rest of her life, the two did not marry until 1892 when Alice's husband finally died.

Vétheuil provided Monet with some outstanding subjects which his genius was able to transform into stunningly new art. His second winter there was initially extremely harsh, followed by a thaw which caused monumental blocks of ice to flow down the river. Monet's series of paintings of these ice-floes not only catches the drama of the whole, but also startles by its extraordinary colours. Few painters had previously thought of painting ice pink. Monet loved painting Vétheuil wreathed in fog (or London, for that matter, once observing that London without its fogs was virtually worthless to an artist).

By the time he married Alice Hoschedé, Monet was financially secure. Paul Durand-Ruel had recovered his financial stability and was again buying Monet's paintings. Americans were increasingly interested in his work, Monet's travels around Normandy, as well as creating extraordinary pictures of the region around his own village, could now be supplemented by painting trips as far afield as the Mediterranean coast. Monet could enjoy in tranquillity his habitual forty cigarettes a day, most of them thrown away half-smoked, as well as his wine, taken undiluted – for he found water scarcely palatable, save in tiny doses after his morning chocolate.

In the 1890s Monet suddenly decided to transform his patterns of work. Unexpectedly he abandoned his extensive travels and began to concentrate on obsessionally and brilliantly painting three single sets of subjects. He was almost always painting three canvases at once, on account of the changing light, but these three sets carried his obsession with the nuances of atmosphere far beyond anything he had previously achieved.

The first set, done in 1890 and 1891, comprised fifteen remarkable paintings of haystacks standing in a field near his Normandy home. Monet was trying to capture 'instantaneity', he wrote, to depict not so much the haystacks themselves as their whole surrounding atmosphere. Initially he had been painting just one haystack scene when he perceived how quickly the light was changing and with it the scene itself. Calling on Alice Hoschedé's daughter Blanche to help him speedily switch canvases, he painted successive impressions of the same – yet imaginatively different – scene, reworking them later for exhibition. In December and January he was able to extend the range of his summer haystack paintings by magically depicting them under snow. Marvelling over them, I have often recalled another literary connotation: Guy de Maupassant's delicious conceit in *Boule de Suif* that snow falls on Rouen 'like a continuous rain of cotton'.

The next year Monet completed a similar group of atmospheric paintings, this time restricted to a group of poplars. They lined the River Epte near his home. Discovering that a farmer was about to fell them, Monet bought the trees himself. Such are the benefits of paying artists properly. In February 1892 fifteen paintings of these poplars, seen from different aspects and distances, depicted in varied colours and subtle shades, were hung in Durand-Ruel's Parisian gallery.

Finally, between 1892 and 1894 Monet was inspired to paint a series of sublime views of Rouen cathedral. Altogether he painted twenty such canvases. Sometimes he transformed the white stone into shimmering purple. All but two of his twenty paintings show the west façade, and not one is in any way a pale copy of another. Five of this superb group of paintings can still be experienced as he intended them all to be seen, hung together, at the Jeu de Paume in Paris. Naturally, without visiting Paris you can see one of Monet's superb depictions of Rouen cathedral, alongside others of his masterpieces, in the musée des Beaux-Arts at Rouen itself.

Monet frequently made use of his extended family's ability to trail around after him lugging half-finished paintings, and the technique admirably suited the changeable Normandy weather. Writing in 1866, Guy de Maupassant said that Monet seen painting was:

like a hunter on an expedition, followed by children carrying five or six canvases each representing the same subject painted at different times of the day and with different effects. Following the changes in the sky he would take them up and put them aside in turn. Watching his subject the painter would lie in wait for the sun and shadows, capturing with a few strokes of the brush the ray that fell or the cloud that passed.

No doubt Guy de Maupassant exaggerated, but only just, for he claimed once to have seen Monet seize in his hands a downpour beating on the sea, dash it on the canvas, and thus paint rain.

The influence of Monet can be clearly seen in several great Rouen paintings by his friend Camille Pissarro. The two had met in 1859, and when Pissarro's home was overrun during the course of the Franco-Prussian War he joined Monet in London. After 1884 he too lived in Normandy, at Bazincourt-sur-Epte near Gisors. The little village of Bazincourt-sur-Epte has much to commend it: peacefulness; the mound of its former château; a pretty parish church incorporating elements from the eleventh century. But Pissarro relished the Normandy coastline more than this charming village. In the Jeu de Paume hangs his delicious painting of the church of Saint Jacques at Dieppe, all greys and blues and yellows. His paintings done in the 1890s of Rouen cathedral and its surrounding markets note, in Monet fashion, the time of the day and the state of the weather. Grey weather for Camille Pissarro usually meant that he painted in pinks and reds, with a touch of green! You do not, of course, need to leave Normandy for Paris to enjoy his works. Pissarro is proudly on display in the Dieppe museum.

Can one overestimate the importance of the Normandy coastline on artists at this time? It inspired the American Whistler and his English pupil Walter Sickert, and before them J. M. W. Turner himself. Sickert's visits to, and work at, Dieppe over thirty years have earned him a rich room of his own in the city art gallery there. André Gide remembered meeting him at Dieppe for a second time in 1904 and noted in his diary that Sickert greeted him with the words, 'Do you remember that when we met for the first time you asked me whether I was greatly upset because you liked my paintings?'

But the grandeur of the Normandy coastline seems above all to have inspired French painters to new heights of sublimity. A year after Pissarro moved to Bazincourt-sur-Epte, Georges Seurat spent a part of the summer at Grandcamp in Normandy. The fishing port of Grandcamp is so tiny – a village of fewer than 450 inhabitants at the last census – that one might erroneously think it insignificant. Yet it commands an awesome barrier-reef, which each day savagely uncovers itself when the waters recede; it derives from a couple of old villages founded by the Normans themselves in the twelfth century; its church, dedicated to St Michael, in its present structure dates largely from the seventeenth century, but boasts a redoubtable sixteenth-century bell-tower and houses splendid eighteenth-century panelling; and once a year on the mid-Sunday of August the villagers of Grandcamp mount their gay and traditional fête.

Seurat loved the spot, especially its wild barrier-reef, and there he painted his first seascapes. In the summer of 1886 he visited Honfleur. Two years later he was once again on the Normandy coast, at Port-en-Bessin, where the sea has gouged its fingernails into the steep cliffs, where fishermen still sit silently on the granite jetties, and where the River Dromme debouches into the Channel.

These visits marked a turning-point in the history of French art. In the Tate Gallery, London, hangs a superb seascape from the time of Seurat's stay at Grandcamp. It glowingly depicts the strange rock which juts out of the sea here and is known as le Bec du Hoc. This painting, and thus the Normandy seascape, has been much underestimated in Seurat's work, for 'le Bec du Hoc, Grandcamp' is one of the first major paintings in which Seurat deployed to the full his celebrated technique known as pointillism. By this means he placed touches of unmixed colour side by side on the canvas to produce a yet greater luminosity than if they had been previously mixed on the artist's palette.

If, in Seurat, Normandy and its coast thus played their part in the development of neo-impressionism, they also played a major role in inspiring the fauvists Kees van Dongen, Raoul Dufy and Georges Braque. Van Dongen probably hovered around Trouville and Deauville mostly because these fashionable resorts attracted fashionable sitters able to pay for his portraits. But both Dufy and Braque were sons of Le Havre, and Dufy also loved to stay and work at Trouville. In the Museum of Modern Arts, Paris, there is a painting of 1906 devoted mostly to street posters and passers-by at this seaside resort. His studio at Le Havre overlooked the harbour, and sketches of the artists and his model are frequently over-shadowed by splashes of colour depicting ships through the open shutters of the window. Today you can see a sparkling collection of more than seventy works by Dufy, which were presented by his wife to the musée des Beaux-Arts André Malraux at Le Havre, a collection now supplemented by works lent by the Museum of Modern Art in Paris.

Braque was, in truth, born in Agenteuil and not in Normandy, but his family moved to Le Havre when he was five and he studied there at the *lycée* and the École des Beaux-Arts. Entrancing holidays in Dieppe in the late 1920s persuaded him to return more or less permanently to Normandy, and he set up a studio at Varengeville-sur-Mer. There in the mid-1950s he executed a series of stained-glass windows for the village church, in whose cemetery both he and his wife now rest. These windows are (in my view) among the rare modern stained-glass in France that one should go out of one's way to see.

In the early 1880s Monet too had loved this stretch of the Normandy coast west of Dieppe where Braque made his home. In 1882 he painted no fewer than eighteen times the coastguard's cottage overlooking a narrow ravine at Varengeville-sur-Mer. In the same year he also painted an extremely rich version of Varengeville church (it hangs in the Barber Institute, Birmingham). Even without Braque's connection, Varengeville-sur-Mer is well worth a visit – its thirteenth- and sixteenth-century church and cemetery set apart, recently restored and containing, as well as the stained-glass windows, Renaissance bas-reliefs of maritime scenes.

But no one visiting Normandy should remotely consider missing a visit to the house at Giverny where in 1883 Monet decided to move with his extended family.

The nearest sizeable town to Giverny is Vernon, and it was on the train from here to Vétheuil that Monet first spotted Giverny. The best way to approach it is still by way of Vernon, which lies beautifully situated on left bank of the Seine. Lying north-east of Paris, close to the south-east border of the *département* of the Eure, the town is easily reached by the Autoroute de Normandie (the A13) and is itself worth lingering in.

If you approach Vernon from the north the route is even more rewarding. The drive along the D135 from Venables to les Andelys comprises eleven scenic kilometres skirting a great loop of the Seine, flanked by rolling hills, sheer white cliffs and the rich forest of Grande Garenne. Old farmers with their sheepdogs add to the glamour of the journey. In summer the lower banks of the river are thronged with fortunate campers.

Les Andelys consists of two charming villages dominated by one of the most entrancing ruins in Normandy. Château-Gaillard rises above the Seine, white as the cliffs on which it stands. Richard Coeur de Lion built it at the very end of the twelfth century as a bastion against King Philippe Auguste. 'I would defend it, even if its walls were made of clay,' Richard is reputed to have declared. 'I shall conquer it, even if its walls are made of iron,' responded Philippe Auguste. In the event, the King of France's words came true. In October 1203 his forces besieged Richard's château and took it, albeit by treachery. So fell the last bulwark of the dukes of Normandy.

Exactly four centuries later much of the magnificent château was demolished on the orders of Henri IV, its stones offered to Cardinal de Bourbon for his new château at Gaillon. In between château-Gaillard had served in 1314 as the jail for Louis X the Headstrong, his wife and her two sisters, who, it was alleged, were grievous adulterers. Louis's wife, Margaret of Burgundy, was strangled here two years later.

What still remains of château-Gaillard offers an unrivalled opportunity to explore a Norman castle at its most arrogant and elegant, a pattern of military architecture incorporating all that the Normans had assimilated from the Saracen castles they encountered on the crusades. The walls of its keep are five metres wide and its moat is fifteen metres deep. You can visit it from mid-March to mid-September, except on Tuesdays and Wednesdays.

As for the villages of le Petit-Andely and le Grand-Andely, the former lies on the right bank of the Seine, was fortified by Richard Coeur de Lion shortly before he built château-Gaillard and boasts lovely half-timbered houses and the church of Saint-Sauveur, built at the end of the twelfth century and the beginning of the next. Inside the church is an organ designed and built by Ingout of Rouen in 1674. In front of the church is a monument to Jean-Pierre Blanchard, the first man to cross the Channel in a balloon. The year was 1785. This benefactor of humanity also invented the parachute and has thus saved countless lives of his successor aeronauts and astronauts.

At le Grand-Andely, which you reach from le Petit-Andely by taking the shady avénue-de-la-République, the widow of King Clovis, St Clothilde, founded a monastery in 511 on the spot where the collegiate church of Notre Dame stands today. The windows of its thirteenth-century nave gleam with Renaissance stained-glass; the mighty organ case dates from the same era; and the south aisle is a thrilling example of Normandy flamboyant architecture. Not far away is a pretty fountain, successor of one dug on the orders of St Clothilde, who would occasionally encourage her thirsty workmen by turning its water into wine. I should have thought such generosity would have sent them to sleep rather than vigorously back to work. The saint, I suppose, knew better.

But this chapter is supposedly devoted to painting rather than the plastic arts, architecture and pious legend. In Notre-Dame at le Grand-Andely are displayed three paintings by Quentin Varin, who was the teacher of Nicolas Poussin, the greatest son of les Andelys. (Poussin was actually born in 1594 at Villars, just outside the twin villages.) In rue Sainte-Clothilde the musée Nicolas Poussin displays his masterpiece, 'Coriolanus griefstricken by the tears of his mother'.

Now drive on to Vernon, which is far older than its present aspect indicates. Neolithic man settled here beside the river. The Romans and the Gauls followed suit. As one might expect, the medieval seigneurs of Vernon built a château to dominate the confluence of the Seine with the Epte. The sole remaining vestige of the château is its late twelfth-century keep, the tour des Archives, from close to which (for access is, alas, forbidden) you have a luscious view of the Seine valley. King Philippe Auguste of France built it after he had gained Vernon by treaty from John Lackland in 1196, and he also built the ramparts, traces of which remain in the town centre. An even finer view of the river is that obtained from the chapel and belvedere of Notre-Dame-de-la-Mer nine kilometres south-east.

Vernon too has a superb collegiate church, also dedicated to Our Lady, its fine central tower dating from the thirteenth century, its nave and west façade from the next, its organ case from the sixteenth century and its Renaissance tapestries from the seventeenth. The statue of the Virgin on the west façade dates from the fourteenth century, the flamboyant rose window from the next. I have lingered long in Vernon church, admiring the works of art proliferating in its chapels, the stained-glass windows, and especially the splendid Louis XVI high altar rescued from the Charterhouse of Gaillon when it was dissolved at the Revolution. I greatly admire the carvings on the organ case, of the musical angels, the sybils and David, musician-king of the Jews. And simply surveying the west façade of this collegiate church is an enormous treat: the rose window over its mighty doorway made up of four smaller roses, a clock on top of that, another blank rose in the steep triangle above, the whole flanked by a couple of traceried towers and everything supported by flying buttresses. To add to the charm, next to this mighty church are some of Vernon's exquisite half-timbered old houses.

Such an important military site as Vernon had its disadvantages. It was bombarded by the Prussians in 1870 and again – much more severely – in 1944, suffering savage damage to its numerous half-timbered houses. At the head of the 43rd Wessex battalion, Montgomery liberated the town on 25 August, and the citizens promptly made him a freeman of Vernon. Happily they have resolutely set about renovating their ancient houses, adding to the charm of the place. The best ones today line the picturesque rue Bourbon-Penthièvre and the rue d'Albuféra.

If you are visiting Vernon and Giverny between Easter and All Saint's Day (1 November), don't fail to call in also at the altogether splendid château de Bizy just outside Vernon. (It lies one and a half kilometres south-west and closes on Mondays.) Built by the architect Coulant d'Ivray for his patron Fouquet, the Duc de Bell-Isle, in the mid-eighteenth century, this classical château boasts magnificent furnishings as well as a park with cascades and fountains, sculptures and shady walks.

Returning to Vernon, cross the river by the pont Clemenceau (noting the pillars of the old medieval bridge and the fifteenth-century mill) to reach the town's suburb, Vernonnet, where again, as you would expect, a twelfth-century château was built to guard the bridge. Its remnants are still there, alas another victim of the campaign of 1944.

Giverny boasts a flamboyant fifteenth-century church dedicated to St Radegone, with a twelfth-century Romanesque apse. Soon after Monet glimpsed Giverny from the train he, Alice Hoschedé and their children were ensconced in a local inn. Then they rented a house whose extensive land sloped down to the lower end of the village.

Monet, increasingly affluent, next decided to buy this house for 22,000 francs. Now he set about creating a magnificent garden, as well as a studio where he could complete his last masterpieces: superb paintings of the very garden he had conceived. In 1893 he succeeded in buying a further plot of land at the other side of the road and the little railway track from which he had first seen Giverny. In 1895 he managed to divert a stream there from the River Epte. Over the stream he constructed a lovely Japanese bridge, and on its waters he created landscapes of water-lilies. At first, he confessed, he had planted his water-lilies simply for pleasure, not intending to paint them. 'A landscape does not get through to you immediately,' he explained. 'Then suddenly the revelation came to me of the magic of my pond.' By 1899 a second studio had been built at Giverny, and in that year Durand-Ruel's Paris gallery displayed Monet's sensational series of paintings of water-lilies.

Fame could not wipe away his misery at the loss of his second wife in 1911. But his daughter-in-law Blanche sustained him, as did his friendship with Georges Clemenceau, who encouraged him to create a final stupendous masterpiece based on his Giverny garden: massive decorative panels of water-lilies, called the 'Décorations des nymphéas'. In spite of suffering from cataracts, Monet began work on the project in 1916, donating the finished work to the French nation in 1925, a year before his death. In 1927 they were installed in the Orangerie, Paris.

Blanche devotedly cared for Monet's house and garden at Giverny until her death afer World War II. Then the neglected garden slowly fell into disrepair; most of Monet's pictures were sold. In 1966, however, Monet's eighty-eight-year-old second son died, and his will turned out to have left the property to the Académie des Beaux-Arts. With the extraordinarily generous help of Monet's American admirers, and under the direction of the curator of Giverny, M. Gérald van der Kemp, the house and gardens have been miraculously restored. Weeping willows, irises, roses, water-lilies, rhododendrons, azaleas and the Japanese bridge are all once again as Monet envisaged them.

The three-kilometre drive from Vernon to Giverny, with the wide river valley rising to the right into wooded slopes, shows exactly why Monet chose this idyllic spot. Monet's house and garden at Giverny are open to visitors from the beginning of April to the end of September, his immense studio now a bookshop whose walls are lined with reproductions of his works – including, of course, the massive water-lilies for the Orangerie in Paris. Here too are displayed marvellous photographs of the great man, with his huge white beard, working in his studio or taking people around his garden, proud as a peacock in his broad-brimmed hat and with a cigarette almost always in his mouth. He stands on his Japanese bridge with an extremely pretty Blanche and a Japanese collector of his paintings, the three of them photographed around the year 1921. In one photograph Monet is pointing at the central part of his 'Déjeuner sur l'herbe', which he began in the 1850s and never finished. Nearby on the studio wall is a fine reproduction of the painting itself.

The garden is vibrant: apple trees trained as a hedge; chickens and hens; gladioli; hollyhocks; cornflowers; aubretia; lilies; tall roses; exotic trees ranging from tamarisks to a yellow-leaved albizzia – all today neatly, unobtrusively labelled. Visitors always stand and stare entranced at the green-painted furniture, the lawns, taking in the delicious scents, the reds, blues and yellows. A cat broods in the sun. Doves perch on the house.

An underground passage (paid for by a generous American) leads to the famous water-lily garden, with its irises and lupins, heather and laurel and fern, weeping willows, bushing azaleas and rhododendrons, and a reconstruction of the Japanese bridge which Monet built in 1895, with wistaria trailing along its sides.

Then it is time to visit the house itself. Every detail, from the ceramic tiles of the kitchen, through the delicate blue décor of the reading room and the pale yellow of the dining room, to the bedroom where Monet died in 1926, has been authentically re-created. The furniture of Monet's bedroom is original. The rooms are filled with reproductions (and the occasional original) of pictures collected by Monet, especially the Japanese engravings, such as Utamaro's triptych beach at Futamigaura, whose influence can be discerned in Monet's own limpidly free portrayal of his Normandy coast. Upstairs in his dressing room is a chrysanthemum by Hokusai. In the next room hangs a stunning picture of a convolvulus and tree frog by the same artist.

And from a photograph of Monet in one of the rooms you suddenly spot that you are standing in that very same room, that the vases on the mantelpiece, beside which he was photographed, are still arranged as in his day, and that over that mantelpiece now – as then – hangs Yoshiku's lovely engraving of 'the bath that gives one's skin the texture of flowers'.

Normandy in flames

An inscription carved after World War II in the military cemetery at Bayeux reads *Nos a Gulielmo victi victoris patriam liberavimus* – 'We who were conquered by William have liberated the land of the conqueror.' This second invasion, however, was a war of liberation, not of conquest. Before describing this thrilling and also bloody episode in Normandy's history, may I try to answer a question raised by this lapidary phrase: were the British and their allies really liberating the same race that had conquered England in 1066, or had not the real Normans disappeared long before? As Hilaire Belloc put the point, the Normans 'were a flash. They were not formed or definable at all before the year 1000; by the year 1200 they were gone.'

The superb Belloc, I believe, oversimplifies. Many historians have stressed the extraordinary ability of these early Normans to adapt themselves to the manners of those whom they invaded. Viking sailors became superb horsemen, riding the steeds that their opponents utilized and wearing the standard armour of north-west Europe. Norman pagans converted to Christianity almost overnight, building superb churches where they had destroyed shrines, founding monasteries and setting out as crusaders instead of scourges of the faithful. Brutal in battle, they also adopted the knightly cult that had developed in the Carolingian courts of the tenth and eleventh centuries. To protect their conquests they developed the castles invented by their opponents: a mound (or motte) defended by a ditch and palisade (or bailey), surmounted by a wooden palisade and tower.

As administrators they took over the basic principles already established in Carolingian feudalism. In England, for example, where their ruthlessness was displayed in a virtually complete elimination of the former English aristocracy, they divided up the country anew between some 180 Norman tenants-in-chief and countless mesne tenants, all of whom possessed their fiefs by agreeing to serve as knights. Thus, at the same time as inheriting the system whereby land-tenure was held in return for service, the Normans transformed it into a pattern of military feudalism which provided William the Conqueror with more than 40,000 knights.

Some historians, following the lead of R. H. C. Davis, have seen this skill at adaptation as eventually destructive of anything that can be called quintessentially Norman. Davis makes the striking point that 'The most puzzling feature of the Normans is the way they disappeared', pointing out that England had an Angevin king from 1154, Sicily a German from 1194, and that in 1204 Normandy was lost to the French. 'Though the heirs of Bohemond ruled over the last remnants of the principality of Antioch till 1287, they no longer thought of themselves as Normans,' Professor Davis continues. 'The people who had dominated so many aspects of Europe in the eleventh and twelfth centuries, in the thirteenth century had simply disappeared.'

The Normans provided England with only three sovereigns: William the Bastard, William Rufus and Henry Beauclerc. In 1120 Henry's only son William the Aetheling was drowned at sea. Henry therefore decreed that his daughter Matilda was his heir, but when he died the Conqueror's grandson, Stephen of Blois, claimed the throne. The subsequent civil war in England ended when Stephen was accepted as king, with the proviso that Matilda's son Henry of Anjou should succeed him. In 1154 he became Henry II, first monarch of the house of Plantagenet.

With the end of his reign the historian Charles Homer Haskins dates the beginning of the collapse of the Norman empire. Only two more men were thenceforth designated dukes of Normandy, both sons of Henry II: Richard Coeur de Lion, who had betrayed his father and ruled from 1189 to 1199; and Richard's brother John Lackland, who ruled from 1199 to 1216.

In July 1189 Henry II himself lay dying in his château at Chinon, abandoned and even attacked by his sons and forced into a humiliating peace with Philippe of France. Still hoping that one son, Count John, had remained faithful, he listened to the list of those who had thrown aside their allegiance. 'May Christ help me,' said the clerk as he read the document, 'the first here written is Count John, your son.' Starting up from his bed, the king cried, 'What, John, my very heart, my best beloved, for whose advancement I have brought upon me all this misery? Now let all things go as they will; I care no more for myself nor for anything in this world.'

Two days later the king's labouring breath cursed his own sons and the day he had been born, and he died constantly repeating, 'Shame on a conquered king.' As had happened with William the Conqueror, his corpse was plundered of its royal apparel, though in pity someone threw over him a 'court mantle' or short cloak. After another two days he was buried in the nunnery of Fontrevault. In the words of C. H. Haskins, 'Thus passed away the greatest ruler of his age; thus began the collapse of the Norman empire.' Did the authentic Normans also disappear with it?

Maybe the Normans live on only as a myth, or rather as several different myths. Sometimes they appear as demons, for these mythical Normans have not always received a good press from those they conquered. In the late eighteenth century, for example, the English radical, Tom Paine, seized on them to castigate what he saw as the evils of an hereditary monarchy:

England since the Conquest hath known some few good monarchs but groaned beneath a much larger number of bad ones, yet no man in his senses can say that their claim under William the Conqueror is a very honourable one. A French bastard landing with armed *banditti*, and establishing himself king of England against the consent of the natives, is in plain terms a very paltry rascal indeed.

By contrast another Englishman named Orderic Vitalis, who lived in the twelfth century as a monk at the abbey of Saint-Évroult-Notre-Dame-du-Bois in Normandy (at that time one of the leading intellectual centres of Europe), took a totally different view from Tom Paine. If ever an historian adored the Normans it was this English monk. He also acutely described their volatile character. 'The Normans are unconquerable, ready for any wild deed unless a strong ruler restrains them,' he wrote:

In whatever group they find themselves, they seek always to dominate the rest, and in the heat of their ambitions they frequently violate their obligations. All this the French, the Bretons, the Flemish and their other neighbours have often experienced. The Italians, the Lombards, the Angles and the Saxons too have learned the same – to their own undoing.

How then do I personally answer the question: where are the Normans today? My answer is that they are to be found virtually everywhere in the English-speaking world, not just in Normandy but wherever Norman blood flows through someone's veins. Consistent with the adulation of Orderic Vitalis, Norman descent is jubilantly asserted by anyone with the remotest claim to it. Even the British royal family (which is basically derived from German-speaking descendants of the house of Hanover, who succeeded the last of the Stuarts in 1714) takes care to trace its ancestry back to William the Bastard. Similarly, nearly all of us who live in the Western world, and especially southern Italians and Sicilians, can claim Norman descent.

In 1914 Henry Adams published for his nephew a beautifully written study of le Mont-Saint-Michel and Chartres. He charmingly and succinctly summed up the history of the Normans since 1058, when the great triumphal piers of the abbey church on the mount were constructed:

Eight years after these piers were built, in 1066, Duke William of Normandy raised an army of forty thousand men in these parts, and in northern France, whom he took to England, where they mostly stayed. For a hundred and fifty years, until 1204, Normandy and England were united; the Norman peasant went freely to England with his lord, spiritual or temporal; the Norman woman, a very capable person, followed her husband or her parents; Normans held nearly all the English fiefs; filled the English church; crowded the English Court; created the English law.

Adams added, 'Since the generation which followed William to England in 1066, we can reckon twenty-eight or thirty [generations] from father to son, and, if you care to figure up the sum, you will find that you had about two hundred and fifty [million forebears], it would not much affect the certainty that, if you have any English blood at all, you have also Norman.'

So, Adams surmised, anyone whose veins pulsated with such blood, and who could go back in the imagination to live again as his or her ancestors of the eleventh century, would find him- or herself ploughing the fields of the Cotentin and Calvados; going to mass in the parish churches of Normandy; rendering military service to the lords, spiritual or temporal, of this region; and helping to build the abbey church at le Mont-Saint-Michel.

I like to concur with him. In consequence, in 1944 the invading Americans, Canadians and British could claim to be liberating not strangers but their fellow Normans.

As anyone who cares to travel along the now-nostalgic beaches and cliffs of Normandy perceives, it was no easy task. In Guy de Maupassant's *Pierre and Jean*, Monsieur Roland delightfully describes to his guests this same Norman coastline, seen across the Seine estuary from Le Havre:

He pointed out Villerville, Trouville, Houlgate, Luc-sur-Mer, Arromanches, the river of Caen and the rocks of Calvados which make navigation difficult as far as Cherbourg. Next he talked of the sandbanks of the Seine, shifting with every tide and leading astray even the pilots of Quilleboeuf unless they took care each day to reconnoitre the channel afresh.

Monsieur Roland then told them that Le Havre separated Upper Normandy from Lower Normandy. The flat coast of the latter slopes down to the edge of the water, and is a country of pastures, meadows and fields, he said. Upper Normandy by contrast boasts a coastline of steep, sometimes precipitous cliffs descending to the sea, a tremendous white wall of clefts and indentations stretching as far as Dunkirk, each cleft sheltering a port or a village: Étretat, Fécamp, Saint-Valéry, Tréport, Dieppe and the rest.

Monsieur Roland's guests become utterly bored, not by the land and seascape but by his droning voice, impertinently disturbing the calm of the vast expanse of air and water and the magnificent sunset, so I shall not continue describing it myself, since my readers will surely visit it for themselves.

In 1944 the calm of this superb coastline was once again impertinently interrupted. Maupassant's mentor Gustave Flaubert had compared these same white cliffs, with their occasional streaks of black and traces of flint, to the curve of an enormous defensive rampart. Part of the invading Allied forces in 1944 would be faced with scaling this rampart, most of them under withering enemy fire.

Winston Churchill had initiated plans for invading Normandy as far back as 1940, after the British Expeditionary Force had been forced by the might of the invading Germans to withdraw from Dunkirk. Churchill's initiative was an extraordinarily pugnacious decision at a moment when Hitler seemed likely to invade and almost certainly conquer Britain within months.

Hitler's own error in invading Russia, and narrowly failing to defeat her, gave Britain a vital respite. At Casablanca in 1943 the Allies agreed to joint operations. The scheme was to be called Overlord, and May 1944 was chosen as the date for putting it into effect. At Cairo in November 1943 Churchill and President Roosevelt agreed that the supreme commander must be an American, General Dwight D. Eisenhower. The British Air Chief Marshal Tedder would be deputy-commander. As for the tetchy, mercurial Bernard Montgomery, the hero of El Alamein, he should command all the Allied ground forces until they had gained their foothold in Normandy, after which his command would be shared with the American General Omar Bradley, both men being ultimately subordinate to Eisenhower.

At least this command structure was clear, even though it offered scope for considerable dissension. Adolf Hitler, by contrast, managed to set up a cripplingly divided structure of command in planning the German defence of Europe. By 1942 the genuine possibility of a joint Anglo-American invasion of Normandy had prompted him to bring out of retirement General Gerd von Rundstedt, who had brilliantly circumvented the Maginot line during the invasion of free France in 1940. Ironically Hitler now charged him with creating just such a vulnerable line of defence – yet far greater in length, stretching from Denmark to Spain – for the protection of Nazi-occupied France.

Von Rundstedt reluctantly complied. Two hundred and fifty thousand conscripts toiled at creating tank traps, building bunkers and block-houses, planting concrete 'dragons' teeth' along the possible lines of attack, digging slit trenches for machine guns and fortifying the Normandy beaches. The general, now Hitler's western commander-in-chief, also set about the hopeless task of building up a German army sufficiently well-trained to withstand a determined Allied attack on these defences.

This became the Atlantic wall. Von Rundstedt was astonished in November 1943 when the increasingly bizarre Führer commissioned Field Marshal Erwin Beit von Rommel with the task of inspecting the wall and, if necessary, suggesting where it might be improved. Although the two distinguished military men were friends, their strategies at this point differed markedly. Von Rundstedt still believed that a mobile force could swiftly deploy itself wherever the British and Americans managed to break through the Atlantic wall; Rommel held that this would prove impossible. Instead a massive army was needed, he believed, to stretch itself along the entire length of the defence in order to destroy the spearhead of the attackers and thus stop them gaining any toehold at all in Normandy.

So Rommel increased the number of dragons' teeth sown along the defences. Submerged at sea were concrete tetrahedra, reinforced with steel and designed to impale attacking ships and landing craft. The beaches were mined. Miles and miles of barbed wire were strung three metres above the ground, charged with explosives to deter paratroops. Rommel's failures paralleled Von Rundstedt's similar lack of success: neither Hitler nor Goering was willing to commit enough troops or air resources to the defence of Normandy.

Although the Pas de Calais is nearer to Britain than the Normandy coast, Normandy seemed much more favourable to the success of the 1944 invasion. The English south-coast ports could accommodate more ships and the hinterlands more British, Canadian and American troops. (In the event, more than a million and a half US troops were billeted in south-west England in preparation for Operation Overlord.) A further consideration was that Normandy was less well-defended than the Pas de Calais. And the Cherbourg peninsula would give the invading ships a measure of protection from the Atlantic seas. None the less it was essential to keep the decision to invade Normandy, and not the Pas de Calais, a total secret in order to keep the German defenders guessing as to where the final assault would come.

Success was by no means guaranteed, as a tragic episode in the war had already shown. Just below the fifteenth-century château at Dieppe is a flower bed in the shape of a maple leaf. It commemorates a disastrous raid on the town, made under withering fire by Canadian troops on 19 August 1942. On the route to Pourville, opposite the golf links, is a museum commemorating this frightful episode in World War II, a sortie which was intended as a 'reconnaissance in force' and ended in slaughter.

The aims of the Dieppe raid included not only reconnaissance. The Allies also intended to force the Germans to pour defensive troops into the Channel port and its environs, thus weakening their forces elsewhere in Normandy. In addition, the Allies wished to test out new assault techniques, in preparation for Operation Overlord itself. On 20 May the 2nd Canadian Infantry Division began training on the Isle of Wight in amphibious operations.

In the early hours of 19 August some 5,000 Canadians, supported by another 1,000 men consisting chiefly of British commandos along with fifty American rangers, attacked the coastline of Dieppe along a sixteen-kilometre stretch. Supported by seventy-four Allied air squadrons and four Royal Navy destroyers, the plan involved four preliminary, simultaneous flanking attacks, followed half an hour later by a massive frontal attack on Dieppe itself and on the two gaps in the Alabaster coast at Pourville and Puys.

Almost immediately the attack went wrong. Secrecy was blown when a small German convoy came across the landing craft on the eastern sector and spiritedly engaged them in battle. The noise of fighting was audible ashore, and the German defences were instantly set on alert. The commandos managed to knock out the German battery at Varengeville, but the south Saskatchewan regiment and the Canadian Cameron Highlanders had no chance of reaching Dieppe. Forced to withdraw, their rearguard surrendered. The rest of these bloodied men, many of them wounded, re-embarked for Britain, leaving their dead behind.

At Puys, four kilometres west of Dieppe, the narrow beach is commanded by high cliffs and proved a death trap for many more. German batteries mounted above the invaders cruelly pinned them down, killing 220 of them (200 of whom died instantly, the rest in agony later). Those who survived the relentless fire of the defenders had no option but to surrender.

The main assault was thus doomed to failure. The heavy losses sustained by the infantry from similarly withering German fire were compounded by errors of intelligence and strategy. At one point the Allied command mistakenly read a message from the invaders to mean that Dieppe was close to capture. They sent in the reserve battalion, to meet vicious enemy fire. Secondly, the tanks of the Calgary regiment landed fifteen minutes late. In consequence the infantry fought ahead without their support. The shingle bogged down the tanks, and the enemy poured salvo after salvo on their immobilized opponents.

Of the 4,963 Canadians who set out on the Dieppe raid of 19 August, altogther 3,367 became casualties – 907 of them dead, 1,946 prisoners of war. These included two men who later received the Victoria Cross. One was Lieutenant-Colonel Cecil Merritt, who under intense fire led party after party across the River Scie. The other was the only chaplain in the Canadian army ever to win this coveted honour, the Rev. John Weir Foote, padre hero of the Dieppe raid. As chaplain to the Royal Hamilton Light Infantry, assigned for the central thrust on Dieppe, he saw his comrades suffer appalling casualties, some of them slaughtered even before they had set foot on shore.

When the order to re-embark was issued, Padre Foote doggedly toiled among the wounded, helping them to safety regardless of the hail of bullets under which he was ministering. Remaining on shore to the very end, Foote was inevitably captured, and spent the rest of the war in German POW camps. Afterwards this humble padre gave his VC to his regiment, arguing that the bravery of all its men had been honoured by the award. He used to say, 'If I did anything of value, it was ministering to the captured troops in the prison camps. The action at Dieppe was the easy part of it.' A quarter of a century later this modest, mellow man of God died in Cobourg, Ontario, at the age of eighty-three.

In the commune of Hautôt-sur-Mer, five kilometres south of Dieppe, 707 Canadians lie alongside 237 of their British colleagues in the Dieppe Canadian War Cemetery. And in the centre of Dieppe itself, the place Canada encloses the Dieppe-Canada monument, not solely as a commemoration of the disastrous raid of 1942 but also as a reminder of all the links between Normandy and Canada, since Samuel de Champlain sailed from Honfleur in 1603 and five years later founded New France.

Painfully conscious of the débâcle of 1942, the Allied supreme command was well aware that Operation Overlord might fail disastrously. This time the build-up to the attack was massive. From 1 April 1944 the Allied air forces began to make sorties over northern France, achieving 200,000 in all before Operation Overlord was finally launched. Each sortie dropped an average of a ton of bombs, aimed in particular at industrial centres and rail connections. The planners took care to bomb the Pas de Calais more than Normandy, so as to reinforce the impression that here would come the eventual attack. Even so, Hitler felt sure that Normandy would be the venue for the invasion, and in May Rommel was instructed to move three divisions there. Yet Allied intelligence consistently leaked false information to the Germans, building up the rumour that General Patton was to lead an army against the Pas de Calais. In consequence the German Panzer divisions were fatally divided, some of the best concentrated where the attack never came.

Then the invasion was delayed by bad weather. The forecast of 5 June indicated that the weather would improve for at least thirty-six hours, and Eisenhower ordered Operation Overlord to begin early the following

morning, with a fleet of over 7,000 vessels crossing the Channel, reinforced by planes carrying 23,000 paratroops.

To trace where the Anglo-American forces landed, start at Caen, at the
church of Saint-Pierre. Built between the thirteenth and the sixteenth
centuries, it initially seems to have nothing to do with World War II. Its
spirited Gothic spire, reaching a height of seventy-eight metres, its
delicate Gothic nave and the luxuriant lacy frieze of its sanctuary speak of
the greatest achievements of religious architecture. Part of the vault was
rebuilt in the flamboyant Gothic style by two masters, Hector Sohier and
Jean Masselin, who worked between 1535 and 1550. Turn around to look
west at the rose window and its embellished clerestory, both dating from
the second half of the fourteenth century. We shall see more of this
church later in this book (consult the index). What is astonishing is that so
much of it was destroyed in the Allied invasion of 1944 and so much has
been meticulously restored.

For a start, on 12 June the steeple was smashed down by a 420-lb shell
and the vault of the nave was completely destroyed (along with an
irreplaceable eighteenth-century organ). By March 1957 both nave and
spire had been beautifully rebuilt. One of the sculpted keystones of the
flamboyant vaulting depicting St Peter, lifesize (if we assume that the real
St Peter stood six feet tall), was also destroyed in 1944. The St Peter you
see today is new, lovingly carved from a seven-ton piece of Caen stone,
the statue itself weighing a massive three tons.

Such brilliant restoration does not mean that the citizens of Caen have
forgotten the war. Caen took over twenty years to rebuild its shattered
self, after the RAF raids and Allied and German shelling which led up to
its liberation on 9 July 1944 had destroyed 75 per cent of the city. Lest we
forget, visit the Caen-Normandy Museum of Peace which opened here on
6 June 1988, exactly forty-four years after D-Day, when Operation
Overlord was launched to liberate Normandy from German occupation.
Open between 1 May and 30 September from 09.00 to 18.00 and for the
rest of the year from 10.00 to 17.00, the museum documents the illusions
of the mid-war years, the black years of occupied France, the total war
being waged outside that country and then the events from 6 June 1944 to
the end of World War II on 8 May 1945.

Reach the Museum of Peace by taking the avénue Maréchal-Mont-
gomery in the northern part of the city (it runs from Invasion rond-point)
as far as the esplanade Général-Eisenhower, which stretches along a cliff
that once sheltered the underground headquarters of the defending
German divisions. The museum itself, a 'functional' building, as its
architects describe it (they should have said 'ugly'), bears a symbolic
wound at its heart. You enter the museum by passing an RAF Typhoon,
almost pitifully tiny by the standards of today's aircraft but crucial in 1944

for the success of the invasion. Inside the museum 'Monty', Allied commander-in-chief until Eisenhower took over in July 1944, is portrayed in the Rolls-Royce which was landed on day nine of the Normandy invasion, alongside the US Sherman tanks, as well as German weaponry – for the present German state lent its help to Caen in creating this museum. (Indeed, Caen is now twinned with Würzburg, that exquisite Bavarian city which also suffered considerably from Allied air raids in 1944.)

After visiting the Museum of Peace, take the D515 north-east from Caen to Ouistreham Riva-Bella. The road runs through Bénouville close to the celebrated Pegasus bridge. Here on 6 June 1944 the 6th British Airborne Division landed, planning to link up with the 3rd British Infantry Division, which had begun landing at Ouistreham Riva-Bella at 07.30 that morning. The British did not expect the vigorous defence put up by the counter-attacking 21st German Panzers. Not until 15.30 that afternoon did the infantry and the paratroops meet up at Bénouville, and only after the infantry division had been reinforced by commandos.

The route turns left at Ouistreham and Riva-Bella (with its museum to the 4th Commandos) to run along the coast as far as Langrune, a region known to war historians as Sword Beach. Between Ouistreham and Lion-sur-Mer the 3rd Infantry Division landed, planning in vain to reach and take Caen that day. A little further on is Luc-sur-Mer. Between Luc-sur-Mer and Lion-sur-Mer there was once a series of curiously shaped fissures which the locals dubbed 'confessionals'. All but two of them have long been filled up with debris; but the remaining two are well worth seeing, as is the twelfth-century bell tower of the church at Luc-sur-Mer itself.

Today the cliffs of Luc-sur-Mer have been classified as a protected natural site, since scientists have discovered there a group of rocky but frail spongy reefs unique in France, covered with fossils and dating back some 160 million years, if not more. The invaders of 1944 had little time to notice such a priceless and delicate heritage, nor to observe the skeleton of a whale washed up on the pretty beach in 1885 and still displayed in the old town. But even in the teeth of battle, culture need not totally disappear. A retired Sussex schoolmaster once told me that during World War I he read Wordsworth during lulls in the fighting around Ypres. I do not think there were enough lulls in June 1944 for such civilized behaviour.

There is space to recall here that in his novel *Les Bains de mer*, Émile Zola describes a bourgeois Parisian family at Luc-sur-Mer, a family too obses-sed with hunting to relish the sea. As one might expect, Zola's own protagonists in *Les Bains de mer* do not find the spot so charming. For him Luc-sur-Mer represents 'the sadness of this maritime coast, the most rebarbative imaginable, with pebbles and pointed stones and rocks piercing the sand, and the village itself peopled with grey and morose houses'. These repellent cliffs made this part of the British sector during the Normandy invasions all the more hazardous. Still, by the end of the day the British had gained their coveted toehold on enemy territory.

Beyond Luc-sur-Mer the D514 runs west through Saint-Aubin-sur-Mer, today a favourite bathing spot with its sandy beach and beckoning row of rocks a little way out in the sea. On 6 June 1944 the variedly jagged and gentle coast that stretches between this peaceful site and Courseulles by way of the village of Bernières was selected for the spearhead of the Allied forces' attack on Normandy, the cost of which is movingly recalled by the orderly British military cemetery at Hermanville-sur-Mer.

Happily the invasion spared the exquisite thirteenth-century bell tower of Bernière's parish church, as well as its fine contemporary nave and choir. It houses a lovely late seventeenth-century stone retable and a rococo altar. But what happened to its stained-glass windows (for the present ones are modern)? Also spared was the pretty classical manor of Quintefeuille, which you see to your right as you leave the village.

Courseulles bears the honour of being the first port officially liberated in 1944. A stele by the beach recalls the moment when General de Gaulle stepped ashore here. Courseulles's oyster farms (the oldest dating from 1796), its boatyards and its fishing smacks, along with the seventeenth-century château in the old part of the town, seem oblivious to the sacrifices involved in those desperate days, until you discover the Duplex drive DD Sherman tank fished out of the sea twenty-seven years after the war and mounted in the place 6-Juin, as well as plaques commemorating the bravery of the British and Canadian troops who came ashore to fight here.

This section of the invasion area, Juno Beach, which you can drive down to from the centre of Courseulles, is followed by Gold Beach, which stretches west as far as Port-en-Bessin. Juno Beach was where the Canadians forced their way into Normandy. Gold was the venue of an attack by British infantry and royal marines commandos, supported by engineers desperately trying to clear the beaches of mines and emplacements. The debris of war is still being uncovered along this coast. Drive on from Courseulles to Gray-sur-Merand, where you will find on display a Churchill tank belonging to the 79th Armoured Division, which was dug out of the sand only in 1976, as well as several concrete German blockhouses littering the beach. Canadians visiting the Normandy beaches ought here to make a diversion along the D79 towards Bernay, to discover their own military cemetery.

Otherwise continue by way of Asnelles (where a monument commemorates the men of the Dorset and Hampshire regiments who landed

here) as far as Saint-Côme-de-Fresné, set on a promontory which dominates Arromanches. The parish church of this little town has a curiously
flat apse. Park by its orientation platform, imaginatively set out on the site
of a former German radar station, for a splendid view of the beaches – the
ones on the left overlooked by cliffs. In the sea are visible the remains of
the Allies' artificial port, created from floating ferro-concrete boxes
weighed down by submerged concrete. Code-named Mulberry, this
artificial port was towed over from Britain to make an improvised
breakwater, just as the Americans made another at Saint-Laurent-sur-
Mer in their sector of the Normandy landings.

Here a plaque lists the incredible cost in lives of these landings, noting,
for example, a cemetery containing no fewer than 21,160 dead German
soldiers, as well as 4,655 British dead at Bayeux, another 11,956 British
warriors buried at Huisnes-sur-Mer, 2,959 Canadians at Batteville-
sur-Laize, 650 Poles at Granville-Langannerie and 9,386 Americans at
Colleville-Saint-Laurent.

At Arromanches are mounted some of the anti-tank guns that killed a
few of these soldiers, and here is a museum commemorating it all. The
massive stone farmhouses between Saint-Côme-de-Fresné and Arromanches reveal what normal life must have been like before this slaughter;
beautiful black and white, brown and golden cattle graze. Some villages
entirely escaped damage, such as Longues-sur-Mer, set above sheer cliffs
where the only danger is of tumbling into the sea where the cliffs are
being steadily eroded. Yet even here arrows point the way to German
bunkers and a blockhouse.

Port-en-Bessin calls itself Normandy's premier fishing port. It marks
the start of Omaha Beach, where in 1944 the Americans desperately
fought to gain a foothold in Normandy. This proved to be the most
perilous beachhead of Operation Overlord. Its lovely sandy beach, quite
different from the rocky approach to Arromanches, is peaceful now, but
then it so bristled with defences, mines, anti-tank guns and concrete
emplacements that in the end the Americans had to take the spot from the
rear. To make matters worse, the US 5th Corps attempted to land without
the amphibious tanks or armoured support vehicles necessary to force
their way ahead of the brave young soldiers. Some attributed the error to
Omar Bradley's inexperience at leading an assault against a powerfully
defended beach. Before midnight on 6 June 1944, 1,500 of his troops lay
dead.

With a little imagination, looking over the beachhead today you can re-
live the problem. The tide was rising; the cliffs rugged; and the
Wehrmacht fought back brilliantly and sacrificially, their artillery constantly shelling the invading Americans. To find the cemetery and the
memorial to those who lost their lives under this withering fire, drive on

via Saint-Honorine-des-Pertes, with its restored thirteenth-century church, to reach Colleville-sur-Mer.

The nearby American military cemetery is superbly situated overlooking Omaha Beach. Once over 23,000 soldiers were buried in this region, but the bodies of some 14,000 of them were taken home to the USA at the request of their loved ones. Of the 9,386 war dead whose last resting place is Colleville-sur-Mer, 307 remain unidentified. Many more remain missing, buried at sea or choked under the sand, and the cemetery incorporates a lovely garden dedicated to 1,557 such men, their names, ranks, organizations and states carved here. As the inscription says, 'They sleep in unknown graves.'

The memorial to those buried here, known and unknown, and to the missing, is a colonnade whose semi-circle at each end terminates in a loggia. Donald De Lue, a New York sculptor, created the bronze statue dedicated to the spirit of American youth – for these were, for the most part, young lives – and around its base are inscribed words from the Battle Hymn of the Republic: 'Mine eyes have seen the glory of the coming of the Lord.'

Nearby is the circular memorial chapel, with France depicted over the altar offering a laurel wreath to those who died liberating her people. On the north wall of the chapel is inscribed:

> Think not upon their passing
> Remember the glory of their spirit

over which are carved the tablets of Moses and the star of David. The inscription on the altar itself reads, 'I give unto them eternal life and they shall never perish.' In the window behind glows again the star of David, a dove at its centre. An angel, a dove and a ship bound for home complete the decoration of this chapel – though peace was found only in death, for those who lie buried outside, and they did not return home.

Walk down a flight of granite steps to reach the orientation table overlooking the landing beaches themselves, and if you will, walk down from here to Omaha Beach.

From Colleville-sur-Mer the road runs on through Saint-Laurent-sur-Mer to Vierville-sur-Mer, a little town still preserving a couple of German concrete blockhouses and what was left of its artificial harbour after the storms of 19 June 1944. It also preserves a well-restored thirteenth-century church. Then the coastal route takes to the celebrated pointe-du-Hoc, which lies just north off the D514. Here under the command of Lieutenant-Colonel James E. Rudder, the American 2nd Ranger Battalion climbed the thirty-metre-high cliffs and took the fortified post which dominates Utah Beach. Their feat is commemorated by a granite pylon which rises from a concrete bunker. Remarkably, in 1979 the French government formally agreed to cede this bit of France to the United States of America.

We have so far visited no German military cemetery or memorial chapel, though no student of those days should forget how valiantly the Wehrmacht defended their occupation of Normandy, its leaders well aware that the Führer back in Berlin was insanely interfering with the judgment of those who knew that the situation was now hopeless. To find one such cemetery by way of a richly picturesque route, drive back to the D514 from the pointe-du-Hoc. Turn left, passing the church of Saint-Pierre-du-Mont, with its Romanesque nave, its thirteenth-century choir and its fifteenth-century porch. Turn right at the next village crossroads and reach the late sixteenth-century château d'Englesqueville, with its exceedingly pretty towers, and the twelfth- and thirteenth-century church at Englesqueville-la-Percée. From here take the D194 west to Criqueville-en-Bessin, where you will find a Renaissance château and a Gothic church. Then drive south-west to reach the D113, which takes you due south to la Cambe.

Just outside the village, west along the Route National 13, you reach the German cemetery to which I am taking us, its graves marked by iron crosses. In the mound at the centre rest those soldiers whose corpses were unrecognizable and unidentifiable. The entrance to this humble cemetery serves also as its chapel.

Continue now along the R N13 to Carentan by way of Isigny-sur-Mer (see the index). Soon in the distance appear a lovely church spire and tower, for Carentan boasts a splendid fifteenth-century church of Notre-Dame, a classical town hall which was once an Augustinian monastery and a fair number of fine houses built in the fifteenth and sixteenth centuries (some of them, in the place de la République, arcaded). From here the R N13 turns north towards Sainte-Mère-Église, notorious due to the film *The Longest Day*, which chronicled its capture by American airborne troops at 04.30 on 6 June 1944, two hours before Overlord was due to begin.

The town thus became the first in France to be liberated in 1944. Its citizens could hardly be expected to know what was happening, and when a preliminary incendiary bomb set a house on fire, the mayor of Sainte-Mère-Église simply called on the part-time firemen to put it out. Unaware of the consequences of their actions, some citizens incautiously opened their shutters as the American paratroops entered the towns and were shot dead by their would-be liberators. Naturally enough, there is a museum dedicated to the parachute regiments (it is said to be shaped like a parachute, but looking at it I am not so sure), and the glider preserved here seems terrifyingly fragile. The stained-glass in the parish church recalls the Normandy landings, and the hôtel John-Steele commemorates a bizarre episode of the invasion when a paratrooper of that name was perilously suspended by his parachute from the church spire until the Germans cut him down and took him prisoner.

On its way to Sainte-Mère-Église the R N13 passes through Saint-Côme-du-Mont, whose parish church with its eleventh-century doorway was sadly damaged in 1944 and has been decently restored. My own choice would be to turn north before then, along the D913 for a final look at the Normandy beaches proper, this time Utah Beach.

This road reaches Sainte-Marie-du-Mont, which the 101st American Airborne Division occupied at the very start of Overlord. Three kilometres north-east you reach la Madeleine and Utah Beach, where a red granite obelisk in a little park commemorates the American forces of the VII Corps. Although the remains of a German blockhouse survive, the Wehrmacht defences here were comparatively weak. Only 210 American soldiers died landing here (compared with nearly 4,000 at Omaha Beach, 1,500 of them, as we have noted, before the end of the first day of the invasion), and by the end of 6 June 1944 over 23,000 men, nearly 2,000 vehicles and 1,700 tons of supplies had safely reached French soil.

The liberation of France was not of course complete, and Normandy was to suffer more until that longed-for moment. In particular the battle of the Falaise gap in August 1944 was described by General Eisenhower as one of the biggest slaughterfields of any sector of war. Although by the time Falaise was taken 1,450,000 Allied soldiers had reached Normandy, the whole operation, fought in the teeth of a German ring of military steel around Caen, took seventy-seven days, while the harvest ripened and no one reaped. When the Germans finally broke out, they left behind 450,000 dead or wounded, as well as priceless stores of weapons and vehicles.

With equal stubborn bravery they defended Domfront and Mortain. The Americans took four days to capture Avranches, and contemporary photographs show the city itself grievously wounded. General Haislip's armoured divisions took Alençon on 12 August, the windows of its cathedral scarcely able to point their shattered tracery to the sky. The Americans entered a devastated Mortain on 13 August. The 30th US Infantry Division was occupying broken Domfront two days later. Then the same American divisions, reinforced by the armoured corps, set off to liberate Coutances and Saint-Lô. The 3rd US Armoured Division invested Rânes. The capture of Argentan between 20 and 21 August proved equally destructive of the patrimony of Normandy architecture.

Altogether a force of 156,000 Allied troops had been needed to set about liberating western Europe from Hitler's Germany. To liberate Saint-Lô alone cost the lives of 8,000 of them. By now Hitler's army was in disarray. When the army command in Berlin ordered Von Rundstedt to counter-attack on Bayeux, the general telephoned Keitel in Berlin to say that the plan was impossible. 'What then shall we do?' asked Keitel, at which Von Rundstedt angrily counselled surrender, exclaiming, 'Fools, make peace! What else can you do?' The fools in Berlin instantly reported the remark to Hitler, and Von Rundstedt was dismissed. (Officially he stepped down three days later on the grounds of ill-health.) The Führer was thrown into another rage when Von Rundstedt's successor, Field Marshal Hans Günther von Kluge, also reported that a German defeat was inevitable.

Serving Adolf Hitler was now an extremely hazardous occupation. Rommel in fact had turned against him, and was actively plotting the Führer's assassination. He managed to persuade the Führer to visit the front on 17 June, to be confronted by a megalomaniac who could speak only of such miracle weapons as the V1 rocket. V1s killed over 5,000 British civilians in June and July 1944, injuring another 35,000 and destroying some 30,000 buildings; but such tactics could no longer win the war. In a phrase matching Eisenhower's, Rommel bluntly told Hitler that Normandy would soon consist solely of brutal 'killing fields'. Hitler countered by insisting that the British and Americans were really planning to invade the Pas de Calais. When the Führer again refused Rommel any reinforcements in Normandy, the field marshal turned on him with the words, 'Do you believe this war can be won?' Hitler screamed back, 'Look after your own invasion front and don't bother about how we're going to continue the war.'

On 17 July a lone British fighter plane managed to knock out Rommel's staff car near the village of Saint-Montgomery-de-Foy. Rommel was invalided into hospital. Three days later a group of courageous Germans attempted to kill Hitler. The plot failed; its leaders were executed; and Rommel, implicated in the assassination plot, was forced to commit suicide.

The Allied generals could also find themselves at odds – their characters did not coinhere. The modest Eisenhower enjoyed mingling with his fellow officers and would spend hours of an evening in the warm company of his lady driver, whereas the arrogant Montgomery was a solitary, living alone in the trailer he had captured from Rommel in the desert. This trailer symbolized both Monty's genius and his faults. Monty was rightly aware that his desert victory of October 1942 had given new hope to his nation, but the knowledge fed his arrogance. Asked once who he thought were the greatest military commanders in history, he replied, 'The other two were Alexander the Great and Napoleon.' As for Field Marshal Alexander of Tunis, one of his long-suffering British colleagues in World War II, Montgomery was apt to praise him with the clipped remark, 'a first-class general – did everything I told him to'.

Montgomery's attitude to senior officers, particularly Americans, was insensitive to say the least, and the two chief Allied leaders were soon at loggerheads. Montgomery deeply resented Eisenhower's assumption of supreme command and subtly let Eisenhower know this. He continued to bear this grudge even when the war was over. On 26 August 1944 Ike signalled Monty to say that all resistance in Paris had ceased. The supreme commander offered an olive branch to his brilliant, fractious English colleague, inviting Montgomery to enter the city at his side. 'If you should like to accompany me,' Eisenhower telegraphed, 'will wait until flying conditions permit you to arrive at Bradley's headquarters. Request prompt reply to Bradley.' Monty's response was curt: 'Regret unable to go with you tomorrow. Thank you for asking me.'

He was still bitter three years after the war, when Eisenhower's lady driver, Kay Summersby – whose relationship with the supreme comman-der was indiscreet, to say the least – published her book *Eisenhower was My Boss*. In his diary Montgomery expressed his indignation that Ike had 'discussed with Kay Summersby, *his woman car driver*, his views on Generals under him and also disclosed to her the most secret matters'. He added, 'Her views on the leading war figures are enlightening, since they are obviously Eisenhower's view; the British come out badly, the Ameri-cans always win.'

Such pettiness happily did not prevent the Allies from winning the Normandy campaign. Even so, the battle did not proceed according to plan. The British forces were detailed to take Caen on the first day of Operation Overlord. Overcrowded beaches and Mongomery's habitual caution meant that the British and Canadian forces did not set off for Caen till the afternoon, only to find themselves fiercely checked by a German Panzer division. This delay was crucial, for on 7 June a second Panzer division arrived. Only after a month of savage fighting did Montgomery's forces finally reach Caen. In the meantime the Americans had taken almost three weeks to capture Cherbourg. Ironically the nickname of their commander, Major General J. Lawton Collins, was 'Lightning Joe'.

The Allies were also miffed at not being totally welcomed by the French, whose exquisite cities they were obliterating. Eisenhower's son John noted that instead of bursting with enthusiasm the French 'seemed not only indifferent but sullen'. The Americans pressed on regardless south towards Coutances and Avranches, while the British pushed towards Caumont. Bravely and fanatically the soldiers of the Third Reich fought back, defending Mortain from 7 August for a desperate five days and valiantly refusing to allow the British and Canadians to walk into Caen unimpeded. Their strength would have been better deployed further south. Eisenhower and Bradley had spotted an opportunity to encircle the enemy, and these valiant, miserable Germans retreated under the most vicious attacks, leaving their dead behind. As Eisenhower wrote after the carnage, 'It was literally possible to walk for hundreds of yards at a time, stepping on to nothing but dead and decaying flesh.'

The liberation of France thus took far longer than anyone had envisaged in planning Operation Overlord, and Normandy was to continue to suffer until that moment arrived. The tightly knit hedges of the Normandy bocage were almost as impenetrable to the Allied tanks as the Atlantic wall. No strategic planner on the Allied side had remotely considered this logistical problem. Nor, with a few exceptions, have exultant Western military historians given the Germans anything like their due praise for the way their soldiers fought back against the invaders, at a moment when – at last – the French resistance had begun to reassert itself.

For the invading Allies were not alone, even though some of their political leaders resented the way the French resistance muscled in at the victory celebrations. When the Allied forces entered Paris on the afternoon of 25 August 1944 they were accompanied by a man to be reckoned with: Charles de Gaulle. Some churlishly objected.

De Gaulle, head of the free French in exile, had cunningly persuaded General Leclerc, commander of the 2nd French Armoured Division, to march with him down the Champs-Élysées. Earlier Leclerc had achieved a masterly political stroke. Choltitz, the German general commanding Paris, had decided to disobey Hitler's instructions that the city should be defended to the last, even if this meant its total destruction. Soliciting the aid of the Swedish consul-general, Choltitz managed to secure a truce with the Parisian resistance. The truce broke down; the resistance rose up in the capital; the beleaguered Germans despairingly defended their HQ; Leclerc's division overwhelmed it; and Choltitz was taken prisoner. In consequence the German commandant of Paris surrendered not to the British or the Americans, but to Leclerc and the leader of the Parisian branch of the French resistance. In vain the US general Gerow forbade Leclerc to march his 2nd Armoured Division down the Champs-Élysées behind de Gaulle. In consequence General Charles de Gaulle, and not the Americans or the British, marched into Paris as its liberator.

These ironic political jockeyings must not obscure the real part played by the French resistance in liberating Normandy and the rest of France from the Germans, but to gauge the total extent of this resistance in World War II has proved a daunting historical task. How do you read the hearts and minds of a nation under occupation? A literary person like myself would probably begin with the regional writers, even so recognizing that writers dissimulate quite as much as anyone else.

One who was uncompromising in his opposition to Hitler was the Jewish writer André Maurois. Born in 1885 at Elbeuf in Seine-Maritime, Maurois took up Anglo-Saxon culture with gusto. His first literary success, *The Silences of Colonel Bramble*, affectionately chronicled the experiences of a phlegmatic British officer on the western front in World War I and drew on his observation of the British soldiers alongside whom Maurois had fought during that bitter war.

Maurois never wavered in his opposition to fascism, and he served on the British side in World War II. By contrast Pierre-Eugène Drieu La Rochelle, son of a Coutances lawyer, was a fascist long before Hitler came to power, inspired by reading Nietzsche's *Thus Spake Zarathustra* to espouse a false heroism. In 1932 he was in Argentina, participating in a conference on the crisis of democracy in Europe. A year later Hitler achieved power in Germany, and Drieu La Rochelle devoted himself to creating a national socialist party in France. The year 1935 found him participating in Nazi rallies at Nuremberg. An heroic combattant in World War I, a profoundly disturbed man who saw that both capitalism and communism were in deep crisis in the inter-war years, Drieu La Rochelle took up fascism as (in his own words) 'the sole way of counteracting the decadence of Europe'. For him, fascism offered the chance of 'reconciling the vigour of the people with the genius of a new elite'. All this hope, he wrote, was held together by 'the genius of Hitler and Hitlerism'.

Throughout the occupation of France this sadly misguided writer still cared for individual freedom, courageously securing the liberation of several fellow intellectuals who had been unjustly imprisoned by the Nazi régime. On 15 March 1944, surrounded by political enemies and perceiving that his fascist friends could no longer give him sustenance, he felt that he had no option but to commit suicide. He lies today a quisling in the cemetery at Neuilly.

Among those Normandy intellectuals who chose exile and resistance abroad during World War II, Max-Pol Fouchet should not be forgotten. Born in 1913 at Saint-Vaast-la-Hougue in the Cotentin, he underwent the singular experience of being baptized not in holy water – for his father was an atheist – but in apple liqueur on a ship named *La Liberté*, symbolically anchored halfway between England and France. In adult life his best friend was Albert Camus, and both worked in Algeria, Max-Pol Fouchet concentrating on socialist politics as well as poetry, the history of art and novels. In 1940 he married an exquisite woman named Jeanne Girardi, who died in a storm two years later. By now Fouchet was active in the French resistance, keeping his contacts with the resistance in North Africa and soon escaping to Britain, whence he broadcast to his beleaguered compatriots via the BBC.

For my part I would infinitely have preferred to be an intellectual opposing fascism in Bush House, the Strand, London (HQ of the BBC World Service), than to risk my life fighting it surreptitiously in occupied France. One maquisard who courageously fought on in Nazi-controlled Normandy was Robert Leblanc. By 1944 he headed a clandestine veritable army of 12,000 Normans pledged to drive the Germans from their soil. He was scarcely thirty years old and ran a *café-épicerie* in the village of Saint-Étienne-l'Allier, which lies between Pont-Audemer and Brionne. The Rouen bocage and the neighbouring forests offered cover for his allies, young men who had no intention of being transported to Germany to work for their enemies, men who were secretly encouraged by their local parish priest, the abbé Meulan.

Helped by Edmond Floquet, the muscular local butcher, Robert Leblanc began training his fellow resistance members in ambushes and stealthy assassinations. By 1943 they were receiving weapons from abroad and were infiltrating a triangle of countryside pointing west from a line joining Honfleur and Rouen. 'I wish to serve France' was Leblanc's simple explanation of what he was doing.

Christmas 1943 marked an escalation of their operations. They stole petrol from the Germans. On 22 January they rescued three French prisoners from the Nazis, aided by maquisards from Alsace who had journeyed to Normandy to offer their services where these were most valuable.

Yet the struggle was costly. One hundred and thirty of Leblanc's maquisards died fighting the Nazis, seventy-one killed in action, another fifty-nine either executed or killed in German concentration camps. The anti-terrorist inspector of police at Rouen, convinced that Robert Leblanc was leading the resistance in the Seine-Maritime, now determined to have him killed. It was too late. On 26 August 1944 Leblanc's maquisards met up with the Allied forces. Leblanc himself was put in charge of a new group of men, the 1st Normandy Infantry Battalion, and successfully led it in the subsequent invasion of Germany itself.

These are heroic tales. Their achievements were surely worthwhile, but they should not blind us to the costliness of it all. Surveying the shrubs and conifers, Japanese roses, French tamarisks, Australian pines, beds of polyantha, European ash trees, golden cypress, whitebeam, buckthorn and Russian olives that surround the American cemetery and war memorial at Colleville-sur-Mer, I once observed to M. Harlan H. Laumeier, its assistant superintendent, that the peaceful spot seemed to me much more like a lovely garden than a cemetery. He rebuked me, courteously but very sharply. It is a cemetery and a memorial, not a park, he insisted. In a park anything goes. 'People come and suppose this is just a spot in which to stroll around. They forget that no animals are allowed in here. This is not a place for bikinis and dogs, nor for chickens or cats.' So M. Laumeier regretted that the cemetery was so accessible from the bathing beach.

I take his point. Yet this is the paradox of the north Normandy coastline: though memories must be preserved, time has passed. We are still travelling through holiday country; the heroic deeds of the past fade as do the exploits of William the Conqueror himself; and tourism – bikinis and all – is part of the life-blood of this place. The dividing line between a war cemetery as memorial and as a tourist attraction is perilously thin.

None the less, even if our first decision to visit the Normandy beaches and the war cemeteries of the region is simply one of natural curiosity, we shall be less than human not to quit them chastened by the pity of war. The best we can do, no doubt, is ponder upon their noble inscriptions, such as the one at the pointe-du-Hoc which reads:

Ici
Des combattants
Demeurent.
La Bataille
Dans son chaos
les a unis
pour
l'ÉTERNITÉ

(Here lie some combatants.
In the chaos of the battle
they have been eternally united.)

Unfortunately we are unable to seek the comments of these illustrious dead on this comforting legend.

A cuisine of cream, cider and Calvados

'An imbecile cannot be a gourmand, for a gourmand is like an artist, like a poet,' asserted Guy de Maupassant. 'Taste is a delicate organ,' he continued, 'perfectible and to be respected, like the eye or the ear. If you have no taste, you lack an exquisite faculty, failing in that ability to discern the qualities of food just as some people have no ability to appreciate the qualities of a book or a work of art. It's like possessing the mouth of an animal – indeed, the soul of an animal.'

The cuisine of Normandy is never far from Maupassant's stories. In a stroke of genius he even managed to describe his chubby trollop, Boule de Suif, as if she were made out of Normandy delicacies. 'Short and round, fat as butter, her podgy fingers with their nipped in knuckles looking exactly like strings of chitterling sausages, she none the less was so fresh, with her ripe breasts swelling under her dress, that her succulence was exceedingly tempting,' he wrote. 'Her face was a red apple, or maybe a peony just about to open.' Maupassant adds that she was reputed to possess other remarkable qualities as well.

Travelling to Le Havre from Rouen in the company of a group of so-called respectable folk, Boule de Suif succeeded in forcing them to pay her some decent regard simply by bringing out a delicious Normandy picnic and offering to share it with them. Chickens in jelly, pies and fruit appeared first. Then they devoured a goose liver pâté, a slice of smoked tongue, Cressane pears, *petits fours*, Pont-l'Évêque cheese and a jar of pickled gherkins and onions.

Clearly Normandy food far exceeds simply the apples and cider

traditionally associated with the province. None the less these remain
central to its richness. The apples derive from Irish monks, for the first
apple trees to be planted here served the great abbeys which they
founded in Normandy in the sixth century. So much did their orchards
prosper in the rich Normandy soil that by the time of Charlemagne royal
regulations governed the way the trees were planted, grafted and
pressed.

Drive throughout Normandy today and you see farmers everywhere
advertising their local cider, though especially in the pays d'Auge. You
can also see for yourself the way the cider is created, if you follow the
cider-route which the canny farmers of the pays d'Auge have established
through some of their most delicious orchards. You reach it from the
RN13 which runs between Caen and Lisieux. Coming from Caen, turn
left along the D16 at Carrefour Saint-Jean. The signposted route begins a
couple of kilometres north at the junction with the D49, indicated from
now on by signs bearing the words 'Route du Cidre' and the outline of an
apple.

Through high hedgerows and luscious orchards you drive north-east to
turn right at the D85 and run down as far as Cambremer. The cider-route
turns north-east again here, wandering through exquisite little spots such
as Grandouet, Saint-Ouen-en-Pin, and then twisting its way by the
former abbey of Val-Richer and the château de la Roque-Baignard till you
reach Bonnebosq. From here it winds more or less westwards, through
Druval, Beaufour and Clermont, to turn south-east again at Beuvron-en-
Auge. After running through Victot-Pontfol it rejoins the D16 where you
started.

If that sounds a mouthful, it isn't once on the road. You can pick up a
leaflet describing the route in every tourist shop of the pays d'Auge. What
the leaflets do not prepare you for are the treats en route. Apart from the
beauty of the countryside, this little tour passes through villages that have
preserved unspoilt little architectural gems. You reach Cambremer by
way of the valley of the River Grandouet, the stream which fills the moat
of the manor of Bais, whose brick and stone entrance dates from the
sixteenth century, as does its lovely dovecote. The village itself boasts a
Romanesque church and pretty wood and brick houses. The church at
Grandouet, a village named after the stream, is by contrast Gothic, with
some good fifteenth-century windows and classical altars.

At Saint-Ouen-en-Pin you should find Guizot's grave in the cemetery
beside the church, before entering the house of God to admire its mid-
seventeenth-century furnishings and a lovely terracotta statue of St Anne
and the Virgin Mary. The paintings in this church all come from the
former abbey at Val-Richer, which has been turned into a mini-château.
Just beyond it the cider-route arrives at another château, that of la Roque-

Baignard, famed as the home of André Gide. You cannot visit this château, but you should go inside the parish church here to admire its superb eighteenth-century furnishings. At Druval, Beaufour and Clermont there are three more fine parish churches, and Beaufour also boasts an early seventeenth-century manor house.

Beuvron-en-Auge is a picture village, its ancient houses nestling around the market place and dating from the fifteenth to the eighteenth centuries. The next stop, Victot-Pontfol, is guarded by one of the loveliest châteaux in the pays d'Auge, with three centuries of building and brick, slate, stone and terracotta combining to form an entrancing ensemble.

No one need travel this route simply in order to buy cider from local farmers, for that you can do virtually everywhere in this region. The originality of this particular route is that by annual competition certain farms are awarded the designation 'Cru de Cambremer'. This is indicated by a placard, marked with those words, surrounded with a blue border and decorated with an apple on a white background. The right to display this sign lasts for one year only (unless the farmer wins the competition again). The designation means that you are welcome to visit the farm's cider cellars and marvel at its ancient presses and huge granite or wooden crushers. In season you may even watch the cider being made, a fascinating process. Apple juice is squeezed from the selected varieties. As it matures it at first turns cloudy, but then clears as the sugar is transformed into 5 per cent alcohol. The tang is always an individual one, differing between farms a mere kilometre from each other.

Taste and buy. As the promotional leaflet of the cider-route rightly insists, 'There is an individuality in these ciders which at first one just cannot place, but this is an attribute of the best of its kind. Ciders must be drunk young! Every year is the right year to drink last autumn's brew.'

When I was a schoolboy in Bolton, Lancashire, one of my English teachers not only introduced me to that celebrated line of Keats which runs, 'To bend with apples the moss'd cottage-trees' but also, after I had exulted over these succulent words, brought to my attention a comment by the redoubtable critic Dr F. R. Leavis that if one pronounced 'moss'd cottage-trees' with sufficient vigour, one's mouth seemed to be actually munching an apple. Whenever these days I drink Normandy cider – especially the sweet (*doux*) variety – I seem to retaste those musty apples weighing down the boughs of those mossed cottage-trees.

In the past the Normandy farmers would brew their own cider from apple trees under which their brindled cows daily grazed. Having bought her Normandy farm in the 1930s, Mrs Robert Henry discovered that 'The secret of having cows in a cider orchard is not to have too many. Even so, when the apples start to form, cows will stretch up their necks and tear at the branches, which is both damaging to the tree and a danger to the animals who, greedily eating too much fruit, can choke.' To prevent such disasters the farmers of those days, she recalled, used to put chains on the cows to keep their heads down, so that they could only graze and not harm the apple trees or themselves.

The variety of apple, as well as the skill of the farmer and the lie of the land, all contribute to these different flavours. The russet-coloured, slightly streaked Reinette is the apple you normally eat rather than transform into cider. Tête de brebis, Saint-Lô, Diard, Tranquil, Domain are some of the traditional varieties of apple crushed each October, their scent filling the orchards in late summer and early autumn. Speedily bottled and corked (*bouché*) after a light fermentation, they form the *cidre bouché* on offer at countless local farms. For me nothing is more delightful than to arrive at a farm selling this nectar (dry, sweet or slightly sparkling) when the farmer – or maybe his merry old goat of a father-in-law – has time to talk.

Even where you find yourself chatting to someone with a strong Normandy accent, the problem of language is far from insuperable. Normandy has a good number of its own words, not found elsewhere in France – *chasse*, meaning little road; *achocre*, meaning maladroit; *goutu*, meaning tasty; *rocailler*, meaning to fish among the rocks – but it has no *patois* as such. As for Normandy pronunciation, the regional variations are few. The Normans do make a difference between the vowels 'en' and 'an', which elsewhere in France are indistinguishable; for example, Caen is pronounced as if it rhymed with *quand*. Few of us are likely to be thrown by such minor peculiarities. The rewards of a conversation with a Normandy countryman and his family are well worth taking the risk of not understanding everything.

Received opinion is that the Normandy peasant is a taciturn man, rarely venturing an opinion unless he immediately, and brusquely, contradicts it. The stereotyped Norman, asked 'Will it rain?', answers instead of yes or no, 'perhaps', adding instantly, 'but on the other hand, some think it won't'.

Whatever the truth in this notion of *une réponse normande* (and the myth is endlessly repeated), I have found Normandy farmers filled with delicious anecdotes, ever ready to chat and tell a tale or two. Whether they are slyly poking fun at me is another matter. The subject of cheese, for instance, today always raises in my mind the question whether the peasants of Normandy are still so delightfully cunning as the ones depicted by Guy de Maupassant. On one farm in the Seine-Maritime I was talking to a farmer about goats' cheese when he told me a story which I half believe, but only half. He bought for his daughter, he said, an ancient nanny-goat as a pet. About six months later this mangy nanny-goat appeared to be pregnant, and sure enough (the farmer claimed) soon a little billy-goat was born. But, the Norman sagely continued, nanny-goats normally carry their infants for no more than two months, and this particular billy-goat had been born more than half a year after the farmer had bought his mother. How then could this wonder have occurred? 'The father must have been a wild stag who tupped the nanny one night,' this voluble farmer explained without batting an eyelid. 'There are many such *cerfs* in the woods near here, all of them fond of nanny-goats,' he added, 'and of course stags and goats are basically the same family.'

Can all this be true, or was a Normandy peasant having a joke at the expense of an English author seeking a little information about goats' cheese? I do not know. All I can do is vouch for the truth of the anecdote, give or take a word or two.

Naturally enough, the cider from these farms offers its unique piquancy to many a Normandy dish. *Sauce au cidre rouennaise* is lavishly poured over game and its strength matches the richest pheasant. To create this sauce a cup of dry cider, some chopped shallots, a fingerful of ground cloves and another fingerful of salt are mixed with cider vinegar and reduced over a hot stove. Next a couple of cups of brown stock are added, the whole reduced to half. The word *rouennaise*, meaning after the Rouen fashion, in this recipe comes, I think, from two puréed livers – duck or pheasant – which are now whisked uncooked into the mixture, along with two tablespoons of butter.

In Normandy kitchens a couple of quartered chickens are frequently simmered for half an hour or so in cider and stock, browned with rich Normandy butter, and then simmered for another half-hour with the addition of chanterelles. A final gesture in the creation of this *fricassée de poulet* is to add for the last five minutes a quarter-cup of thick Normandy cream. Often the phrase 'pays d'Auge' appears on a menu when you are offered a chicken dish, for this part of Normandy breeds the finest such fowl. *Coquelets pays d'Auge* involves cooking the chicken along with golden apples, *crème fraîche* and dry cider.

On the matter of cooking with cider, you should particularly look out in Normandy for *jambon au cidre*. Normandy ham used to be packed in sea-salt for a couple of months, before being washed clean in water, and you can still buy *petit salé de porc*, though whether this has been created by the traditional method is none too clear. For this dish three slices of ham require three cups of cider, as well as a clove. The cider is brought to the boil, the ham and clove added and the whole simmered for half an hour. Then the ham slices are taken out and fried in butter, before being served with a sauce made from the same butter into which has been stirred a little cider vinegar.

Expect, therefore, to find cider enriching countless dishes on the menus of Normandy hotels and restaurants: *dorade de beurre au cidre*, which is that most delicate of sea-bream gently cooked in cider and Normandy butter; and *andouillettes au cidre*, which some people relish though I am not one of them. Almost always, however, *au cidre* indicates gastronomic bliss. Staying near le Mont-Saint-Michel, I was once disappointed when the menu offered not *jambon au cidre* but *jambon braisé au madère* as a starter. My reaction was premature, for the dish was delicious, cooked in the thick cream sauce of Normandy enriched with sliced *champignons de Paris*.

Remember too that the phrase *au cidre* can be deadlier than it seems. Around Flers and throughout the Orne a speciality is known as *lapin au cidre*. The humble rabbit is certainly part of this dish, along with onions, garlic, *bouquet garni*, shallots, fresh Normandy cream, all the rabbit's blood and (as the menu promises) cider – in this case *cidre brut*. What one should also know is that along with half a litre or so of this cider, the chef will have added up to a quarter of a litre of Calvados.

The name Calvados derives from a Spanish galleon, invading England in 1588 and wrecked on the coast of Normandy. Dubbed 'El Calvador', the name was applied to the spot where the doomed man-of-war ran ashore and then in 1789 to this whole Normandy *département*. Already the Normans had been creating an *eau de vie* from apples, and this soon took the new name of the region.

To make the liqueur now known as Calvados the Normandy farmer, instead of bottling his cider, leaves it on its lees in the cask for up to two years before distilling it. Then the juice is drawn off and distilled once again, before being left in oaken casks with the apple cores. Calvados, unlike cider, can keep for years, the best improving with age. This heartwarming *eau de vie* thus enters the lists of wine merchants as a dated vintage. The phrase *appellation réglementée*, signifying specifically where the Calvados was made, has in consequence become important. Today there are ten regional *appellations réglementées* in Normandy, and one Calvados even qualifies for the soubriquet *appellation pays d'Auge contrôlée*, in the fashion of fine French wines. This designation means that in this one Calvados district the liqueur has been distilled not once but twice, producing a flavour as enticing as it is powerful.

Not that the Normans, though they relish their unique liqueur and create it with enormous skill, take all this wine lore too seriously. For over 400 years they have been blithely drinking a goblet of Calvados in the middle of a meal (a habit known as *le trou normand*, which they roughly translate as 'the Normandy refresher') to facilitate digestion and make a new hole in the stomach for several more rich courses. The Calvados deglazes (so to speak) the fatty elements of what has gone before and tickles the stomach for what is to come. Everyone drank a *trou normand* at Emma Bovary's wedding feast. And the prince of gastronomes,

Curnonsky, who managed till he was eighty-four to live more or less continually replete (and even then died only by falling through the window of his Paris apartment), sagely observed that although the custom of taking a glass of Calvados in the middle of a meal 'incontestably hastens the digestion of the first part, enabling one to attack the second half with greater gusto, none of this prevents one taking another snifter of the same Calvados as a digestive at the end of one's repast'.

In Normandy legend, Calvados can do more than improve the digestion. Indeed, to the Norman mind it seems a remedy for almost any ill. One of Normandy's most delightful fairy-tales is called *le chaudron de Flambourg*. The cauldron in question belongs to the mischievous fairy Malegf, who sits on the rocks, makes a hearth, sets on it an enormous cauldron, puts on top of the cauldron his alembic, or still, and blows the fire into life. Two peasants, Cadetdouble (who has a little fishing smack) and Doublecadet (who possesses one cow), watch him. Three days later Cadetdouble is amazed to see that the noxious vapours from Malegf's cauldron have turned the azure sea orange, that the *crevettes* are now multicoloured, the grass red and the milk from Doublecadet's cow blue. Everything has been poisoned.

Doublecadet and Cadetdouble work out a plan. Shyly on Sunday morning they both approach Malegf with a great platter of violet, green, orange and white *crevettes* and some azure cheese. The fairy thanks them and gobbles it all up. That night he becomes so ill as to believe he is dying. He calls to the two peasants for help. They empty his horrible cauldron, wash it out with clean water and fill it with autumn apples. From the pure apple juice they make *eau de vie* and rub it all over Malegf until he revives, crying, 'Truly, the *eau de vie* of Normandy is a marvellous remedy.' Malegf repents of the evil he has done and promises never to create the noxious vapour again. To keep him occupied the two peasants kindly give Malegf a mirror, after which he is so busy trying to trap the sun in it that he has no time to get up to any more mischief.

As well as healing sick fairies and restoring the gourmand's appetite in the middle of a hefty meal, Calvados in the 1920s and 1930s became reputed for rousing jaded Parisians from slumber and lethargy in the early morning. It reached its height of popularity in the capital as a result of World War I, for the returning combatants took it back in their hip flasks instead of water. A *café-calva*, created from thick black coffee and a generous dollop of Calvados, was guaranteed to waken the most effete of young men and women. Another use for this estimable liquor was to *flamber* a dish besides one's table. None of this makes for the snobbery so regrettably attached to other drinks.

A further indication that the Normans do not treat their Calvados with excessive solemnity is their habit of making cocktails out of it. A Calvados sour, I am told (for I prefer my liqueur neat), is a delicious blend of the chilled *eau de vie*, shaken with the juice of half a lemon, a teaspoonful of sugar and a few drops of grenadine. The cocktail dubbed 'Normandy golden dawn' is even more striking (I almost wrote 'strikingly vulgar' but for my objection to wine snobbishness): one glass of Calvados mingled with equal parts of orange juice, apricot liqueur and gin, served chilled. As for *porto flip normand*, I cannot imagine anyone guzzling hungrily at an egg yolk mixed with half a glass of port and half a glass of Calvados, the whole topped with grated nutmeg; yet many pour it down with abandon.

Some Calvados needs cherishing. In creating the liqueur the first rough alcohol, known as the head or *tête*, is discarded. So is the tail (*queue*), the final, inferior *eau de vie*. Only the *coeur* or heart is allowed to go forward as true Calvados. The cellar masters over the centuries have developed skills at blending the different *cuvées*. A great Calvados can age for up to fifty years in oak from the Limousin, slowly losing its alcohol content and gradually adding a yellower, darker hue to its original tint, and sliding down the throat with a gentler charm.

Far more acceptable to me is the use of this splendid liqueur in cooking. I adore delicate liver pâtés, and *ramequins de foie au calvados* means that chicken liver pâtés have been laced with the delicious apple liqueur. Similarly, in Normandy *pâté de foie en terrine* indicates a pork pâté enriched with Calvados and (more rarely) also with truffle juice.

Obviously Calvados will go well with the apples from which it is created. *Tarte tatin flambée au calvados* also reminds us that setting food temporarily alight with Calvados is still acceptable in Normandy. Again, tart apples are made into a pie with short flaky pastry, and then the dish is flamed with the liqueur just before serving. As for *poulet vallée d'Auge*, this is a casseroled chicken, cooked on the top of the oven with the addition of a cup of thick cream. After thirty minutes a quarter of a cup of Calvados (for a 900g (2lb) chicken) is poured over the dish and blissfully ignited.

Crêpes also benefit from being *flambées au calvados*. *Crêpes calvados* will be filled with sautéed apples and a Calvados sauce. What is not so obvious, until you have tried it, is a Calvados omelette. Technically speaking this is an *omelette soufflée*. You take four egg yolks and beat them in a bowl along with a pinch of salt and a cupful of sugar, adding a quarter of a cup of rich cream. Next beat the whites of six eggs until they are firm, before folding them into the previous mixture. The whole should be baked in a buttered dish for half an hour (or a little less) in an oven that you have preheated to 140°C (275°F). Just before you serve the *soufflée*, liberally pour Calvados over it and set it on fire.

Finally, Calvados is strong enough to take on that most recalcitrant fowl when it comes to cooking: the goose. Whereas the pays d'Auge prides itself on its chickens, Alençon boasts of its fat grey geese. The dish to look for is *oie en daube à la normande*. The bird will have been stuffed with minced pork mixed with apples and Calvados. Its offal will have been blended with carrots, shallots and onions to make a sauce. While cooking, the goose will have been kept moist by liberal doses of cider. Almost certainly it will be served with an apple purée.

The third, and least known abroad of these Normandy apple drinks, is the delicious apéritif Pommeau. Pommeau is created from the must of cider, that is to say the juice before fermentation is complete, which is added to Calvados and then matured for at least one year in barrels of oak, thus ensuring a powerful alcoholic kick that you scarcely notice as it mellowly warms your whole being. The liquid slowly becomes a seductive amber colour. It somehow retains the very smell of the apple orchards at the time of the harvest.

In Normandy they serve it cold, at 5–8°C (41–7°F), but never chilled. As well as livening up the taste buds before a meal, I have often been offered it to accompany my *tarte aux pommes* at the end of the meal. And of course the kitchens of Normandy use Pommeau in cooking. Traditional Pommeau dishes include *jambon au pommeau*, ham served up in a Pommeau sauce made from a white roux and a third of a litre of the amber apéritif. If you see on a menu *fraises au pommeau*, the strawberries will have been macerated in Pommeau and sugar for three hours or so in a refrigerator.

I am extremely fond of quails cooked with grapes. Two of them have just the right amount of rich flesh to enable me to eat a few more courses as well, without becoming bloated. In Normandy the dish is further entrancingly enriched as *cailles au pommeau*.

A visit to a Normandy distillery is one of the great treats of this region. Even if you are not on the cider-route itself, don't neglect the invitation. Just north of Lisieux along the D48, for instance, the Distillerie du Moulin de la Foulonnerie at Coquanvillers is entrancing. Its massive oak barrels and spotless alembics are open for viewing every single day of the week during the summer season till three in the afternoon, and its *cidre bouché*, Calvados and Pommeau ready for tasting. (It closes at weekends from 15 September to 30 March.) A little further north at Pont l'Évêque the cellars and barns of Père Magloire, holding 2,000 casks of maturing alcohol, are even more delightful. They belong to Debrise Dulac and Co., who have set up there a museum of Calvados and old-fashioned crafts. Here you can see, for example, an ancient mill once used for crushing the apples, as well as a former wine press that is at least 150 years old.

If you are in the area around Domfront, which is famed for its delicious pears as well as apples, you can also sample *poiré* or pear brandy. Here, in consequence, expect further gastronomic marvels, such as *gourmondaise domfrontaise*. Usually served warm or hot, this consists of fresh pears baked with pear brandy and topped with cream.

The town of Pont l'Évêque, where the distillery of Père Magloire is situated on the route de Trouville, has given its name to one of the most celebrated Normandy cheeses. *Le Pont l'Évêque* is a lovely soft cheese whose invention dates back before traceable gastronomic history. Lauded in the *Roman de la Rose*, where it is called by its earlier name of 'Angelot', this cheese originated in the valley of the Touques. Today *le Pont l'Évêque* is so renowned that it must be made under the most stringent regulations. First and foremost, all the ingredients must come from Normandy. Next, it has to contain some 45 per cent fat. Thirdly, the milk should be fresh from the cow, still warm when cheese-making starts. Finally, it has to have spent up to three weeks maturing in the traditional square moulds. In the late nineteenth century *le Pont l'Évêque* was so popular among the workers of Normandy that it was dubbed 'the working man's meat'.

The milk of Normandy is crucial to all its cheeses, and richer than any other in France. Three litres ($5\frac{1}{4}$ pts) of its curds are needed to create 600g (1lb 6oz) of *le Pont l'Évêque*. Nearly twice as many are required to make the same amount of yellow, crusty *Livarot*, the second oldest Normandy cheese and again a product of the pays d'Auge. It too takes its name from a town. Though small, Livarot on the D579 south-west of Lisieux boasts some pretty wooden manor houses and a fine Gothic parish church. Look out for a former cheese shop where from March to November (except on Mondays) you are offered a guided tour of the intricacies of cheese-making, can visit the cellars where the cheeses mature and, of course, are invited to sample and buy.

In fact *Livarot* is widely produced in southern Normandy, traditionally at Orbec-en-Auge, Vimoutiers and Saint-Pierre-de-Dives as well as at Livarot itself. It is one of the few Normandy cheeses still created throughout the autumn and winter months by many local farmers and sold by them on the local markets, as opposed to being produced in bulk in factories. Drained and salted, the cheeses mature for up to a hundred days in humid cellars, kept from touching the cold stone slabs by cane baskets. Bound with strips of reed, *Livarot* is now ready for sale, marked *appellation contrôlée* and kept succulent by its red crust.

North-east of Lisieux is a small town which since the 1950s has been responsible for the revival of a little-known Normandy cheese that had almost been forgotten. Moyaux, on the D264A, seems an unlikely spot to have pioneered such a revival, though it is an exquisite village, its Romanesque church, the lime trees around its market square and its old houses guaranteed to bring out anyone's camera. This is the centre of an industry devoted to the cheese known as *pavé d'Auge*, soft and delicious, requiring even more full-cream milk than *Livarot*.

Almost as ancient as *le Pont l'Evêque* is a cheese from the pays de Bray – *Neufchâtel*, first mentioned in history in a document of 1050 when Hugues de Gournay allowed the abbey of Ligy to tithe it. *Neufchâtel* must contain at least 45 per cent *matière grasse*. Neufchâtel-en-Bray itself, lying amid rich pastures on the left bank of the River Béthune, has long been reputed for its fine cheeses. By the tenth century its farmers were selling them under the soubriquet *les Bondons* – a name still prized here and proliferating on the Wednesday and Saturday morning market stalls. The secret of the cheeses' fragile charm is said to be that in the cellars of Neufchâtel-en-Bray they mature on strips of rye. And when Neufchâtel-en-Bray holds one of its fairs (as on the second Sunday of April and November), the farmers sell their cheese specially moulded into the shape of a heart.

The pays de Bray offers two other magical Normandy cheeses: *brillat-savarin* and *les petits-suisses*. *Brillat-savarin*, named after the great Parisian revolutionary politician and gastronome, is made in the region of Forges-les-Eaux from triple Normandy cream.

Les petits-suisses, yet more renowned, was invented at Gournay-en-Bray which, like Neufchâtel-en-Bray, is surrounded by lush pastures and lies on its own river, this one the Epte. This region probably produces more milk than any other in Normandy. In 1850 a perceptive local farmer decided to make a new kind of cheese out of unstirred *crème fraîche* added to double-cream milk. *Crème fraîche*, thick and sweet, is one of the glories of the Normandy cuisine and a natural development of its supremely rich milk. Though it is today found in every French supermarket, in 1850 the farmers all made their own, skimming the cream from the milk and leaving it in a covered pot in their cool cellars until, after a few days, it had thickened of its own accord. The cheese created from *crème fraîche* became immensely popular. Today at Gournay-en-Bray the celebrated factory of Gervais-Danone pours out the many varieties of *les petits-suisses* developed over the past century – *demi-sel*; *aromatisés*; *aux fines herbes*, and the rest. I have known people crudely add sugar to their *petits-suisses* and buttoned my lip, lest my reproof insult them.

Lastly Normandy is the home of the orange-yellow *Camembert*, a Normandy cheese scarcely older than *les petits-suisses*. Not far from Vimoutiers, in the village of Camembert situated south-west on a flank of the Viette valley, you can see a statue of a young farmer's wife, Marie Harel. Her farmhouse is still there, just above the church. Here in 1791 Marie was concealing a priest from fanatical republicans, and together they invented what is today one of the most celebrated cheeses in the world. It did not achieve this worldwide fame until the 1890s, however, when an ingenious woodworker named Georges Leroy invented the now-ubiquitous circular boxes made of laurel. Thus packed, *Camembert* was ready to conquer the world. The French frequently tell a possibly apocryphal story of the second Vatican Council. Having difficulty explaining exactly where his diocese was situated, the Bishop of Sées in desperation finally explained that it was not far from the village of Camembert; and that was sufficient for all the other assembled princes of the Church.

Unlike the other superb Normandy cheeses, *Camembert* requires no more than 2.2 litres (3¾ pints) of milk to produce 600g (1lb 6oz). Ask the locals what gives it its peculiar refinement and they will either suggest the oat baskets in which it matures or the unique microbiological conditions of their cellars. The finest *Camembert* is made in winter. Although throughout France imitations are created, the mark *appellation contrôlée* tells you that you are tasting genuine Normandy cheese.

Naturally today *Camembert* appears on virtually every French cheese board. In the Auge valley chicken breasts, awash in melted butter and stuffed with *Camembert*, are served as *suprêmes de volailles camembert*. But I like best the Normandy fashion of serving *Camembert* warm on toast, along with a green salad that has been drenched in walnut oil.

Crème fraîche, cider and cheese cannot alone constitute a regional gastronomy. Where the marquetry board that is Normandy gains is in its remarkable variety of vegetables, game and meats. Its contented pigs have for centuries provided cooking-lard as well as ham. (Though I describe them as 'contented', I must add that I was sitting with a Normandy farmer one day when a power cut nullified the strands of electrified fence that kept his pigs in order. In a trice they sped away, across fields, through the courtyard, into the woods, the little pigs squealing with joy as they anarchically escaped with their elders.) From the Danes the Normans inherited a skill at transforming some of their rich milk into a butter that is renowned throughout France. The Danes too were breeding massive cattle before the Normans began farming their territories in France.

Green beans soon arrived here, certainly by the time William the Bastard conquered England. By the seventeenth century Mme de Maintenon was reporting that after the high-born ladies of Normandy had eaten in the company of the king, they would consume a few of these green beans before retiring, in case indigestion stopped them sleeping.

When you order *soupe aux peis de mai* in Normandy you are offered an ancient, simple and extremely satisfying recipe. It requires 500g (1lb 2oz) of fresh green beans, a bunch of sorrel and chives, some chervil, a couple of potatoes, butter, salt, pepper and of course *crème fraîche*. While the potatoes are being peeled and the sorrel chopped, the green beans are blanched for five minutes in just over a litre (1¾ pints) of lightly salted water. Then the beans are drained, leaving the water for cooking the potatoes. Now the beans are chopped and buttered. Halfway through cooking the potatoes, the chef adds the sorrel, chives, pepper and the green beans. At the last moment a large lump of butter is added to the mixture and lots of thick cream poured in. The leaves of chervil are placed directly in the soup bowls, into which this *soupe aux peis de mai* is poured.

The remarkable variety of vegetables available for the Normandy chef and kitchen arrived in the province at diverse times and in diverse ways. Whereas carrots were enjoyed by the Gauls (though in those days they are said to have been white) and cabbages arrived with the Roman legions, the artichoke reached France and Normandy only in the early seventeenth century. It immediately began to flourish in the fields around Caen. Cauliflower and asparagus soon followed. For centuries the red-currant was the Norman peasant's sole fruit. His staple diet was bread, mostly stale bread, and especially made from buckwheat, which was tax-free.

Life slowly improved, with strawberries and pears appearing at his table. Today the typical large Normandy farm, alongside its fifty or more hectares of apples, will also grow five hectares of strawberries, nine of blackcurrants, one and a half of redcurrants and two of raspberries. The Norman capacity to assimilate new ideas had not disappeared. Indeed, the art of cider-making itself came from the Moors, who brought it to Spain, using not apples but dates (which the Spaniards then replaced with apples), hence the derivation of 'cider' from *sicera* or date-drink.

New utensils began to supplement the simple cooking pot, and Normandy lore began to fill up with references to food and cooking. The traditional tale of *La Fée des Lozis* describes the prince fighting his way through the forest, hacking down brambles and dragons alike, to rescue the captive princess. His helmet turns out to be a cauldron, his breastplate a huge oval dish, his knee-pads a couple of cake moulds topped by a salmon dish round each leg. When evening comes the prince takes them all off and puts them back in the kitchen cupboard.

Exulting in the produce of the rich Normandy soil, Guy de Maupassant re-created the legend of le Mont-Saint-Michel, endowing St Michael with all the cunning of a Normandy peasant who relishes the generosity of the soil. In Maupassant's story, St Michael and the devil are neighbours, but after several centuries the saint grows weary of Satan's tiresome company and builds himself a magnificent, isolated dwelling on the mount. To keep the devil away he surrounds the place with treacherous quicksands.

Unfortunately for St Michael, though Satan lived in a humble cottage, he ruled over all the pastures, the fertile valleys and prosperous hillsides round about le Mont-Saint-Michel. After fasting for a few years, St Michael decided he ought to come to terms with his rich neighbour. After six months' thought he called on the devil, who was having lunch by his cottage door. Satan immediately ran forward, kissed the saint's robe and offered him a bowl of soup. Then said St Michael, 'I've come with a proposal. This is it. Give me all your lands.'

Before the flustered devil could speak, St Michael continued, 'Listen. I'll do all the work. I'll plough, plant and fertilize, and then we shall share the crops equally between us.' The devil, a naturally lazy creature, pricked up his ears. He promised to agree if St Michael would also give him some of the delicious red mullet caught around the mount. So they shook hands and spat to one side to demonstrate that they had made a bargain.

St Michael asked one other question: when it came to dividing the harvest, did Satan want that part growing above ground or the food that grew underground? 'I'll take everything above ground,' Satan cried. Six months later he looked out over all that St Michael had grown. All he could see were carrots, onions, turnips, salsify, everything that grew a juicy savoury root below ground and above it leaves fit only for cattle. In a rage Satan told St Michael that he wanted to renege on the bargain. Everywhere he went he called St Michael a swindler.

The saint decided to visit Satan again to apologize. 'It wasn't my fault,' he explained. 'Let's be friends again. To make things up between us, next year why don't you take everything below ground and I'll have what grows above?' 'Done!' agreed Satan. The next year this saint's lands were covered with oats, linseed, maize, red clover, peas, cabbage, artichokes and everything else that blossoms above ground. Satan was deeply hurt. He took back all his lands and resolved never to talk to St Michael again.

For a full year St Michael sat on his lonely mountain-top, watching the devil planting and reaping. The saint grew increasingly angry that he could no longer trick Satan and decided to pay him a vicious lesson. Satan was invited to dinner at le Mont-Saint-Michel the following Monday. Being even greedier than he was lazy, the devil instantly accepted, put on his best clothes and set off to eat with his enemy.

The meal was magnificent. First chicken livers, kidneys and meatballs, then a couple of red mullet cooked in *crème fraîche*; next a turkey stuffed with wine-soaked chestnuts; then tender, salted marsh lamb served with the most succulent vegetables; and finally delicious warm biscuits oozing butter. After each course they made room for more food with a glass or two of Calvados, and St Michael also plied the devil with sparkling dry cider and powerful red wine. Satan ate and drank so much that suddenly his bowels opened.

St Michael rose in mock-anger. 'How dare you soil my home?' he thundered. Seizing a stick, he began to pursue the terrified devil through the halls, around the pillars, up staircases, from gargoyle to gargoyle until they reached the topmost terrace and the miserably sick guest had nowhere else to run. The saint came running up behind him and administered such a tremendous kick that Satan shot through the air like a javelin and crashed down just outside the town of Mortain.

Sadly the devil rose to his feet, limping and permanently crippled, and looking back at the deadly abbey as it stood out in the far distance against the setting sun, he realized that he would always be overcome in this unequal battle against St Michael. He limped away, making for distant lands, leaving to his arch-enemy all his fields, his hills, his valleys and his pastures.

That, concludes Guy de Maupassant, is how the cunning, tricky, deceitful and underhand peasant of lower Normandy tells the tale of how St Michael, patron saint of Normandy, vanquished the devil. Maupassant adds, 'Another people would no doubt have dreamed up an entirely different account of the battle.'

No doubt the devil and St Michael relished Normandy vegetable soup. To assume that soup is more or less the same throughout France would be to underestimate both the quiddities of regional cuisine and, in particular, the juiciness of the produce of Normandy. A further essential ingredient of soup in this province is *graisse normande*, a hearty mixture of beef and pork fat, clarified with a small amount of *bouquet garni* and seasoned with salt and pepper.

Leaving aside the *graisse normande* for a moment, Normandy vegetable soup might begin with three peeled and chopped potatoes, and three or four washed and sliced carrots, thrown into two litres (3½ pints) of water and left to cook for half an hour. During this time the cook would be peeling off the outer leaves of a cabbage, cutting what is left into eight or so pieces and blanching them for twelve minutes in salted boiling water. The blanched cabbage is then thrown into the cooking pot, along with a generous handful of green beans, a couple of sticks of celery, some parsley and a large spoonful of *graisse normande*. This is now cooked on a low flame for an hour and then served, sometimes incorporating slices of bread.

No one would add any more salt or pepper – the *graisse normande* has contributed enough. Nor, at another season of the year, would anyone expect to find exactly the same vegetables in the soup, for potatoes might readily be replaced by kidney beans, and the carrots by runner beans. Only the *graisse normande* would invariably undergird the whole Normandy dish.

Blessed with such an abundance of materials, the cuisine of the province developed a new richness. Alongside its countless apple dishes, *rissoles de poires* became a Normandy delicacy, the pears steeped in the Benedictine so happily re-created in the province. The traditional apple tart triumphantly held its own, but other apple dishes became richer. The overpowering *omelette vallée d'Auge* was, and still is, created from eggs, apples, butter, sugar, Calvados and *crème fraîche*. Combinations of potatoes and pear were tried out and found successful, as in the extremely filling *pommes de terre aux poireaux en blanquette*. Today roast duck is generally served here with a Calvados-enriched apple-jelly sauce. Partridge and apples often appear on Normandy tables wrapped in puff pastry. And you can even start a meal with *la pommeraie glacée*, cold apple soup.

Sampling the gastronomy of a region, I find it fascinating to explore what people ate here in the past. When King François I came to Normandy in 1520 to look at his new port at Le Havre, his chefs were able to buy partridges and ducks, chickens, capons and rabbits. They purchased a couple of sheep and four mutton chops, as well as a goodly number of tarts. Their accounts show that they spurned the cider of Normandy and drank wine from the Loire valley instead.

A hundred and fifty years later Louis XIV arrived in the province with a great train of courtiers and some of his favourite women. Again the local drink was scorned, but the list of game, meats and vegetables was yet more impressive than that ordered for his royal predecessor. Pears, peaches, nuts and grapes, cauliflowers and melons as well as *petits pois* now graced the king's table. The main difference was fish. François I's list contained none. Louis XIV bought smelts and turbot, flounder and sole. He also ate oysters.

Today seafood dishes abound in Normandy. From Fécamp, Dieppe, Cherbourg, Honfleur and Le Havre the fishing smacks set sail, returning with mackerel, cod, sole, lobsters, shrimps and the rest. Fertile beds of mussels, oysters and scallops are found at Villerville, at Isigny-sur-Mer and at Dives. Eat oysters near le Mont-Saint-Michel and you can still taste the salt of the sea. Courseulles-sur-Mer is famed for them, just as Saint-Vaast-la-Hougue justly boasts of its clams.

My favourite way of eating mussels is in the rich soups of the Languedoc, dishes not available in Normandy. My second favourite is found on many a Normandy menu, served in short-crust pastry. Perhaps this preference is partly because in both dishes someone has already done the messy job of taking the mussels out of their shells and removing their beards. In the Languedoc there is also the bonus of garlic, and in Normandy the added zest of double cream and black pepper. Normandy chefs seem to revel in the device of wrapping fish in pastry, and I delight in eating the result, especially when liquid apples have enriched the dish. *Chausson aux crevettes*, for instance, is a shrimp-filled puff pastry with a cream sauce, drenched in Calvados. Eel stew in Normandy (*matelote d'anguilles*) will bear the unmistakable hint of cider. A *marmite dieppoise* will include halibut, sole, haddock, monkfish, shrimps, mussels and *crème fraîche*.

In Normandy *demoiselles à la crème* are small lobsters in a rich cream sauce. Since it will by now be clear that Normandy chefs long ago learned to add an unusual tang to their fish dishes, no one will be surprised to come across, say, a consommé of langoustine enlivened with a hint of ginger. If such tricks are not authentically Norman, the langoustine certainly will be. And in the pays de Caux, a favourite dish of pike-dumplings (*quenelles de brochet du pays de Caux*) is by contrast quintessentially Norman, as the half-litre (18 fl oz) of *crème fraîche* included in the recipe makes abundantly clear. These *quenelles* are also served with *sauce normande*, made out of butter, stock, shallots, mushrooms, cider and yet more *crème fraîche*.

I always try to eat fish when I am staying in or near Avranches, for there my *matelote*, my brill or my salmon chauvinistically reminds the Englishman in me of a note made by Stendhal on his visit to Normandy in the late 1830s. 'Whilst I was taking lunch in my inn at Avranches,' he wrote, 'I learned that this region is haunted by a crowd of Englishmen who must ever be on the move since they have the misfortune of being outrageously expert at fishing with hook and line. They use artificial flies that far too brilliantly deceive the idiot fish, whether salmon or trout.' Stendhal found the local Normans overwhelmed with jealousy at the Englishmen's good fortune. 'They have completely severed social relationships with these English fishermen,' he reported, 'and I understand are even brooding about hauling them before the law.'

On another literary note, Flaubert in *Madame Bovary* enthuses over a restaurant with 'a little fountain gurgling in a marble basin in which, among watercress and asparagus, three lobsters were sluggishly stretching out towards a pile of quail lying on their sides'.

In this great novel seafood plays a part singularly unnoticed by many critics, and especially as an accompaniment to love-making, which is only right. At one delicious moment Emma Bovary and her lover Rodolphe sit at a table in a low-ceilinged restaurant with black fishnets hanging outside. There are many such today. Should one imitate the two entranced and doomed lovers?

They ate fried smelt [a sort of small, sparkling salmon], and then cherries in cream. Then they lay down on the grass in a secluded spot and kissed underneath the poplars. Could they have lived for ever, they asked, like a couple of Robinson Crusoes in that little glade which in their ecstasy seemed to them the most magnificent in the whole world? Many times before they had seen trees, blue skies and grass and heard flowing water with a breeze rustling the leaves; but never before had they admired it all. It was as if nature had not existed till that moment and had begun to be beautiful only after they had gratified their desires.

Well, I do not claim always to have enjoyed a Norman meal to quite such an intensity; but to eat *sole normande* at any time gratifies most of my desires. Oddly enough, it was not invented by a Norman. The chef who devised it, Antonin Carème, was born in Paris in 1784 and died there forty-nine years later as one of the most creative restaurateurs of all time, having produced several masterpieces of culinary writing (*Le Maître d'hôtel français, Le Cuisinier parisien, L'Art de la cuisine au dix-neuvième siècle, Le Pâtissier royal parisien* and *Le Pâtissier pittoresque*). This genius devised the method of poaching sole in a fish stock, covering it with alternate layers of oysters and Paris mushrooms, pouring over it a mushroom and mussel sauce and garnishing the whole dish with puff pastry. Then he paid Normandy the compliment of naming his magnificent creation *sole normande*.

In Normandy the recipe would certainly be enriched with *crème fraîche* and cider. As an alternative which genuinely derives from this province, try *sole dieppoise*, where the fish will again have been poached in a fish stock (with the addition today of white wine) but will be surrounded by prawns and accompanied by a fish and prawn sauce. Often too in Normandy I have eaten fish enriched with Calvados. Trout, offered as *la truite farcie sauce normande*, will have been stuffed, probably with whiting mixed with mushrooms and Normandy cream, and then served with a sauce made from double cream, the yolk of an egg, some lemon juice and Calvados.

A great chef's influence spreads like the ripples on a lake, and Antonin Carème's creation has subsequently influenced a great many fish dishes. At the hôtel de la Poste, Falaise, for instance, while my wife ate a *dorade*, I was served not *sole normande* but hake cooked in the same fashion. I also took a fish dish as an hors-d'oeuvre, a delicate terrine of salmon, one half of it white, the other pink, while my wife tucked into *huîtres de la Manche*.

Raymond Queneau's novel *Pierrot mon ami* has a magical passage revealing this ripe Norman taste for food. 'They all sit down in the dining room around a lobster mayonnaise, commenting about it for a short while before tucking in. Then the lamb chop arrives, inside which are discernible cloves of garlic so big they might well be cooked maggots.'

The variety of Normandy cuisine still amazes me, not least because it none the less remains recognizably Norman. Although it is quite hard to stop a French restaurateur whisking away the menu once you have chosen your first two courses, I once managed to copy down some of the dishes on offer for lunch at a far from pretentious hotel in Rouen. These included a terrine of two sorts of fish *à la crème d'estragon*, a salad of *haricots verts*, carrots, tuna fish and crab; a selection of cold pork and ham (*assiette de cochonnailles*); the inevitable warm chitterling sausages; turkey in a cream sauce (*blanc de dinde à la normande*); a fillet of bream served on a fondue of pears; poached skate with capers; smoked salmon served with whipped cream. I hadn't finished writing down the puddings when my first course appeared, though the list included an apple sorbet *au calvados*.

For my second course I had chosen the *blanc de dinde à la normande*, which turned out to be flanked by apples and pears and soaked in a splendid sauce of *champignons de Paris* and Normandy cream. My pudding was *délice aux pommes*, a warm apple and Calvados concoction, served with vanilla ice cream.

At Rouen I suppose I ought to have chosen one of the two dishes acknowledged as the greatest achievements of Normandy cuisine, noblemen among food besides which the rest are mere courtiers – though glittering courtiers. *Caneton à la rouennaise* (or, as it sometimes appears on menus, *caneton à l'ancienne*) is made from a duck that has been strangled instead of having its throat cut – the manner of death preserving as much of its blood as possible. The carcase should have been pressed and its blood and other juices added to a sauce made from the duck's liver and finely chopped shallots, mixed in butter and cider. Regrettably more pretentious restaurants in Normandy have started replacing the cider with cognac and champagne. Happily I cannot afford to eat in these places.

The particular duckling you are about to eat is unique to this region (though the breed spills over into Brittany). Most of them come from the outskirts of Yvetot, with another centre for raising them in nearby Duclair. The variety arises (so they say in Normandy) from the unusual warmth of this part of the province, which brings domestic ducks on heat at the precise moment that wild ones are about to migrate. In consequence the two mate, creating the *caneton normand*, a uniquely succulent blend of the qualities given to this duck by both domesticity and freedom.

Its wings are often rolled in breadcrumbs and then grilled, while the breasts will have been thinly sliced and cooked on a spit for about twenty minutes before being flambéed. Alternatively (and better in my view) the *caneton* is cooked for an hour and a quarter or so in an oven that has been preheated to 230°C (450°F). In such cases the chef or farmer's wife will have pricked its skin to provide the maximum amount of fat while the bird is cooking and will have seasoned it with salt, pepper and Calvados.

The other classic Normandy dish I shall never eat, since I abhor tripe. But if you can stomach eating stomach, order *tripes à la mode de Caen*. It is said to have sustained the Vikings themselves. In Caen an annual tripe competition awards the so-called Tripière d'Or (shaped like an earthenware pot) to the finest tripe dish of the year. *Tripes à la mode de Caen* need up to twelve hours' cooking and have to rest in the middle of this, so that altogether two days' preparation is required. Leeks, carrots, sliced onions, cider and Calvados are all part of the recipe. I have no idea what the final product tastes like. I only know that many restaurants recommend a glass or two of Calvados in the middle of the meal, so as to get it all down.

Rouen, and the very best of the rest

In the village of Canteleu, perched on the summit of a hill north of Rouen, you can still find the powerful *belle vue* from which Guy de Maupassant described the city: 'one of the most magnificent skylines of the world', as he put it, 'a city of churches, of Gothic bell towers sculpted like ivory curios'. Maupassant gazed enraptured at the new *flèche* of the cathedral which he considered the most superb of human creations, and the thousand smoking chimneys of the manufacturing districts. Before him he saw 'the winding, undulating Seine, sown with little islands, bordered on the right with white cliffs crowned with a forest and on the left with immense fields stretching in the distance to further forests'. As in his day, the great river remains a working artery, with ships and barges at anchor and others tailing each other ('*à la queue leu leu*' as Maupassant comically put it) as they sail downstream from Rouen to Le Havre.

Canteleu, possessing its own pretty Renaissance and classical château guarded by a statue of Henri IV, stands on the chalky cliff road (la Corniche, as the French call it), high above the River Seine, offering panorama after panorama of the river and Rouen, rendered yet more picturesque by the mid-nineteenth-century Gothic basilica of Bonsecours. Canteleu also boasts a celebrated cemetery bell which is rung whenever the people of the Roumois feel the need for a celebration.

The Celts were probably the first to settle around Rouen. Then the Romans Christianized the region. St Vitricius, who was elected Bishop of Rouen around 380 while still a layman, had enlisted as a Roman soldier at the age of seventeen, but on his conversion to Christianity renounced violence. In consequence he was flogged and then sentenced to death. Freed by some obscure miracle, he devoted himself to learning, befriending such contemporary luminaries as St Martin of Tours and St Paulinus of Nola. A tireless preacher to the heathen, he brought a new discipline to his fellow clergy and much improved their own learning.

His successor St Mellon built Rouen's first cathedral in the early fourth century. The Normans destroyed the old one in their pagan days and in the twelfth century, having become Christians, built another. Soon most of it had perished by fire, but the tour Saint-Romain on the north side dates from this twelfth-century building, embellished by the addition of an upper storey in the fifteenth century. Basically, however, Rouen cathedral is a Gothic masterpiece.

John Ruskin was entranced by Rouen cathedral and said so in *The Seven Lamps of Architecture*. Judging that in general 'the most delicate niche work and best mouldings of the French Gothic are in gates and low windows well within sight', he added that since the very spirit of that style was exuberance, 'there is occasionally a burst upwards and blossoming unrestrainedly to the sky, as in the pediment of the west front of Rouen, and in the recess of the rose window behind it'. The elaborate flower-mouldings, all but invisible from below, enraptured him by the way in which they added 'a general enrichment to the deep shadows that relieve the shafts of the advanced pediment'; while in the earlier and grander north and south gates, he relished 'a very noble proportioning of the work to the distance, the niches and statues which crown the northern one, at a height of about one hundred feet from the ground, being alike colossal and simple; visibly so from below, so as to induce no deception, and yet honestly and well finished above'. In short, Ruskin wrote, the decorations of Rouen cathedral were both 'full of expression, and as delicately wrought as any work of the period'.

The south tower of Notre-Dame cathedral at Rouen, dubbed the 'butter tower' – since it was built with conscience money paid by Christians who needed a dispensation to indulge themselves with butter during Lent – is complex and thrilling, and a lacy network of pinnacles and gables joins it with the north tower. The fifteenth-century lantern is topped by a nineteenth-century cast-iron spire, the tallest in France. (It replaced the lovely wooden spire which you can see in the paintings of Turner and Cotman and which was struck by lightning in 1822.) Fifty-six bells hang here. Over the entrances on either side are stunning thirteenth- and fourteenth-century carvings. Those of the north porch rise to a magnificent rose window.

Two of the porches of the west façade were carved in the thirteenth century, and in spite of damage you can still make out scenes from the lives of St John and St Stephen, John the Baptist's tussle with Herod and the Christ in majesty. The superb Gothic stonework of the cathedral front is mostly the work of Roland le Roux, sculpted in the early sixteenth century, though the tree of Jesse in the tympanum was carved by Pierre des Aubeaux.

The early fourteenth-century nave has eleven soaring bays, each four storeys in height. To stand amid the piers of the lantern is thrilling. Look left to exult in the fourteenth-century stained-glass in the north rose, well restored and luscious. The thirteenth-century chancel is impressive both by its apparent simplicity and by the majestic upward sweep of its lines.

The fourteenth-century Lady Chapel, a masterpiece in its own right, also houses two splendid tombs. One is Gothic, sculpted in the fifteenth century for Diane de Poitiers's husband Louis de Brézé (by whose head Diane weeps). The other is early sixteenth-century Renaissance, the last resting place of two cardinal-archbishops, Georges d'Amboise, minister to Louis XII, and his nephew.

Rouen cathedral in fact shelters the last remains of a remarkable number of men and women illustrious in the history of Normandy, including (in the chapels of the ambulatory) Duke Rollo, Richard Coeur de Lion, Henry the Young King and William Longue-Épée. The crypt, which remains virtually as it stood in the eleventh century (even retaining its well), contains the heart of Charles V.

No one could miss the medieval stained-glass of the ambulatory and Lady Chapel, most of it dating from the thirteenth century. Graceful, freely drawn figures are a feature of Normandy glass at this time (as you can see also at Fécamp abbey and in Évreux cathedral). Rouen even offers one of the rare names of a thirteenth-century glassmaker, for around 1235 a man named Clement who came from Chartres signed one of the ambulatory windows *Clemens vitrearius carnotensis*.

Some of the lovely windows of Rouen cathedral have evidently been moved around from time to time. In the third and fourth chapels on the north side of the nave, incorporated in a series of composite windows dubbed *Belles Verrières* in the fifteenth century, is an earlier portrait of St John the Baptist. Scholars conjecture that it must have come from one of the bays removed in the early years of the fourteenth century to create the side chapels.

I am pleased to learn that the fourteenth-century clergy of Rouen cathedral were not so obsessed with being up-to-date as to jettison anything created a century before. Yet for my part I like simply to enjoy the lusciousness of it all, without wanting to untangle history too much or poke my nose into handbooks on stained-glass making. Let me add just one further detailed point, borrowing the words of Catherine Brisac of the French historical monuments commission, who insists that to appreciate fully the high standards of stained-glass making in the fourteenth century you must visit Normandy, and particularly Rouen and Évreux:

The series of legendary archbishops in the chapel of the Virgin at Rouen cathedral, which dates from the beginning of the century, reveals those tendencies peculiar to the fourteenth century and the transformations that had been accomplished. The sixteen figures are sheltered beneath tall niches enriched with naturalistic decoration and stand out against damascened backgrounds. The draughtsman-ship and elegant modelling of the faces contrast with the heaviness of the drapery, which reflects the actual material of the costumes. The overall effect is much lighter, not only as a consequence of the repeated use of white glass, but also through the extensive use of very pale or lightly coloured glass. Such innovations were made possible by a high degree of painting skill; the outline is reduced to a thin and sinuous line emphasized by a wash which was applied with a brush and then enlivened by details worked with a stylus. The decorative elements were equally innovative, using motifs copied from nature, in which flowers inter-mingle with parrots and angelic musicians.

This magical cathedral of Notre-Dame, which Monet painted twenty times in one year, is matched in airiness by the splendid thirteenth-century church of Saint-Ouen, built over two centuries after 1315, and by the flamboyant architecture of the church of Saint-Maclou, brilliantly and almost completely restored since its damage during the war. Whereas Ruskin had found the architecture of Rouen cathedral 'honest', entirely without what he called architectural deception, he considered the pierced buttress and the pinnacles of the lantern at Saint-Ouen a flagrant 'barbar-ism', since they clearly had no architectural function at all. Having an ogee curve, the buttress, he wrote, 'looks about as much calculated to bear a thrust as the switch of a willow; and the pinnacles, huge and richly decorated, have evidently no work to do whatsoever, but stand round the central tower, like four idle servants, as they are – heraldic supporters, that central tower being merely a hollow crown, which needs no more buttressing than a basket does'.

'In fact, I do not know any thing more strange or unwise than the praise lavished on this lantern,' Ruskin continued; 'it is one of the basest pieces of Gothic in Europe; its flamboyant traceries being of the last and most degraded forms; and its entire plan and decoration resembling, and deserving little more credit than, burnt sugar ornaments of elaborate confectionery.' Ruskin was wrong. The central tower is a masterpiece of equilibrium, vividly contrasting with the stern west towers and a tiny remnant of another tower built in the eleventh century. The elegant belfry manages to support a ring including a bell weighing four tonnes.

As for its stained-glass, to quote Catherine Brisac again, 'The windows in this ancient abbey church, rebuilt between 1318 and 1339, represent the most outstanding series of French stained-glass windows from the first half of the fourteenth century. Endowed with exceptional stylistic unity, they are the product of a single workshop and reflect formulas which, although perhaps introduced from Paris, were interpreted by local artists.' At this precise moment the Normandy school of stained-glass making had reached its apogee and over six centuries later at Saint-Ouen, it can still make us gasp at its achievements.

In the Middle Ages the waxmakers held a market by the south side of the cathedral, and their memory is preserved in the name of the south porch, the porte des Cieres. The south façade is graced by a magnificent rose window set in a flamboyant gable sculpted with Old Testament kings and queens. Walk round the apse to see its superb flying buttresses and its deliciously placed chapels, graceful and seemingly protected by the might of the square central tower. Inside Saint-Ouen all is airy and perfectly balanced, even a massive nineteenth-century organ failing to intrude on the rest but taking its due humble place.

As for the partly Gothic, mostly flamboyant Saint-Maclou, built in the fifteenth and early sixteenth centuries, two doorways of its splendid west façade are triumphs of Renaissance carving, matched inside by the Renaissance organ case, dating from 1521, and a spiral staircase carved a few years earlier. Fifteenth-century stained-glass windows, rococo confessionals and exquisite chapels enrich this gem.

Nearby (entered at no. 184, rue Martainville) is its so-called cloister, now the headquarters of the Beaux-Arts in Rouen. In spite of its name, this was never really a cloister. The carved skulls, crossbones and the dance of death in its sixteenth-century courtyard give a clue to the fact that here were buried those who died of the plague, and the so-called attic on the first storey remained a charnel house for several centuries afterwards.

The rue du Gros-Horloge, flanked by half-timbered houses, leads from Rouen cathedral under an archway carrying the city's famous Renaissance clock, with its fourteenth-century bell tower and medieval bells, to the place du Vieux-Marché. Here in May 1431 Joan of Arc, after her imprisonment in the castle of Rouen (which is survived today only by its keep), was burned to death, and her ashes thrown into the Seine.

Joan, supporting the dauphin Charles VII against the English, had led a force which routed the army of Sir John Fastolf. She was captured by her enemies in May 1430. On 14 July Pierre Cauchon, then Bishop of Beauvais and an ally of the English, in his own name and that of the King of England, demanded that the maid be handed over in return for 10,000 francs. On 21 November the deal was done. In January the following year she became his prisoner at Rouen.

For two months Joan was daily interrogated, refused permission to hear Mass and frequently chained in her cell. Guards watched her day and night, since she refused not to try to escape. The judges at her trial

were Cauchon and the vice-inquisitor of Paris, the charges being in
essence that she insisted on giving more importance to what she supposed were God's personal words to her than to the commands of the
Church. She was found guilty.

On 24 May in the cemetery of the church of Saint-Ouen Joan was forced
to listen to a long sermon attacking her sovereign Charles VII. Faced with
death, she faltered and signed an abjuration of all she had stood for. She
was taken back to prison and forbidden to wear male attire. Two days
later her resolve had returned. Her captors found her once again dressed
as a man, and she declared to them that both St Catherine and St Margaret
had upbraided her for the 'treason' of her abjuration.

Her martyrdom was now certain. 'Be of good cheer! Now we have her,'
Cauchon is said to have exulted to the Earl of Warwick. On 29 May the
two judges and thirty-nine assessors unanimously recommended that
the maid be handed over for execution by the secular authorities.
Cauchon, in an unusual act of clemency, now allowed her to make her
final confession and to receive Holy Communion. The following day she
was led to the place du Vieux-Marché. She asked a Dominican monk who
was comforting her to shout out his assurances of salvation, so that she
could hear them over the roar of the flames, and to hold a crucifix high
enough for her to see it to the end.

Joan was not twenty years of age. She died holding on to her vision and
her Christian faith. When the flames extinguished themselves the execu-
tioner found her heart intact among the ashes, as he prepared to throw
what remained of her into the Seine.

Nearly twenty years later Charles VII entered Rouen. One of his first
acts was to order a new inquiry into the guilt or innocence of the maid of
Orléans. Cardinal Guillaume d'Estouteville who carried it out found her
innocent. In 1456 Pope Calixtus III annulled the proceedings and the
sentence. On 16 May 1920 Pope Benedict XV declared Joan of Arc a saint.

Today the place du Vieux-Marché is ultra-modern, designed by Louis
Arretche (who created here the 20-metre-high cross as a national monument of reparation to the maid of Orléans), as is its church, dedicated to St
Joan of Arc herself. It houses some sixteenth-century stained-glass
windows which once graced a church demolished by the bombardment
of 1944.

In spite of its modern design, the place du Vieux-Marché, like many
other squares and streets in the old parts of the city, incorporates some
lovely timber-framed houses, its peacefulness belying this savage episode in Normandy history. In the face of the dreadful damage of 1944,
Rouen deserves enormous praise for setting about restoring the exquisite
houses in the old city on the right bank of the river, houses dating from
the fifteenth to the eighteenth centuries and often opulently carved.

Apart from nearly 800 of these restored half-timbered houses, Rouen's secular buildings include the Renaissance Palais de Justice or law courts, once the seat of Normandy's parliament, built in the first quarter of the sixteenth century and embellished with delicate carving. The balustraded, turreted façade was finished in 1526. And recent excavations have unexpectedly revealed that the courtyard was once the site of a Jewish synagogue. The former archbishop's palace near the cathedral was built in the fifteenth century and by quaint contrast with these law courts seems stern and hostile. You enter through an eighteenth-century arch in the rue des Bonnetiers.

The old city is also proud of its medieval bell tower. You can climb it between 10.00 and noon and 14.00 and 18.00 (except Tuesdays and Wednesday mornings, and only between Palm Sunday and the first Sunday in October). A fifteenth-century spiral staircase winds up by way of rooms containing bells and the mechanisms of ancient clocks, until you reach the top with its splendid view of the whole city.

Two other fine churches add their architectural spice to Rouen: the Gothic Saint-Patrice, with another set of splendid stained-glass windows, these ones fired between 1538 and 1625; and Saint-Romain, built in the seventeenth century for the Carmelites and itself containing Renaissance stained-glass.

Seek out too the hôtel de Bourgtheoulde at no. 15, place de-la-Pucelle, built by Guillaume de Roux just as Renaissance architecture was overcoming the Gothic in Normandy. It is a fascinating mixture of gables and arches, friezes and galleries, the round arch of its doorway deliciously crocketed and surmounted by a couple of merry lions holding a coat of arms.

As France's second capital city, Rouen happily bursts with art galleries and exhibitions. The musée des Beaux Arts in the place Verdrel, as well as holding a major international collection of paintings, also displays masterpieces of the celebrated Rouen pottery. Naturally the great Normandy artists such as Poussin, Géricault, the Barbizon school and the impressionists are splendidly represented (see these names in the index to this book). The museum closes on Tuesdays and Wednesday mornings, otherwise opening from 10.00 to noon and 14.00 to 18.00. It incorporates the nearby former church of Saint-Laurent, an excellent flamboyant building oddly filled today with beautiful pieces of wrought-iron, bronze and steel. This unique collection (known as the musée Le Secq des Tournelles) comprises 15,000 works in all and opens from 10.00 to 12.00 and 14.00 to 18.00, except on Tuesdays, Wednesdays and public holidays. Another fascinating museum, with the same opening hours, was set up in 1984 in the late seventeenth-century hôtel d'Hocqueville and is devoted to ceramics.

Naturally Joan of Arc has her museum in the place du Vieux-Marché, tricked out with waxworks. The museum of antiquities is housed in a seventeenth-century convent at no. 198, rue Beauvoisine. Rouen's famous literary son Pierre Corneille is remembered not only by a museum in the house where he was born (between rue de Fontenelle and the place du Vieux-Marché at no. 4, rue de la Pie) but also in the Pierre-Corneille house which his father bought and left to his son in 1639. This house stands eight kilometres from Rouen (by the N138) at Petit-Couronne. (There are guided tours between 10.00 and 12.00 and 14.00 and 17.00, though the house closes on Thursdays.)

As for Rouen's greatest novelist, the Gustave Flaubert museum is in the eighteenth-century hôtel-Dieu at no. 52, rue Lecat. Since Flaubert's father was a surgeon, the house is filled not just with memorials of the novelist but also with the tools of a nineteenth-century surgeon's trade. It opens between 09.00 and 12.00 and 14.00 and 18.00, except on Sundays and Mondays, also closing on public holidays.

Finally, the decorated former offices of finance, built in the cathedral square in 1500, houses Rouen's tourist office. The city market is held all day on Mondays, Tuesdays, Fridays and Saturdays, and an annual fowl and horse fair takes place on 23 October.

L'Aigle

L'Aigle boasts one of Normandy's quainter yet entrancing churches, dedicated to St-Martin, its two towers quite disparate – one twelfth-century, with a later spire and carrying the church bells, the other magnificent and flamboyant, built at the beginning of the sixteenth century. The gargoyles are a great treat. The statues in the niches of the Renaissance side-aisle are modern and pleasant. Don't miss the quite superb Renaissance aisle inside and a couple of sixteenth-century stained-glass windows which far outmatch the other modern ones. The gilded retable dates from the eighteenth century.

In the church square are some of the charming wood and brick houses that grace l'Aigle, as well as the so-called house of Mary Stuart, which was in truth built for Marie d'Aubray in the sixteenth century.

In the château built by Hardouin-Mansart at the end of the seventeenth century there is a museum dedicated to June 1944, displaying waxworks of the war leaders, along with their recorded voices. It closes on Mondays and from 11 November to Palm Sunday. See also l'Aigle in the index to this book.

Six kilometres north of l'Aigle is Saint-Pierre-de-Sommaire whose church houses a polychrome Madonna sculpted in the fourteenth century, as well as a frieze painted in the seventeenth century depicting twenty-three scenes from the life of Jesus.

Alençon

Much of Alençon, with its magical flamboyant church of Notre-Dame containing sixteenth-century stained-glass and boasting a splendid sculpted Transfiguration above its central arcade, is described elsewhere in this book. Next to the church is the maison d'Ozé, built in 1450 and later named after the first prefect of the Orne. The rue du Bercail, which leads west from the north-west corner of the church, possesses fine Renaissance houses. So does the Grande Rue, which runs north–south through Alençon, passing the west façade of the church and reaching another fine house of God, Saint-Léonard, finished in 1509.

Alençon's town hall was built in 1783; its elegant cornmarket dates from the nineteenth century, and the splendid prefecture (near the birthplace of St Thérèse of Lisieux – see the index) was begun by the architect Charles Fromont de la Besnardière in 1630, with two wings added later – one in 1680, the other in 1773. The musée des Beaux-Arts et de la Dentelle in the former Jesuit college (which dates from 1630) offers an opportunity to compare Alençon lace with the masterpieces of other lace-making countries.

As far as its urban architecture is concerned, the city falls into two parts: the quarter around Saint-Léonard, where the houses are mostly fifteenth- and sixteenth-century; and the quarter around Notre-Dame, comprising mainly seventeenth- and eighteenth-century buildings.

Alençon is famous for its white geese and the dishes made from them. Look out too for the succulent rabbit dish, *sanguette de lapin*. The town hosts a daily market and an important grain fair at the beginning of February.

Les Andelys

Château-Gaillard (see the index to this book) can be visited from mid-March to the end of November between 09.00 and 12.00 and 14.00 to 18.00. The oldest church of the town, Saint-Sauveur, has a chancel dating from the late twelfth century and a nave built early in the next century. The nave of the twin-towered Notre-Dame also dates from the thirteenth century. The pattern of the exterior walls was created later – the south side in the sixteenth century flamboyant style and the north side seventeenth-century Renaissance. Four mighty piers were built inside in 1675 to hold up the dome. The organ case, splendidly decorated with (among others) King David playing his harp, dates from 1573.

Eight kilometres away, along the D1, you reach the village of Écouis, whose twin-towered church, dating from 1310 apart from the eighteenth-century roof, houses splendid statues.

Argentan

See the index. As for food at Argentan, do not miss here the grilled pigs' trotters and *truite à la crème*. The farmers of the Orne and Ure valleys bring their weekly produce to the Tuesday market.

Arques-la-Bataille

Arques-la-Bataille, as we have seen elsewhere in this book, is famous for a crucial victory won by Henri IV in 1589 over the forces of the Catholic League. Its ruined twelfth-century château is well worth a visit, as also is the early sixteenth-century church of Notre-Dame. Its belfry and the fine woodwork inside are Renaissance additions, and both the chancel and transept were enriched in the Normandy flamboyant style. The splendid rood dates from 1540, and the high altar is protected by an equally splendid sculpted stone enclosure.

Arques-la-Bataille, with a nose attuned to tourism, has set up a sailing school on the lakes of the Varenne. Its traditional feast takes place each Whit Monday.

Avranches

See the index. If you cannot stand the chitterling sausages of Avranches, try its white puddings, made from mutton and sometimes enlivened with mashed fish. The people of Avranches are equally proud of their soup, *potage avranchinois*. They make it from onions, *bouquet garni*, flour, butter, *crème fraîche* and tomatoes, from which the seeds have been carefully removed. *Potage avranchinois* is a smooth soup, since everything is liquidized before serving, and the dish is usually garnished with chervil.

Balleroy

In the first half of the seventeenth century François Mansart built for Jean de Choisy a distinguished château (as well as its chapel, now Balleroy's parish church) which you can visit from the beginning of March to the end of October – except on Wednesdays – between 09.00 and noon and 14.00

and 18.00. The stately rooms are beautifully decorated from the same century to house a series of royal portraits. And the garden was designed by Le Nôtre.

Barfleur

Although Barfleur was a port before the Vikings arrived in Normandy and, in the Middle Ages, was the principal harbour of the Cotentin, it developed its present jetties only in the mid-nineteenth century and remains an unspoiled seaside resort.

The fine eighteenth-century buildings in the rue Saint-Thomas include the splendid former Augustinian priory, dating from 1739. The church of Saint-Nicolas was built in the previous century and houses some fine sixteenth-century statues as well as the relics of St Mary Magdalen Postel, who founded the Sisters of Mercy, died in 1846 and was canonized in 1925.

Barfleur chefs are proud of their lobsters and also claim to cook the most delicious cauliflower in France.

Bayeux

Apart from the Bayeux tapestry (see the index), Bayeux boasts a magnificent half-Romanesque, half-Gothic cathedral, based on a crypt which Bishop Odo completed in 1070. (The frescos in the crypt were painted four centuries later.) As you drive to the city down the D6 your first sight consists of the twin spires of the cathedral and its dome and *flèche*. Its central tower dates from the fifteenth century, with a nineteenth-century bonnet, as the locals call it. Designed by an engineer named Flachat, it replaced an earlier bonnet that was about to cave in. The two Romanesque towers are supported by thirteenth-century buttresses, and in turn support Gothic spires. Over the main doorways are carvings of the passion of Jesus and the Last Judgment, while the tympanum over the doorway to the south transept depicts the murder of St Thomas à Becket.

The interior is inspiring, 102 metres long, the transept 11.5 metres wide. Massive pillars and arcades support an airy upper storey; little carved figures peer at you. On the right transept are some restored fifteenth-century frescos depicting the Trinity and the Annunciation, near which a nineteenth-century fresco illustrates the murder of Thomas à Becket. Another medieval fresco shows St Nicholas doing his customary good works – stopping people boiling and eating children, secretly popping dowries through windows to help poor would-be brides, saving sailors from drowning.

The high altar dated 1771 is by the engraver Philippe Caffieri. Here too is a treasured bit of one of St Thérèse's fingers. Aristide Cavailé-Coll built the majestic three-manual organ in 1852. And the chapter house is exquisite, basically twelfth century, but with graceful fourteenth-century vaulting and a set of carved medieval monsters. But I like best of all the delicate early thirteenth-century chancel, with its forty-nine Renaissance choir stalls, sumptuously carved in 1588.

Among the most celebrated Bishops of Bayeux were Nicolas of Oresme (see the index), Pierre Cauchon, who was responsible for the condemnation of Joan of Arc, and Thomas Basin, who helped to rehabilitate her. Just before the French Revolution this rich diocese included twelve monasteries, two convents and 620 parish priests, and its bishop was Claude Fauchet, court preacher to King Louis XVI. Siding with the Revolution and chosen Constitutional Bishop of Bayeux in 1791, this shifty cleric was guillotined on 31 October 1793.

The pedestrianized 'old Bayeux' boasts numerous lovely houses dating from the fifteenth to the seventeenth centuries, as well as a botanical garden. Many of these houses overhang the street. The fifteenth-century Grand Hôtel d'Argognes has a passage leading into a tree-filled court-yard. Further on a classical archway, seemingly about to collapse, is engraved 'Halle du Viande' and dated 1784.

The market place in Bayeux is surrounded by shady plane trees and ornamented by a fountain which always seems decorated with flowers. Market days are Wednesday and Saturday mornings. Books, flowers, vegetables, fruit, clothing, leather goods and baskets deck its stalls. In 1987 I picked up here a 1967 edition of the *Nouveau Larousse gastronomique* for only 200 French francs.

The city of Bayeux also has a museum dedicated not to the Normandy landings but to the battle that followed, which lasted until 22 August 1944. It is situated on the boulevard Fabian-Ware, and has curiously irregular opening times, though you can usually get in between 10.00 and noon and 14.00 and 18.00. An interesting collection of Bayeux porcelain is displayed in the musée Baron-Gérard.

If you are driving along the D572 between Bayeux and Saint-Lô (or vice versa) look out for the signs for Cerisy-la-Forêt, a mere six kilometres from the main road. Its eleventh-century abbey is in part a picturesque ruin, with its slender decorated pilasters exposed to the open air. Its church, frescoed in the fifteenth century and blessed with an exceedingly delicate three-storeyed apse, still functions as a house of God. I know this because I once sat outside on the ancient walls when the hydrangeas were in bloom and treated myself to a picnic of cheese, fresh bread and a glass of *cidre bouché*, listening to the amplified voice of the priest as he performed the marriage ceremony for a young couple inside the church. The French do not hire expensive wedding cars but decorate their own instead. The one outside Cerisy-la-Forêt that day was enhanced with a couple of brooms, two dolls dressed as a bride and groom, and placards reading *Convoi des anges heureux* and *Vive les mariés*.

Beaumesnil

See under Bernay.

Le Bec-Hellouin

As we have already seen, this entrancing ruined abbey was once the intellectual centre of northern European Christendom. Though philosophical, such men of God fascinate me but I do not wish to bore my readers and so must make a swift canter through the Normandy successors of Vitricius, simply indicating how they enriched the literary and intellectual patrimony of this region. Here Lanfranc built up a library of over 160 volumes, and others added to it. In the twelfth century Philippe d'Harcourt, Bishop of Bayeux, contributed another 113 volumes. Leaving aside books used for the holy offices and the celebration of the Mass, a count in 1421 discovered some 700 volumes on the monks' reading desks. When the brilliant reforming Maurists recatalogued the library at le Bec-Hellouin in 1671 they classified some 5,000 volumes. The invention of printing enriched the library. Although in 1792 when the monastery was dissolved only eight monks remained, they possessed over 5,000 printed books, not counting pamphlets.

All that remains intact from the ancient buildings of this amazing monastery is its fifteenth-century bell tower, a stunning reminder of what the whole ensemble must have looked like, now represented only by the abbey church's ruined blind arcades and the stumps of its once lovely pillars. You can climb the 201 steps of the tower for a fine view over the valley.

We owe the present lovely monastic buildings largely to the Maurists and their successors (see Maurists and le Bec-Hellouin in the index). Guided tours take place at various times between 10.00 and 17.15, except on Tuesdays.

Bellême

Bellême, surrounded by vestiges of its medieval ramparts, perches 225 metres above the Perche forest. At its heart the walled town boasts lovely classical houses and the seventeenth-century classical church of Saint-

Sauveur (go inside if only to see its splendid font, sculpted in 1684, and then stay to admire the rich decoration and the grandiloquent eighteenth-century pulpit). The 'Ville Close' retains some fine eighteenth-century houses, and one or two earlier ones.

Bellême butchers specialize in white puddings.

Bernay

In 1013 Guglielmo da Volpiano, the Cluniac abbot of Fécamp, founded an abbey here whose church, with a seventeenth-century dome, stands opposite what were once the abbey buildings and now form the seventeenth-century town hall. The oldest extant example of Normandy's great Romanesque churches, Notre-Dame-de-Bernay has carved capitals of high quality. The Maurists rebuilt the monastery in the early eighteenth century, and their lovely buildings now house the town hall, the prefecture and the tribunal.

Two other churches should be seen at Bernay. The fifteenth-century basilica of Notre-Dame-de-la-Couture in rue Kléber-Mercier has a vaulted wooden ceiling and the venerated sixteenth-century statue of Notre-Dame-de-la-Couture. It also contains seventeen stained-glass windows dating from the end of the fifteenth century and another, dated 1632, depicting the seven sorrows of Mary.

The church of Sainte-Croix, begun in the fourteenth century, is no longer used for worship but houses works of religious art brought from le Bec-Hellouin, as well as the tombstone of Abbot Guillaume d'Auvillars, who died in 1418. Over the high altar is a sculpted Nativity dating from 1683.

Broglie and Beaumesnil (see the index) are respectively only 11 and 13 kilometres from Bernay, the former reached by the N138, the latter by the D140.

Beuzeville

Admirers of the modern stained-glass maker Decorchemont, who died in 1961, can see nineteen of his windows in the medieval Gothic church of Beuzeville.

Broglie

See under Bernay.

Caen

Although much of Caen was newly built after World War II, it retains charm and much historical and architectural interest, and some of its old streets, such as the pedestrianized rue Froide and part of rue Caponnière, escaped intact. Other fine houses, such as the late fourteenth-century maison des Quattans (no. 31, rue de Geôle) have been extremely well restored, and the nineteenth-century dock is today entirely given over to pleasure craft.

Caen is first mentioned in a document of 1026 as one of four villages where the River Orne meets the River Odon. It owes its prosperity to William the Bastard, who started building the château. His successors added its keep and rebuilt the walls. Despite considerable damage in 1944, it is today entrancing – encircling a garden, guarded by two cannons which were given by the republic of Senegal, and housing both the musée des Beaux Arts (a magnificent collection, local, national and international, in a vast new building) and the Normandy museum, a collection of local crafts. The exchequer was built in the twelfth century as the great hall of the château. The castle's chapel of Saint-Georges was founded in the twelfth century and mostly rebuilt in the fifteenth.

The Abbaye-aux-Hommes (see the index), dedicated to St Stephen, escaped damage in 1944, having been despoiled by the Protestants during the Wars of Religion and restored in the next century. The view from the place Louis-Guillouard of its three-storeyed apse abutting on to the classical monastic buildings is thrilling. Walk round to see the majestically Romanesque façade of the church, with two elegant eleventh-century towers rising from it. The lantern tower in no way conflicts with this Romanesque austerity, though it was rebuilt in the seventeenth century. The chancel, dating from the beginning of the thirteenth century, is an extremely early example of Normandy Gothic. Its stalls are seventeenth-century, and both the decorated clock and the organ date from the next century. The exotic marble high altar was made in 1771.

Though the early eighteenth-century convent, designed by Guillaume de la Tremblaye, is now Caen town hall, you can follow a guided tour beginning on the hour between 09.00 and 17.00 (except for 13.00). The view across the municipal gardens of this delicious building, 105 metres long, stretching alongside the Romanesque apse of the abbey church, is breathtaking.

The Abbaye-aux-Dames, unlike its sister church, did suffer during the 1944 invasion. It had lost its spires long before, during the Hundred Years War. Yet this church, dedicated to the Holy Trinity, remains a Romanesque masterpiece, its huge nave graced by pointed twelfth-century arches, its chancel by eleventh-century groining, its transepts beautifully decorated. In this chancel lies the Conqueror's wife (see Mathilde in the index), who founded the church in 1060. Do not neglect to descend into the unspoilt eleventh-century crypt. The chapter house, which is reached by the south transept, dates from the thirteenth century.

By the place Louis-Guillouard stands the romantic ruin of the church of Vieux-Saint-Étienne. Caen has more churches than anyone is likely to visit at one stay: the eleventh-century Saint-Nicolas; the Jesuit church of Notre-Dame-de-la-Gloriette, built in the 1680s and boasting a splendidly decorated high altar under a baldachin of 1797 (originally created for the Abbaye-aux-Dames); the fourteenth-century flamboyant church of Saint-Jean; Saint-Sauveur, half-Gothic, half-Renaissance, with a Romanesque bell tower. But no one should miss the church of Saint-Pierre.

Rising just below the château in rue Saint-Pierre (which boasts, at nos 52 and 54, two superb half-timbered houses), its Normandy Gothic spire dates from the early fourteenth century. The nave of Saint-Pierre, finished in the early fifteenth century, displays soaring ribs and splendid, foliage-carved keystones. The rose window gleams blue and red above the organ loft. The flamboyant choir and the luxurious sanctuary seem to have been built only yesterday (which in some respects happens to be true). The apse is magnificent, restored by the city of Caen at the beginning of this century, its vaulting matching the finest in Europe.

Two of the pillars of the nave should on no account be missed. One, the second on the left, has a capital in which rabbits disport themselves in a field of cabbages. Even more delightful are the carvings on the capital of the third pillar on the left. Glorifying divine love, they also mock carnal lust. The philosopher Aristotle is saddled and bridled, whipped by a woman. Virgil, who carnally desired the daughter of a Roman emperor, hangs helplessly in a basket, halfway up to the window of her bed-chamber. Lancelot vainly seeks Guinevere, and Sir Gawain lies in the perilous bed, wounded by Cupid's arrow.

Other carvings depict the unicorn, pursued by huntsmen, and taking refuge in a virgin's lap – a symbol, according to the medieval bestiaries, of the Blessed Virgin bringing succour to fraught humankind. A pelican feeds its young on the flesh of its own beast – another medieval symbol of Christ sacrificing himself for his flock. Samson, tearing apart the lion's jaw, symbolically repels evil. A phoenix rises reborn from the flames – symbol of the death and resurrection of Jesus.

Finally, pay a visit to the nearby tourist office of Caen, a lovely Italian Renaissance building which a merchant named Nicolas le Valois d'Escoville commissioned in the 1530s (hence its name, the hôtel d'Escoville). Turrets, an extremely elegant staircase, a loggia and splendid classical and biblical carvings (David and Goliath, Perseus rescuing Andromeda, and the like) decorate his home.

Caen holds two weekly markets, on Fridays in the place Saint-Sauveur, and on Sundays in the place Courtonne. Its two hypermarkets are Carrefour and the massive Continent (on the road to the côte du Nacre), often filled with tourists stocking up on a one-day trip across the channel.

After sampling *tripes à la mode de Caen* try here a *matelote* of sole.

Canteleu

See under Rouen and in the index.

Carentan

Carentan's town hall was once an Augustinian priory, begun in the mid-seventeenth century and finished in 1717. Although the church of Notre-Dame is principally a fifteenth-century building and houses some entertaining gargoyles, it boasts a Romanesque west doorway and a fourteenth-century tower resting on a twelfth-century crossing.

I have eaten here delicious frog's legs, supposedly garnered in the neighbouring marshes, but (I suspect) imported from China like most French *grenouilles* these days.

Carrouges

Set on its 417-metre eminence in the midst of a lovely park, the brick and granite château of Carrouges, which can be visited from 10.00 to 12.00 and 14.00 to 17.30 (except on Tuesdays) has preserved its square fourteenth-century keep and its irregular courtyard with towers and balustrades and impressive sixteenth-century living quarters. Unlike many French châteaux now open to the public, it is also sumptuously furnished.

The weekly market at Carrouges takes place on Wednesdays, and there seems to be a fair every other month.

Caudebec-en-Caux

The 'beck' of Caudebec-en-Caux happens to be the Seine itself. Walk from the river up the rue de la Boucherie to reach the tourist information office and the thirteenth-century gabled house of the Knights Templar, now a museum of medieval and Renaissance Caudebec-en-Caux.

Further on stands the church of Notre-Dame with its lovely rose window and flamboyant porches. It houses sixteenth-century stained-glass, a seventeenth-century font, and a modern organ with more than

3,000 pipes, as well as some powerful fifteenth-century statues brought here from the abbey of Jumièges. The Lady Chapel is famous for its mighty keystone, said to weigh seven tons. The church tower, rising to a height of 54 metres, is crowned by an octagonal *flèche*. Some of the chapels are adorned with stained-glass from the fifteenth and sixteenth centuries, one of them (in the fifth chapel on the left) given by the English and fittingly depicting their patron saint, St George.

The rest of Caudebec-en-Caux was severely damaged by fire in June 1940, though some of its charming old houses survived around the church. One sole tower remains from the ramparts which were built to protect Caudebec-en-Caux in 1364, and the moat is still fed by the Rivers Ambion and Sainte-Gertrude.

This summer resort has long been inhabited, for archaeologists have dug up Roman and Gaulish coins nearby. The banks of the rivers here are beautiful. Market day is Saturday, and during the first two weeks of September the place is alive with a national equestrian festival.

Cerisy-la-Forêt

See under Bayeux.

Cherbourg

Haunt of artists, bitterly fought over by the defending Germans and three American divisions in 1944, Cherbourg has regained its loveliness and composure. The Emmanuel-Liais park, laid out in 1827, managed to save from damage its delightful collection of exotic trees and plants. The baroque theatre of 1882 also escaped the bombardment. The pedestrianized centre of the town has kept its narrow shopping streets and its fish market.

Cherbourg also has its share of architectural treasures. In 1145 Mathilde, the daughter of Henry I of England, founded here an abbey which flourished till 1774, when its exquisite buildings became an army and naval barracks. Today the abbey du Voeu lies partly ruined, but the chapter house, the refectory and cellar are still enchanting and intact.

The Normans, having destroyed Cherbourg's church in their pagan days, founded a new one, the church of la Trinité, in 1055. The English repeatedly despoiled it in their attacks on Normandy, and the church had to be almost entirely rebuilt in the fifteenth century, hence the present magnificent flamboyant building. Inside, as well as some bas-reliefs carved at the crossing, the nave gallery is sculpted with a grisly dance of death (restored in the nineteenth century).

The museum of the Liberation is reached by the avénue de Paris, and the art gallery, the musée Thomas-Henry, is in the Centre culturel in the rue Vastel and is open every day except Tuesdays from 10.00 to 12.00 and 14.00 and 18.00. Apart from its collection of works by Millet (see the index) its chief treasure is Fra Angelico's 'Conversion of St Augustine'.

Naturally at Cherbourg you should eat shellfish, cod baked with onions and potatoes, and whiting cooked in cider. Cherbourg chefs also boast of their delicate mutton dishes.

Clères

The château at Clères, basically nineteenth-century though founded in the fourteenth, today houses in its park a splendid zoo, mostly inhabited by birds but enlivened by deer and several kangaroos. It opens from 09.00 to 18.00 during the summer (closing an hour earlier in the winter months). A further delight at Clères is the Normandy car museum, which has the same opening times.

Conches-en-Ouche

Conches-en-Ouche has preserved one of the finest sets of Renaissance stained-glass windows in Normandy, housed in the fifteenth-century church of Sainte-Foy. Though technically flamboyant, the architecture of this church has decided not to go over the top, so to speak, and is pleasingly gentle.

Admire the fifteenth- and sixteenth-century houses in the church square, before taking a picnic to enjoy the splendid view from the gardens which surround the ruined château's keep (which you reach through the archway of the town hall). Its well is still visible. Nearby stands one of several delightful old houses which add to the charm of this little town: the half-timbered maison de Richesses de l'Eure, today given over to exhibitions.

Coutances

Coutances cathedral, which dominates the skyline as you drive into the city, was founded by a companion of the Conqueror, Geoffroi de Montbray, ten years before he set sail for England. When a fire destroyed most of his church in 1218, a Gothic one rose on the spot, incorporating parts of the earlier Romanesque towers, which reach up almost eighty metres. Its lantern, fifty-seven metres high, is one of the marvels of Normandy architecture, with an octagonal cupola reaching up to forty-one metres.

Its side chapels date from the late thirteenth and early fourteenth centuries.

The west end is absolutely regular. The interior is regular too, every bulge on one side matched on the other. A classical organ is supported by four Corinthian columns and two bearded caryatids, each one with a hand on his head and the other hand coquettishly on his waist. Some splendid medieval stained-glass decorates the choir, and the little chapel behind the silver-gilt high altar is prettily decorated with diaper work, painted flowers and leaves, red, white and green stripes and sheaves of corn. Yellow and green devils appear in a stained-glass depiction of the Last Judgment. Opposite, a thirteenth-century window depicts the murder of Thomas à Becket and a noble St George killing a green dragon. The garish twentieth-century glass behind the organ cannot compete.

South-east of the cathedral is the former episcopal palace, built with eighteenth-century elegance. To the south-west are the terraces of the public garden (laid out in 1860 in the so-called English style, that is with landscaped trees and flower beds), which look out over the valley of the River Bulsard and three thirteenth-century arches of the city's former aqueduct.

Further south from the cathedral, along rue Geoffroy-de-Montbray, is the church of Saint-Pierre, an attractive lantern-towered Renaissance building begun in the fifteenth century and finished in the next. By contrast with the cathedral, its flamboyant spire is gloriously asymmetrical. And north of the cathedral the church of Saint-Nicolas, rebuilt in the eighteenth century, now serves as a museum of local traditions and farm implements.

Part of the charm of the old streets of Coutances, especially those south of Saint-Pierre, derives from shops set up in its old artisans' houses, some of them dating back to the fifteenth century. The city hospital south of these incorporates a fifteenth-century hospice where you can see a collection of traditional medicinal jars.

At Coutances sample ham cooked in cider, or *tripes à la crème*.

Deauville

See the index.

Dieppe

'Commodious' was John Evelyn's word to describe Dieppe when he visited the port in 1644. He also noted that 'This place exceedingly abounds in workemen that make and sell curiosities of Ivory and Tortoise shells, in which they turne and make many rare toyes; & indeed whatever the East Indys afford of Cabinets, Purcelan, natural and exotic rarities are here to be had with abundant choice.' These ivories were carved from the tusks of elephants brought from West Africa by Dieppe mariners. You can admire many such ivories in the fifteenth-century château set high on the cliffs, which now serves as Dieppe's museum. There too (except on Tuesdays when it closes) is displayed a fine selection of works by Camille Pissarro, Renoir and Georges Braque, as well as a room devoted to Walter Sickert. Dieppe's fame as a fashionable seaside resort in the mid-nineteenth century is also commemorated here in a comical collection of early bathing costumes.

To sail into Dieppe is undoubtedly the most entrancing way to enter Normandy, for the ship ties up in the bustling centre of the town. The harbour front is crammed with fishing smacks, and on disembarking you are immediately among brasseries and fish restaurants, with stalls selling cooked shrimps. The sea front boasts a slightly faded Edwardian gentility – Edwardian being the *mot juste*, for among the hotels near the casino and along the boulevard de Verdun you spot such names as the Epsom and the Windsor alongside the hôtel Les Arcades, the hôtel de l'Univers and the rest.

Inevitably the fish meals at Dieppe are delicious. *Marmite dieppoise* is composed of turbot, sole and angler fish, cooked in cream and wine, with a stew of leeks, onions and celery. Dieppe scallops are succulent. And the town has flourished as a tourist shopping centre, specializing in jewellery, cheeses and sugared almonds (which are called here *spécialités dieppoises*). The Grand'Rue, like the rest of Dieppe, far from being devoted simply to the knick-knacks of the tourist trade, boasts also its cake shops, *épiceries* and *charcuteries*. If you want to stock up at one of France's monster supermarkets, drive to Mamouth, four kilometres outside the town on the N27.

On Saturday mornings, starting at 07.00, a market sets up its stalls along the main street. Cheeses, garlic, mushrooms, flowers, onions, fish, fruit, herbs, butter, cream, vegetables, clothing and shoes are sold from stalls which continue around and beyond the church of Saint-Jacques. The market closes down by 13.00.

The church of Saint-Jacques has a fourteenth-century porch over which is an impressive rose window. The nave itself dates from a century earlier, but has been much decorated. Look out for the stone screen in the fifteenth-century chapel of the Holy Sepulchre and the flamboyant vaulting of the chapel of the Sacred Heart. Behind the church of Saint-Jacques stretches the pretty restored fishermen's quarter known as Sainte-Catherine.

Dieppe also boasts a saline and mud bath centre. Sole, mackerel and

3,000 tonnes of *coquilles Saint-Jacques* are fished annually at Dieppe, many finding their way into the town's restaurants. Markets take place on nearly every day of the week.

Georges Braque is buried eight kilometres away in the little cemetery of Varengeville-sur-Mer (see the index), where you can also in summer visit another testimony of British influence on this coast, Les Moutiers with its lovely park and gardens, all the work of Sir Edwin Lutyens.

Continue along the white cliffs of the Alabaster coast for a charming trip as far as Le Havre. The route passes through Veules-les-Roses, a village which once lost its entire adult menfolk in a storm. Today white cabins line the sea front, and Veules-les-Roses nestles in the wooded valley of the stream from which it derives its name. Its sixteenth-century church, Saint-Martin, boasts a square thirteenth-century tower. The organ case dates from 1628, and the church houses some fine fifteenth-century statues. I do not believe that the painting of Jesus being mocked is by Grünewald, as some claim, but it is moving all the same.

Veules-les-Roses has created a garden incorporating a sixteenth-century Calvary around the ruined church of Saint-Nicolas.

Dives-sur-Mer

To imagine William the Bastard setting sail in 1066 to conquer England from Dives-sur-Mer on the east bank of the River Dives is difficult, for today the river has silted up and the pretty town no longer opens on to the sea. Yet its citizens revere the memory of the conqueror, witness the sixteenth-century hostellerie de Guillaume le Conquérant, and the little enclave beyond it, dubbed 'William the Conqueror village' by the artisans who sell you their trinkets there. The church of Notre-Dame-de-Dives, though basically sixteenth-century Gothic, retains a few Norman features, in particular the mighty Romanesque pillars of the crossing, as well as a plaque listing William's companions.

Nearby is the sixteenth-century market hall, opposite which stands the manor of la Falaise, built in 1695.

Domfront

Domfront we have already visited, paying however insufficient attention to the lovely Romanesque church of Notre-Dame-sur-l'Eau, built out of granite in 1020 and housing thirty-seven medieval tombs and a sixteenth-century statue of the Virgin Mary.

The town's Saturday market is a delight, and *rillettes*, *boudins*, pears and pear brandy are gastronomic specialities of Domfront.

Eight kilometres away along the D962 and the D22 you reach Lonlay-
l'Abbaye, whose church, basically Romanesque and once part of an
eleventh-century abbey, has a Gothic chancel built out of granite and a
fifteenth-century porch.

Duclair

Rightly celebrated for the succulence of its ducklings, Duclair ought also
to be famed for incorporating in the church of Saint-Denis seven pink
marble columns from a pagan temple where the Gauls and the Romans
once offered sacrifices. Its stained-glass windows are mostly sixteenth-
century, though the ubiquitous Max Ingrand has contributed some of his
own mediocre twentieth-century glass as well. From the twelfth-century
belfry rises a sixteenth-century spire. The church is filled with statues,
including a rare wooden Trinity dating from the fourteenth century, and
statues of St John and Mary in her Assumption. A fifteenth-century
sculpture depicts Jesus on the cross, flanked by his mother and St
John.

Écouis

See under les Andelys.

Elbeuf

The Gallo-Roman tombs in the museum of Elbeuf, housed in the town
hall, a museum which rarely opens (usually Wednesdays and Saturdays
from 14.00 to 18.00, but not always), indicate how long this region has
been settled. Elbeuf possesses two fine churches: the Gothic Saint-
Étienne, dating from 1517 and incorporating some excellent sixteenth-
century stained-glass; and the eighteenth-century Saint-Jean, with contemporary furnishings and a sixteenth-century stained glass depiction of
the tree of Jesse from the earlier building that stood here.

The restaurants of Elboeuf will serve you young juicy pears.

Étretat

Beloved of nineteenth-century artists, Étretat is set between two remarkable cliffs, known as the Amont and the Aval. In part its church dates
from the eleventh century, but the most entrancing sight at Étretat (or, to

be exact, just outside the resort) is the Manneporte, which you see best from the cliffs at the porte d'Aval.

In 1927 two French airmen tried to fly across the Atlantic from the Amont cliff. They drowned in the attempt, and there stands their memorial. Their names were Charles Nungesser and François Coli, and their museum opens from Easter to the end of September between 10.00 and noon and 15.00 and 18.00. Close by is the chapel of Notre-Dame-de-la-Garde.

The Romanesque church of Notre-Dame has an early Gothic lantern tower and a twelfth-century doorway carrying a tympanum of 1866. Étretat is remarkable for its surrounding cliffs and promontories, and from here the Alabaster coast stretches for ninety-five picturesque kilometres as far as Dieppe.

Étretat's market is held on Thursdays, and the town hosts fairs on the first Sunday after Easter and the first Sunday in August. Gastronomic specialities here include *rillettes* of rabbit, bass from the River Eure, and chicken cooked in *morilles* (when this mushroom is in season).

Eu

Eu was a Roman port. Here Duke Rollo died and here too William the Bastard met his future victim Harold and also married Mathilde. The St Laurent to whom the church of Notre-Dame-et-Saint-Laurent at Eu is half dedicated turns out to be an Irish monk, St Lawrence O'Toole, who died here in the twelfth century and lies entombed in the contemporary crypt.

The present Gothic nature of this spacious building stems from Viollet-le-Duc's nineteenth-century restoration, but this ace-restorer preserved the difference between the 13th-century Gothic of the nave and the fifteenth-century apse. Seek out the fifteenth-century entombment of Christ in an ambulatory chapel, under its flamboyant canopy.

Henri, Duke of Guise, built the château at Eu in 1578, and in its much altered state this was the favourite residence of King Louis-Philippe, who reigned from 1830 until 1848. Now the Louis-Philippe museum, it can be visited with a guide from the beginning of April to the end of September. The finest room must be the bedroom, inhabited in the second half of the seventeenth century by the Duchess of Montpensier.

Guise himself, assassinated in 1588, lies in a marble tomb (close to that of his wife) in the chapel of the Anguier college, which he founded in 1582, though the chapel was not built for another forty years.

Eu is today a tourist centre, given over to horseriding, fishing, and hiking in its forests and woods. Every Wednesday it holds a market.

Évreux

Beginning as a Gaulish village set on the plateau above the River Iton, Évreux was first missionized in the fourth century by the redoubtable St Taurin (see St Taurin in the index). The cathedral of Notre-Dame-d'Évreux was founded in the sixth century, rebuilt in the twelfth, and rebuilt again after a fire in 1260. A second fire of 1356 was then followed by a long delay in restoring the cathedral again, with the result that Évreux cathedral is a rich mélange of styles.

The flamboyant lantern and the Lady Chapel date from the fifteenth century and the superb façade of its north transept dates only from the sixteenth century, the work of Jean Cossart. In consequence great Romanesque arches support the cathedral's Gothic tracery, and fourteenth- and fifteenth-century stained-glass vies in beauty with fifteenth-century wrought-iron grilles and Gothic and Renaissance wood-work. Notice that the figures in the fifteenth-century stained-glass in the Lady Chapel include a tree of Jesse, as well as King Louis XI and the peers of his realm. The glass of the north rose window vigorously depicts the Last Judgment. At the Revolution all the cathedral's statues were destroyed and its sculpted north porch was mutilated. World War II did yet greater damage, necessitating a scrupulous restoration. Happily the stained-glass and the pulpit of 1674 (which came from the abbey of le Bec-Hellouin) were saved.

To the south of the cathedral stands the former bishop's palace, a rich flamboyant building with a staircase tower and dormer windows, now housing the city museum. Inside are some fine Roman remains, including a first-century statue of Jupiter and a third-century statue of Apollo (their heads are splendid, Jupiter nobly bearded, Apollo extremely beautiful), and to wander among the rich furnishings of a prince of the Church is a great delight.

The relics of St Taurin are housed in a splendid thirteenth-century silver-gilt reliquary in the church of Saint-Taurin, which you reach by walking west from the cathedral across the River Itan, along the boulevard J.-Janin and continuing along the rue Joséphine. The church itself is a masterpiece, part Romanesque, part Renaissance but mostly built in the fourteenth and fifteenth centuries.

Évreux also boasts a late fifteenth-century clock tower, forty-four metres high and carrying a two-ton bell affectionately dubbed Louise. Seven kilometres east of the city you reach Vieil-Évreux. Here were excavated the statues of Jupiter and Apollo now found in Évreux's museum, as well as a Roman amphitheatre.

The *pâtisseries* of Évreux serve particularly pungent *brioches*.

Évron

Although Évron seems sleepily industrialized, its basilica is magnificent, with a mighty square Romanesque tower, four massive Romanesque bays in the nave and the rest fourteenth-century Gothic. The chapel of Notre-Dame-de-l'Épine is rich in statues, metalwork and tapestries.

Falaise

See the index.

Fécamp

Now a busy harbour for tourists who prefer to sail their own boats to Normandy rather than use the cross-Channel ferries, Fécamp was famous in the early Middle Ages for its monastery, which claimed to possess a drop of blood from the Saviour's crucifixion. Today the precious blood is annually displayed on the Tuesday and Thursday following Trinity Sunday in the abbey church of La-Trinité, against which abut the former abbey buildings which now serve as the town hall.

Some time after the crucifixion of Jesus, so legend tells, a relative of Joseph of Arimathea, who lent the Saviour his tomb, poured this drop of holy blood into a bottle and threw it into the sea. It washed up at Fécamp and was enormously prized by the monks who rescued it. In the early eleventh century they built here a magnificent Romanesque abbey. Like most such abbeys in Normandy, it was ravaged by fire, this time in the twelfth century, though two chapels were spared and can still be seen in the otherwise early Gothic church that replaced their earlier house of God.

When the abbey was suppressed at the Revolution, the church of La-Trinité was spared by becoming Fécamp's parish church. Vast and beautiful, its lantern tower reaches a height of sixty-five metres. In the sixteenth century the monks commissioned an Italian, Girolamo Viscardo, to create a marble high altar to house their precious drop of Christ's blood. Its lovely wooden baldachin was added 200 years later and is matched by the carved stalls. Fine though these are, they are bettered by the sixteenth-century screens of the chapels around the chancel, some of them sheltering the tombs of medieval abbots (one of whom, Guglielmo da Volpiano, first abbot of Fécamp, lies in a seventeenth-century tomb).

Three later additions grace this huge church, which was substantially finished by 1220: the stone screens in the chapels behind the high altar; the flamboyant chapel of Our Lady; and the classical west end created in the eighteenth century. During July the enlightened tourist board of Fécamp sponsors musical concerts in the abbey.

We also owe a singular debt to a nineteenth-century merchant of Fécamp. The remarkable liqueur *Bénédictine* derives its name from the fact that it was invented by a Benedictine monk, Don Bernardo Vincelli, in the early sixteenth century. In 1863 this Fécamp merchant rediscovered the original formula of alcohol, cognac, sugar, honey and twenty-seven aromatic plants, matured in oak to produce this superb elixir.

The *Bénédictine* museum, a Gothic-Renaissance building in the rue Alexandre-le-Grand, is not only crammed with monastic remains but also has a section devoted to the liqueur which Vincelli created in 1510 and which that Fécamp merchant re-created four and a half centuries later. Guided tours of the distillery, which is housed in a splendid nineteenth-century building, take place from 09.30 to 11.30 and from 14.00 to 17.30 (between Easter and 11 November) and naturally include a tasting.

Fécamp's municipal museum (at no. 21, rue Alexandre-le-Grand), which opens from 10.00 to 12.00 and 14.00 to 17.30, has a room dedicated to the history of sailing ships, with some fine maritime paintings along with fishermen's nets; and the town's fishermen still catch the juicy cod and herrings served in Fécamp restaurants.

La Ferté-Bernard

This pretty and once-fortified town is enriched with a marvellous flamboyant church, Notre-Dame-des-Marais, built in the second half of the sixteenth century. Busts of the Roman emperors oddly decorate its south aisle, and the gallery also supports statues of the King of France and the peers of his realm. The clerestory glitters with Renaissance stained-glass windows.

Of the medieval fortifications only the porte Saint-Julian remains. Go through it and along the rue de l'Huisne to savour some of the Renaissance houses of la Ferté-Bernard.

Its museum of folklore opens from 14.00 to 17.00 in the tourist season.

Flers

See the index; and try the town's noted *rillettes*, often enriched with a little cider. The museum of the Normandy bocage opens from Easter to 15 October between 14.00 and 18.00. Market days at Flers are Wednesdays and Saturdays.

Forges-les-Eaux

See the index, which also contains a reference to the celebrated cheese of this town, *Coeur de Bray*. Forges-les-Eaux also sponsors horseracing in the summer season. Do not miss the Thursday market; even if you have no need to buy a cow or a calf, wait till the afternoon to buy your cheese and fruit.

Gaillard

See the index under château-Gaillard.

Gisors

See the index. The château of Gisors, overlooking the town, is a superb example of a Norman fortress and can be visited from 10.00 to 16.00. The tour takes a couple of hours, which ought not to leave the visitor too exhausted to explore the lovely Gothic church of Saint-Gervais-et-Protais, with its fabulous façade, especially if you pause in between for a meal of Gisors' celebrated *truites à la crème*.

Giverny

See the index.

Gournay-en-Bray

See the index, under Gournay-en-Bray and *les petits-suisses*. The main market sets up its stalls here on Tuesday mornings, with a smaller market selling fowl opening on Friday mornings.

Grandcamp

The fishing port of Grandcamp is so tiny – a village of fewer than 450 inhabitants at the last census – that one might erroneously think it insignificant. Yet it commands an awesome barrier reef which each day savagely uncovers itself when the waters recede; it derives from a couple of old villages founded by the Normans themselves in the twelfth century; its church, dedicated to St Michael, in its present structure dates from the seventeenth century, but boasts a redoubtable sixteenth-century bell tower and houses splendid eighteenth-century panelling; and once a year on the mid-Sunday of August the villagers of Grandcamp mount their gay and traditional fête.

Granville

A town founded on a defensive rock by the English in order to besiege le Mont-Saint-Michel, Granville has endured a bloodthirsty history. Its finest and most violent hours occurred in November 1793, when the town defended itself against an army of some 5,000 royalist *Vendéens* (or *chouans* as they were called here), engaged in their hopeless revolt against the French Revolutionaries. Such was the valour of the men of Granville that the siege lasted twenty-eight hours, and twenty-six republicans lay dead before the *chouans* retreated, leaving behind their own dead. So grateful was the Convention that the town was officially dubbed Granville-la-Victoire.

The poet Charles-Théophile Féret, who relished Normandy as 'the paradise of the Vikings', also remembered in a poem of startling imagery the savagery of this particular episode in the history of Granville:

> From a crusty field on the cliffs of tawny beaches,
> We watched an iron Granville float,
> And the long rock, with its domes and spires
> Seemed like a breast-plate smoking in the sea.
>
> An irritated crimson along the horizon prolongs
> The deadly horror of the headland for the poor *chouans*,
> The ocean spits out their drunk and soaked-up blood.
> The *Vendée* hangs like haunches of beef at a stall.
>
> There, under the grass which springs like spiky lances under our feet,
> Sleep soldiers in their Breton hats,
> Heavy from the villainous bullets deep in their leathery flesh,
> Embedded in their necks like brass rosaries.
>
> Our Lady of Auray is no republican
> And she refuses to pardon her stubborn sons.
> So the dead feed the grass of hatred,
> And the living in the red night stir up their firebrands.

The *chouans* were later betrayed by Napoleon, who promised those who surrendered safe conduct and then had them summarily shot. Féret mused that the passions roused by this cynical betrayal lived on deep in the hearts of his fellow Normans, nurturing an anger which not even the all-cleansing sea could extinguish.

You would scarcely think this at Granville today, peaceful and welcoming (though traces of the ancient garrison remain, despite numerous efforts, both by the French and the English, to demolish them). The former Logis du Roi, for instance, now houses the local museum but has not lost its fortified demeanour. You should certainly walk around the remaining ramparts which surround the upper town, and along the powerful cliffs to see why the English chose this once-tiny fishing village as the site of their defensive and offensive foothold.

At one end of this walk stands the sixteenth- and seventeenth-century granite church of Notre-Dame; at the other is the place de l'Isthme, which offers in exceptionally fine weather a view as far as Jersey and is now abutted by entrancing public gardens.

Four bells are mounted outside the spire of Granville church, and if you go inside before taking your walk, its rewards include a pulpit of 1727, the thirteenth-century statue of Our Lady of Cap Lihou and a thirty-six-voiced Romantic organ. In its chapel of Saint Clement (patron saint of the town and of its fishermen) modern stained-glass windows from the factory at Fontenay sing his honour and model ships beg his aid. The brown stone vaults stand out against the white plaster.

From the wall adjoining the church square there is a restful panorama over the cranes of the harbour as far as the curving headland, over the moored yachts and fishing smacks protected by the breakwater, the ambience only slightly broken by the refrigerated container-base. The lower town is lively, with lobster pots and stalls and shops selling fish and cheese. This is a region of pony-trap races, and in the fields outside Granville graze frisky stallions and lissom mares.

From here a further exhilarating outing is to the northernmost point of the bay of le Mont-Saint-Michel, the Pointe du Roc, reached by a narrow isthmus. Curiously enough, although the views from here are superb, you cannot see le Mont-Saint-Michel itself. On the way to the point and its lighthouse you pass a formidable barracks, built in 1750.

In spite of the disappointingly narrow beach, for the most part Granville today lives off tourism (as its aquarium, waxworks museum and frequent boat trips to the granite Chaussay Islands indicate), off its commercial port and off fishing. The lighthouse and the old fishermen's houses (dating mostly from the sixteenth to the eighteenth centuries) add their picturesque notes to the town. The most notable houses stand in the rue Saint-Jean, which runs from the place de l'Isthme, in particular the house known from a terracotta bas-relief as the house of Adam and Eve (at no. 3); no. 37, built in the sixteenth century and reputed to have been the scene of illegal Catholic Masses in one of its cellars during the Reign of Terror; the powerfully built house of Fortuné de Boisegobey (a prolific, long-forgotten novelist) at no. 39; the late seventeenth-century hôtel dit

Ganne-Destouches at no. 45; and the hôtel des Picquelin, which was built
in 1737 and stands at no. 61. Three more splendid hôtels grace the rue
Notre-Dame.

Finally Granville's tourist industry admirably promotes summer concerts and festivals and the resources of a local yacht club add more
modern pleasures to the traditional fêtes and religious spectacles of the
town. Codfish *à la Granvillaise* is the local treat.

Hambye

Hambye abbey retains a Romanesque abbey church with a spacious
Gothic chancel, as well as the cloister, a frescoed hall of the dead, a Gothic
chapter house, and the monks' warming room, all enriched by medieval
sculptures. In the tourist season you can visit the abbey between 10.00
and 11.30 and 14.00 and 18.00, except on Tuesdays.

Harfleur

Harfleur's glory is the hall-church of Saint-Martin, founded by Robert the
Devil, rebuilt in the fifteenth and sixteenth centuries. Its retable of 1630 is
but one of the rich furnishings inside this church.

Le Havre

Guy de Maupassant's story *Pierre and Jean* entrancingly describes Le
Havre as it was in the days of steamships and the Southampton packet
(which was named *Prince Albert* after Queen Victoria's late consort).

Long and low, its two sloping smokestacks astern and a couple of yellow-painted
paddle-boxes protruding on its sides like rounded cheeks, the packet was sailing
into the harbour at full-speed, her passengers covering her decks and lying under
parasols. Striking foam from the water her speedy, noisy paddlewheels made her
seem in a hurry, as if she were some important courier; and her steep bows sliced
the sea to port and starboard into powerful waves which rose and then curved,
sluiced thin and transparent along her sides.

Other steamers approached the short white dock from every point of
the compass, swallowed one after the other into their moorings. Fishing
smacks, tugs towing capacious sailing ships with slender masts and white
or brown canvas outlined against the sky all approached the harbour,
which seemed to devour them like some greedy ogre before its satiated
stomach disgorged out to sea a new fleet of steamers, schooners, brigs
and three-masters.

These ships were, I think, the reason why Stendhal took Le Havre for 'the most exact copy of England that France has to offer'. The customs house seemed to him an inferior version of the one at Liverpool. The steamers, billowing brownish coal smoke which, as he settled into his room, filled the rooftops with a deep obscurity, reminded him with enormous pleasure of London.

Is Le Havre today English? Certainly the British populate it, especially our yachting fraternity – which is a paradox, since in September 1944 we viciously destroyed most of it when Bomber Command obliterated the centre of the town and killed 3,000 of its citizens. The master of reinforced concrete, Auguste Perret, who fortunately died in 1954, rebuilt the place de l'Hôtel-de-Ville and the church of Saint-Joseph. For spiritual refreshment visit one of the town's older houses of God, the church of Saint-François, which was begun in 1551.

Do not miss the musée André-Malraux (open except on Tuesdays from 10.00 to 12.00 and from 14.00 to 18.00) above all for its collection of works by Dufy, Jongkind, Pissarro and Boudin (see their names in the index, and also Le Havre itself). You can find a market every day somewhere in Le Havre.

Honfleur

Look up Honfleur in the index, for its remarkable church of Sainte-Catherine and the Eugène Boudin museum in the place Erik-Satie. (It opens between Palm Sunday and the end of September, from 10.00 to noon and from 14.00 to 18.00, except on Tuesdays.)

Honfleur's esplanade also boasts the seventeenth-century pilgrimage chapel of Notre-Dame-de-Grâce. Naturally, fish soups and fish dishes feature on its menus.

Jumièges

See the index; and do visit its ruined abbey, with a seventeenth-century abbot's lodging, twelfth-century cellars, the ruins of the eleventh-century abbey church of Notre-Dame and vestiges of the twelfth-century chapter house.

Jumièges is now served by the parish church of Saint-Valentin, begun in the eleventh century and finished in the sixteenth. Filled with statues, lit with splendid sixteenth-century stained-glass, it still boasts a Romanesque nave. And the ruined church of Saint-Pierre in Jumièges, built in the tenth century, is the only Carolingian building remaining in Normandy.

Lassay

Lassay is noted for its fortified château, built over several centuries, which can be visited from Easter to mid-September from 14.30 to 18.30.

Lessay

Lessay's Romanesque abbey church, half demolished by the raids of 1944, has been meticulously restored.

Lillebonne

See the index. Lillebonne's market takes place on Wednesday mornings.

Lisieux

Although much of Lisieux is described elsewhere in this book, the cathedral of Saint-Pierre can easily be neglected because of the overwhelming impact of St Thérèse and her basilica. To miss it would be a pity, for it was begun in the eleventh century, finished two centuries later, buttressed by thrilling arches in the fifteenth century and boasts the so-called paradise doorway. Bishop Pierre Cauchon, who condemned Joan of Arc, commissioned the flamboyant rebuilding of the Lady Chapel behind the high altar.

At Lisieux restaurants specialize in the delicate chicken of the Auge valley.

Lonlay-l'Abbaye

See under Domfront.

Louviers

Louviers' chief claim to fame is its thirteenth-century church, dedicated to Our Lady and partly transformed in the late fifteenth century into a riotous piece of flamboyant architecture. Its south wall is breathtaking and its south porch superb, partly flamboyant in style, partly Renaissance in its sculptures. This should not stop one walking round to the west doorway, whose porch is an early Gothic delight of the thirteenth century.

Inside the church are carvings in wood of the arrest of Jesus and the ecstasy of the Blessed Virgin Mary. Other bas-reliefs in the church of Notre-Dame, carved and gilded at the end of the fifteenth century, illustrate more scenes from her life. Look for the sixteenth-century stone statue of the mother of the apostles James and John, who appear as children at her side. Another sixteenth-century group depicts the entombment of Jesus. The splendidly carved pulpit dates from the eighteenth century and was brought here from the Dominican monastery of Évreux.

Since Louviers lived off textiles until 1970, as one would expect its civic museum has a large section dedicated to this now defunct industry. You will find the museum in the place Ernest-Thorel, and it opens from 14.00 to 19.00, except on Tuesdays. The restaurants in the town take a pride in serving spring cabbage.

Luc-sur-Mer

In his novel *Les Bains de mer* Émile Zola describes a bourgeois Parisian family at Luc-sur-Mer, a family who are too obsessed with hunting to relish the sea. Today the cliffs of Luc-sur-Mer have been classified as a protected natural site, since scientists have discovered there a group of rocky but frail spongy reefs unique in France, covered with fossils and dating back some 160 million years, if not more. Between Luc-sur-Mer and Lion-sur-Mer there was once a series of curiously shaped fissures known to the locals as 'confessionals'. All but two of them have long been filled up with debris; but the remaining two are well worth seeing, as is the twelfth-century bell tower of the church at Luc-sur-Mer itself.

As one might expect, Zola's own protagonists in *Les Bains de mer* do not find the spot so charming. For them Luc-sur-Mer represents 'the sadness of this maritime coast, the most rebarbative imaginable, with pebbles and pointed stones and rocks piercing the sand, and the village itself peopled with grey and morose houses'. Today it is charming.

Mayenne

Dominating the town and the river is the medieval château; and the charm of Mayenne is enhanced by its Gothic basilica of Notre-Dame.

Le Mont-Saint-Michel

See the index.

Montivilliers

The abbey of Montivilliers survived the vicissitudes of the Middle Ages, the Wars of Religion and seventeenth century, only to suffer grievously at the Revolution. What survives is a superb abbey church, dating from the early twelfth century, with a nave rebuilt in the fifteenth and a Renaissance crossing that supports a Romanesque lantern. Its furnishings and statuary are sumptuous and mostly date from the seventeenth century.

Many of the streets of Montivilliers are crammed with ancient houses including the manor of Epaville, built in the seventeenth and eighteenth centuries. In the fifteenth-century cemetery of le Briscaret is a Gothic cross and a seventeenth-century chapel.

Mortagne-au-Perche

Once fortified, Mortagne-au-Perche (whose name derives from the Gallo-Roman 'Mauritania') today retains from its former ramparts only the twelfth-century gate of Saint-Denis. The upper double-storey was added to the gate a hundred years later.

Straggling up its hillside, its classical houses mingling with modern plastered façades, Mortagne-au-Perche is scarcely the most beautiful town in France (as it claims to be); but it is well worth a visit. The church of Notre-Dame, dating from 1494 to 1535, is half-flamboyant, half-Renaissance in style. Its mighty square tower was built in the sixteenth century and added to in the eighteenth. The choir stalls date from the eighteenth century. Each Saturday a market sets out its stalls in the shade of the church.

On the corner of the market hall and the rue Sainte-Croix you find the entrance to the public park, with an immense view of the surrounding countryside and a bronze statue of the young Neptune. Fittingly, for this was once percheron country, he sits astride a fine horse. Mortagne-au-Perche preserves the memory of these majestic horses in its percheron museum (in the porte Saint-Denis), open from July to September between 15.00 and 18.00, except on Sundays and Mondays.

The town has preserved numerous delightful old houses, and is also the home of a confraternity dedicated to black and white blood-sausages (*la Confrérie des Chevaliers du Goût Boudin*). On the Saturday following the third Thursday in Lent it hosts an annual festival dedicated to these delicious concoctions of pigs' blood, onions, sage, pearl barley and the secret ingredients which each butcher adds to his own creation. Here then (since this is also apple country) is a traditional Normandy black-pudding recipe. Four reasonable-sized potatoes should be cooked and mashed with 25g (1oz) of butter. Meanwhile 450g (1lb) of sliced and peeled apples are also cooked and made into a purée. A large onion is sliced and cooked in butter. Finally, slice 275g (10 oz) of black pudding, spread the apple purée on the bottom of an ovenproof dish, place the black pudding on top of it, cover this with the mashed potatoes, except for a hole in the middle where you place the onions. The dish should now be browned under a grill and served immediately.

Saturday is market day at Mortagne-au-Perche.

Mortain

Mortain was much reduced by the bombardments of 1944, yet preserved its thirteenth-century church of Saint-Évroult, as well as the lovely twelfth-century Cistercian abbey situated just outside the town and known as the abbaye Blanche.

Adeline de Mortain founded the abbey for Benedictines in 1105, though its monks soon went over to the Cistercians. Although the abbey is now a seminary, guided tours of the cloister, the thirteenth-century chapter house and the twelfth-century abbey church take place between July and September from 10.00 to 18.00, with a two-hour break at noon.

The chapel of Saint-Michel rises from a hillock 314 metres above the town and houses a number of lovely fifteenth- and sixteenth-century statues in wood and stone. Around Mortain, in rich countryside which you can see from the heights behind this chapel (where there is an orientation table), graze some of the finest of Normandy's cattle, whose steaks grace the tables of the town's restaurants.

Mortemer

The abbey of Mortemer was Normandy's first Cistercian foundation, set in a remote forest as was the custom of this reforming monastic order. Under the patronage of both Henry I and Henry II of England, the monks built a huge church. At the time of the Revolution the abbey buildings were sold as national goods. All that remain today are the romantic ruins of the church, the cloister, the dormitory and the chapter house.

Le Neubourg

Magnificently situated on a plateau surrounded by the waters of no fewer than five rivers, Le Neubourg possesses a fourteenth-century cemetery chapel, a former Benedictine abbey founded in 1638, and the fifteenth-century church of Saint-Pierre-et-Paul, which now houses many of the abbey's treasures.

The town also boasts substantial remains of its medieval château. Not far away (west along the D137) is the splendidly preserved and restored château d'Harcourt, with its powerful ramparts still defended by eight out of twelve towers and surrounded by a park filled with ancient trees. You can visit this château in summer between 14.30 and 18.00, except on Tuesdays.

Take the D road east from château d'Harcourt to reach Sainte-Opportune-du-Bosc, where you can visit another superb château, this one built in the late seventeenth century, open from 10.00 to 20.00 and much given in summer to *son-et-lumière* spectacles.

Neufchâtel-en-Bray

See the index. Like the town iself, the celebrated cheeses of Neufchâtel-en-Bray are also described elsewhere in this book. The town markets take place on Saturday and Wednesday mornings, the latter devoted to cattle.

Nogent-le-Rotrou

The former hospice of this town is where Henry IV's Protestant counsellor Sully, seigneur of Nogent-le-Rotrou, has his tomb, not wishing to lie in the neighbouring catholic church of Notre-Dame – though this thirteenth-and fourteenth-century building with its mid-seventeenth-century organ is delightful enough. In Sully's mausoleum are found his statue and that of his wife, sculpted by Barthélemy Baudin.

Walk up the rue du château to reach the château itself, high above the Huisne valley. It boasts a huge, square thirteenth-century keep, as well as a powerful gateway. Inside, the château, which you can visit, except on Tuesdays, from 10.00 to 12.00 and 14.00 to 18.00 (17.00 between November and April) is enlivened by a museum of local history.

Leaving the château, the rue de-la-Fuye leads towards the old bailiff's house and the former Cluniac abbey of Saint-Denis. The maison du Bailli stands at no. 47, rue Saint-Laurent and was built in the sixteenth century for the bailiff of the abbey. Behind it stand the fifteenth-century monastery chapter house, the twelfth-century chancel of its church and the cloister. The flamboyant church of Saint-Laurent close by contains a lovely fifteenth-century entombment of Christ, but alas is frequently closed.

Nogent-le-Rotrou is blessed with several elegant fifteenth- and six-teenth-century houses and one other church of singular interest. Saint-Hilaire, with its sixteenth-century tower, stands to the north of the town on the banks of the River Huisne. Its chancel was built in the thirteenth century as a passable copy of the Holy Sepulchre in Jerusalem. The town is also celebrated for its *escargots*.

Orbec

Orbec lies prettily in the Auge valley, blessed with some picturesque old houses in its main street, the Grand'Rue, and guarded by the mighty sixteenth-century tower of the church of Notre-Dame, which was rebuilt after the Hundred Years War. Its Renaissance organ console came from the abbey of le Bec-Hellouin.

Orbec's cultural centre is situated in a former Augustinian priory, which was founded in 1632; and its municipal museum and town hall occupy a fine half-timbered building of 1568.

Ouistreham Riva-Bella

See the index.

Pacy-sur-Eure

As well as boasting a virtually unchanged thirteenth-century church, Pacy-sur-Eure is noted for the trout and salmon served in its restaurants.

Pont-Audemer

Pont-Audemer (see the index) straddles the River Risle. Its parish church is dedicated to St-Ouen and its west façade still awaits completion, even though the church was begun in the eleventh century. The aisles, with their splendid keystones, date from the Renaissance, as does the excellent glass in their windows. Max Ingrand has added his modern glass to the chancel and over the organ.

In *Madame Bovary* Flaubert described the well that gives its name to the auberge du Vieux Puits at Pont-Audemer. Now a hotel and restaurant, its menu inevitably includes *truite Bovary*.

Pont-de-l'Arche

Once of great strategic importance due to commanding the river crossing, Pont-de-l'Arche boasts the sixteenth-century church of Saint-Vigor, whose interior is rich with furnishings, some fine stained-glass windows and a resurrection painted by Le Tourneur in 1640.

Pont-l'Évêque

See the index.

Pontorson

William the Bastard founded the solid granite church as a thanks offering when part of his army escaped foundering in the quicksands of Coueson, supposedly as a result of the direct intervention of the Virgin Mary. Its present form is basically twelfth-century Romanesque, enlivened inside by Gothic vaulting. Inside too are a fourteenth-century font and eighteenth-century stalls.

Seek out the pretty sixteenth-century façade of the hôtel Guiscard-de-la-Ménardière in the rue Saint-Michel. At Pontorson I was once served a *truite* so delicious that I asked the hostess what the chef's secret was. She answered simply, 'The cream, *monsieur*.' See also the index.

Saint-Céneri-le-Gérei

Apart from its charming situation on a great loop of the River Sarthe, tiny Saint-Céneri-le-Gérei is distinguished by a Romanesque church containing some not very well-restored, but notable, frescos dating from the second half of the fourteenth century. The chapel of Saint-Céneri contains not only a venerable statue of the saint but also the block of granite he used for a bed. Part of the old château-fort and its mottes can be seen in the village.

Saint-Évroult-Notre-Dame-du-Bois

Today this village has become a centre for tourism, promoting camping, fishing and forest walks.

Saint-Germer-de-Fly

This picturesque village eight kilometres south-east of Gournay-en-Bray boasts an abbey church built in the 1150s. Part of its nave was destroyed during the Hundred Years War, to be rebuilt in brick. Its west door dates from 1640 and its lantern tower from 1754.

Saint-Lô

After looking up Saint-Lô in the index to this book, visit the church of Notre-Dame, whose two thirteenth-century spires struggled through the onslaught of the Allies in June 1944 and now point victoriously to the skies. Its fine rood-loft dates only from the eighteenth century. The windows contain fifteenth- and sixteenth-century stained-glass.

Charlemagne built a defensive wall around Saint-Lô. All that survives is the Poudrière tower, just behind the town hall.

At Saint-Lô between 10.00 and 11.00 and between 14.00 and 16.30, from mid-February to mid-July, you can visit one of Normandy's finest stud-farms, the Haras de Saint-Lô, founded in 1806 under the orders of Napoleon himself. There is a demonstration of dressage here every day at 10.00 between 25 July and 5 September. The civic museum displays beautiful tapestries.

The citizens of Saint-Lô wash down salmon from the River Vire and lamb chops with cider.

Saint-Martin-de-Boscherville

Of the medieval abbey of Saint-Martin-de-Boscherville survive a twelfth-century chapter house, enlarged in the seventeenth century, and the monastic church, dedicated to St-Georges, which was built between 1080 and 1125 except for the thirteenth-century vaulting. Look for the carved Romanesque capitals of the west façade. Abbot Antoine le Roux, who died in 1535, lies here beneath a magniloquently decorated slab. The carvings in the chapter house represent both the rule of St Benedict and scenes from the Old Testament.

Market day here is Saturday morning.

Three kilometres south-east you reach the château de la Rivière-Bourdet, a splendid early seventeenth-century building, with a dovecote dating from 1668 and gorgeous classical stables built in the eighteenth century.

Saint-Michel-de-Montjoie

See the index.

Saint-Pierre-de-Sommaire

See under l'Aigle.

Saint-Pierre-sur-Dives

Until June 1944 Saint-Pierre-sur-Dives boasted a wooden market hall pegged with chestnut stakes dating back to the eleventh century. The reconquest of Normandy destroyed it, and the town has brilliantly restored it all.

The abbey church here is partly thirteenth-century and partly fifteenth-, both the lantern and the chancel dating from the earlier period. Even earlier is one of its west towers, dating from the twelfth century, the other from the fifteenth. Inside is a lovely gilded and sculpted seventeenth-century high altar, and the church has retained its thirteenth-century terracotta floor. Next door the charming thirteenth-century chapter house is still intact.

Five kilometres south-east along the D511 you reach château Vendeuvre, built in 1750, whose historic exhibition of miniature furniture can be visited from May Day to the beginning of September between 14.00 and 19.00.

Saint-Sauveur-le-Vicomte

The eleventh-century Benedictine abbey which you see as you drive into Saint-Sauveur-le-Vicomte from the south-east is almost entirely a reconstruction, for it was partly demolished at the Revolution. An enlightened citizen named François Halley bought it and began to restore it in 1831. World War II caused new damage, and the abbey was finally restored in 1954.

In the town itself you can visit the powerful château, whose twenty-five-metre-high keep was built in the fourteenth century. Inside the huge round tower of the château can be traced the pitiful scratches of those whom it once imprisoned. Another tower defends the north-east flank of the château. It opens from 10.00 to 12.00 and 15.00 to 18.00 except on Tuesdays.

Saint-Vaast-la-Hougue

Apart from its bastion, perched on a triangular rock, Saint-Vaast-la-Hougue is noted for its seafood, particularly its lobsters.

Saint-Wandrille

In 649 St Wandrille founded his celebrated abbey in the Fontenelle valley. The saint, who had learned Celtic monasticism at Bobbio in Italy, was clearly both a formidable and a kindly person, for legend tells that a royal forester named Becto, consumed with jealousy at Wandrille's popularity, once rushed at the saint, lance poised to strike him dead, only to fall at the holy man's feet virtually paralysed. St Wandrille took his enemy back to his own cell and nursed him into health.

Today, after centuries of scholarship, spiritual inspiration and ecclesiastical dominance, his abbey lies romantically ruined. The cloister retains one fourteenth-century wing and three from the next century, housing an exquisite Renaissance lavabo and decorated with superb flamboyant sculpture. The ancient abbey church consists today of a few stumps and columns; but the monastery has been recolonized and lives again (see the index). Guided tours take place between 10.00 and 12.00 and between 15.00 and 16.00.

Sainte-Opportune-du-Bosc

See under Le Neubourg.

Sées

See the index. Saturday is market day at Sées, and the city hosts several fairs throughout the year. Races, concerts, campsites and fishing facilities amply cater for tourists.

Tancarville

Since 1959 Tancarville has boasted not only its fine fifteenth-century château which dominates the Seine, but also a superb bridge, fifty-one metres above the river and 1,410 metres long.

Touques

See the index.

Le-Tréport

See the index. The view from its cliffs is celebrated. You can buy food from its market stalls most days of the week (though not Sundays and Mondays), and a general market is held every Tuesday and Saturday.

Trouville

See the index.

Valognes

At Valognes your first objective should be its fifteenth-century museum of cider and its museum of *eau de vie*, which open from mid-June to the end of September from 10.00 to 12.00 and from 14.00 to 18.00 (except for Sunday mornings and Wednesdays). Citizens of Valognes seem to breakfast off black coffee and Calvados.

Next visit the eighteenth-century hôtel de Granvil-Caligny (if you can, for it opens erratically), once the home of Barbey d'Aurevilly (see his name in the index), a charmingly preserved Normandy patrician house of yesteryear. A yet finer house which you can also visit is the classical hôtel de Beaumont, with a colourful terraced garden. (It opens between July and mid-September from 11.30 to 18.00, except on Wednesdays.)

Eel is a local speciality, tasting even better when served in a restaurant housed in one of the town's numerous sixteenth- and seventeenth-century dwellings.

Varengeville-sur-Mer

See under Dieppe.

Verneuil-sur-Avre

Verneuil-sur-Avre is approached through such flat country that the astonishing tower which the citizens have affectionately dubbed la Madeleine is visible long before you reach the town, entrancing your aesthetic senses, chunky all the way up, and then suddenly narrowing and flying a lazy flag at the top.

The many half-timbered houses of this unspoiled town, some of them corbelled, spread out from its two fine churches, the church of Notre-Dame and the church of Saint Mary Magdalen (la Madeleine), whose sixty-metre-high flamboyant tower was built in the fifteenth century and is enriched with twenty-four statues. Its organ and pulpit were both built in the eighteenth century, and some of the windows boast glittering early sixteenth-century stained-glass. The statuary is abundant and diverse, and includes a fifteenth-century Madonna about to give Jesus an apple, and a touching sixteenth-century entombment (with a beautiful young St John comforting the Virgin Mary).

The church of Notre-Dame boasts a stern central spire and a mélange of styles, including (from the exterior) a brown-stone Romanesque choir and a nineteenth-century Gothic south porch. A fine collection of Gothic statues is displayed inside among the soaring proportions of the church.

Henry I of England gave Verneuil-sur-Avre its round twelfth-century keep (la tour Grise), and you can still walk round some of the ancient fortifications of the town. The Benedictine abbey of Saint-Nicolas is a lovely classical building, its cream walls contrasting with the brown roofs. It is probably invidious to single out just one of the lovely houses, but no. 136 in the rue des Tanneries is a deliciously sculpted Renaissance home.

The restaurants of Verneuil-sur-Avre serve fowl cooked in cider and frogs' legs served in cream sauce.

Vernon

See the index.

Veules-les-Roses

See under Dieppe.

Vieil-Évreux

See under Évreux.

Villedieu-les-Poêles

See the index.

Villequier

Sweet Villequier, overlooking the Seine, would merit a visit quite apart from being the scene of a poignant nineteenth-century tragedy, the death by drowning in the river here of Victor Hugo's daughter Léopoldine and her husband six months after their marriage, a sorrow which the bride's father expiated in a series of moving poems entitled *Les Contemplations*. The victims lie buried in the cemetery of the fifteenth- and sixteenth-century church at Villequier, with its timber roof and its sixteenth-century stained-glass windows. Here too lies Victor Hugo's own wife, Adèle. The Victor Hugo museum displays letters between the writer and his daughter from happier days.

The church of Villequier, dedicated to St-Martin, was built in the fifteenth century. One of its stained-glass windows depicts a sixteenth-century sea battle. Its flamboyant tower rises to thirty-three metres, not including the tiled *flèche*. Two kilometres north-west, château Villequier, built in the style of Louis XV, overlooks the valley. And nearby is the regional nature park of Brotonne.

Vimoutiers

See the index.

Vire

See the index.

Yvetot

Yvetot, which appears in the index to this book, has an extraordinarily dreadful concrete church, built between 1956 and 1963 and illuminated by stained-glass windows designed by Max Ingrand.

The municipal museum houses a fine collection of ivories and of eighteenth- and nineteenth-century terracotta reliefs and sculptures. Yvetot's market sets itself up on Wednesday mornings. Try the rabbit pâté in the restaurants.

Bibliography

Henry Adams, *Mont-Saint-Michel and Chartres*, Houghton Mifflin, Boston and New York, 1913.

Michel Barberousse, *La Normandie: ses traditions, sa cuisine, son art de vivre*, Librairie Hachette, Paris, 1974.

Michel Baudot, *Normandie Bénédictine*, Les amis du Bec-Hellouin, Pacy-sur-Eure, 1979.

Dominique Behage, *Gastronomie Normande*, Éditions SAEP, Colmar, 1986.

Georges Bernage, *La retraite allemande*, in *39/45 Magazine*, hors série no. 4, Éditions Heimdal, Bayeux, Mars–Avril 1988.

Marie-Henri Beyle, *Mémoires d'un Touriste*, tr. into English as *Chronicles of a Voyage*, Austryn Wainhouse, New York, 1958.

Christine Bonneton (ed.), *Normandie: écologie, économie, art, littérature, histoire, traditions populaires*, Ch. Corlet, Condé-sur-Noireau, 1978.

Amélie Bosquet, *La Normandie romanesque et merveilleux. Traditions, légendes et superstitions populaires de cette province*, Gérard Montfort, Brionne, 1978 edition (first published 1845).

Max-André Brier and Pierre Brunet, *L'architecture rurale française. Normandie*, Berger-Levrault, Paris, 1984.

Catherine Brisac, *A Thousand Years of Stained Glass*, tr. Geoffrey Culverwell, Macdonald, London, 1986.

Michel de Brouard (ed.), *Histoire de la Normandie*, Privat, Paris, 2nd edition 1970.

R. Allen Brown, *The Normans*, The Boydell Press, London, 1974.

Alain Coursier, *Normandie*, Regio-guides Duculot, Paris, 1981.

R. H. C. Davis, *The Normans and their Myth*, Thames and Hudson, London, 1976.

David Eisenhower, *Eisenhower at War 1943–1945*, William Collins, London, 1986.

L'Eure, in *Richesses de France*, J. Delmas & Cie., Bordeaux, 1967.

Régis Faucon, *Sur les pas de Guillaume le Conquérant*, Nouvelles Éditions Atins, Paris, n.d.

Gustave Flaubert, *Bouvard et Pécuchet*, L. Conard, Paris, 1923.

—— *Madame Bovary. Moeurs de province*, L. Conard, Paris, 1927.

H. de Formeville and Noël Deshays, *Histoire de l'ancien Évêche-Comté de Lisieux*, 2 vols, E. Piel, Lisieux, 1873.

Pierre Gascar, *Normandie*, Arthaud, Paris, 1967.

André Gide, *L'Immoraliste*, in *Mercure de France*, Paris, 1927.

Claude Guermont and Paul Frumkin, *The Norman Table: Traditional Cooking in Normandy*, Charles Scribner's, New York, 1955.

Nigel Hamilton, *Monty. Master of the Battlefield 1942–44*, Hamish Hamilton, London, 1983.

Mrs Robert Henry, *The Golden Visit*, J. M. Dent, London, 1979.

John House, *Monet*, Phaidon Press, Oxford, 2nd edition, 1981.

Robert Hunt and David Masson, *The Normandy Campaign*, Leo Cooper, London, 1976.

Images de Seine-Maritime, in *La revue géographique et industrielle de France*, Paris, 1963.

Gérald van der Kemp, *A visit to Giverny*, tr. Bronia Fuchs, les Éditions d'Art Lys, Versailles, 1980.

Édith Languille, etc., *La Manche. Bocage Saint-Louis et pays de Coutances*, Hélio-Cachan, Chilly-Mazarin, 1970.

Pierre Lebique, *Contes et légendes en Pays Normand*, Laurence Olivier, Caen, 1981.

Pierre Leprohon and Arlette Marinie, *La Normandie*, Éditions Minerva, Geneva, 1982.

Jean Mabire, Marie-Claire Bernage, Claire Méheust and Nicolle Villeroux, *Histoire secrète de la Normandie*, Albin Michel, Paris, 1984.

Guy de Maupassant, *Oeuvres complètes*, M. Gonon, 2 vols, Paris, 1971.

Brigitte et Jean-Pierre Perrin-Chattard, *Les meilleurs recettes normandes*, Ouest France, La Guerche-de-Bretagne, 1978.

Marcel Proust, *À la recherche du temps perdu*, vol. II *À l'ombre des jeunes filles en fleurs*, Éditions de la Nouvelle Revue Française, Paris, 1918.

V. Sackville-West, *The Eagle and the Dove: St Teresa of Avila, St Thérèse of Lisieux*, Michael Joseph, London, 1943.

Eugène de Saint-Denis, *Du Mont-Saint-Michel au cap de la Hague. Promenades littéraires*, Éditions OCEP, Coutances, 1981.

Jean Selz, *Eugène Boudin*, tr. Shirley Jennings, Bonfini Press, Naefels, Switzerland, 1982.

Louis Serbat, *Lisieux*, Henri Laurens, Paris, 1926.

David M. Wilson, *The Bayeux Tapestry*, Thames and Hudson, London, 1985.

Émile Zola, *Zest for Life*, tr. Jean Stewart, Elek Books, London, 1955.

Index